# Songs In The Whirlwind

# JUNE MASTERS BACHER

**HARVEST HOUSE PUBLISHERS**
Eugene, Oregon 97402

Scripture quotations are taken from the King James Version of the Bible.

**SONGS IN THE WHIRLWIND**

Copyright © 1992 by Harvest House Publishers
Eugene, Oregon 97402

Bacher, June Masters.
    Songs in the whirlwind / June Masters Bacher.    (The Heartland heritage
series : no. 2)
        ISBN 1-56507-000-3
        I. Title.    II. Series.
    PS3552.A257S66        1992                                                        92-6983
    813′54—dc20                                                                        CIP

**Printed in the United States of America.**

For those who journeyed with me through those years of struggle, stripped of all but dreams, hope, and faith in a "better tomorrow." Ours was a generation of endurance, the fabric of our American heritage. For we are not hopeless victims. We can march on heart-to-heart in loving optimism. Blessed are those who remember: You can care!

*Think not for an idle moment*
*Human hearts take shape alone;*
*We are formed and we are fashioned*
*By God's hand and those of others*
*In life's journey we have known.*

—June Masters Bacher

# Contents

*The Lord hath appeared of old unto me, saying, Yea, I have loved thee with an everlasting love.*

—Jeremiah 31:3

*[I am] the Lord God, merciful and gracious, long-suffering, and abundant in goodness and truth, keeping mercy for thousands, forgiving iniquity and transgression and sin.*

—Exodus 34:6,7

*Lives of great men all remind us*
*We can make our lives sublime,*
*And, departing, leave behind us*
*Footprints on the sands of time...*
*Let us, then, be up and doing,*
*With a heart for any fate;*
*Still achieving, still pursuing,*
*Learn to labor and to wait.*

—Excerpt from
"A Psalm of Life," by
Henry Wadsworth Longfellow

# 1

# *From Darkness into Light*

Marvel was with Frederick Salsburg when he died. Surely, the going-on-16 girl told herself in that one panicky moment when she knew the end was near, this was a judgment from on high. Later she was to realize that nothing happens without divine purpose....

"How filled with irony—the timing. This *is* the Fourth of July?"

It was difficult to hear the hoarse whisper of the frail man who, until now, had given no evidence of being alive. Marvel leaned closer, started to remind him to save his strength, then decided against it. Instead, she asked if he was comfortable.

"Of course not" was the reply. But the words were not said irritably. "I have medication—for the pain—"

"Would you like more? Where—"

Frederick Salsburg lifted a wan hand in protest. "It makes me sleepy. I—I—want to be wide awake—aware. But there *is* one— one thing—"

"Anything that will help," Marvel said, surprised to find she meant it. Without waiting for an answer, she squeezed out the cloth in the water basin and made it into a cooling compress for the hot forehead. The frail hand gripped hers in a frightening way.

But his words led her to know she had nothing to fear. "I don't want the shades drawn, the room dark. I like to feel—I—I'm leaving behind a—this—world of darkness—entering a—world of light."

It was then that she knew. A momentary anger filled her heart. How could they? Grandmother had to have known he wouldn't live through this day—planned it—*trapped* her! Had she known when she telephoned to insist that Marvel be their guest at the hotel this holiday week before plunging into her busy summer? It was a trick.

She wanted to run, to escape—to be anywhere with anybody other than here with this man! Until he spoke again.

"I asked every—everybody else to leave—to leave *you* here. There is something—im—port—ant that I must do—and I—need—your help."

*Why me, Lord?*

Marvel moved to adjust the blinds, and immediately the room was flooded with sunlight. Her heart felt lighter, too—removed somehow from the world of darkness he had mentioned.

Returning to her chair at his bedside, "I'll do what I can, Uncle Fred," she said.

"Uncle—" Frederick Salsburg's raspy whisper was one of wonder. "You—you called me—*uncle*—"

"You *are* my uncle." Marvel's voice left no doubt, because there was none in her heart. Through Jesus Christ she could love this man, could comfort him, reassure him, help him through whatever anguish or remorse he must endure—and handle the assignment he was about to give her. "What would you like me to do? And yes, I will do it."

"Don't send—for the others—the reverend—or any—any lawyer. I've made—arrangements—I—I—just—want t'make—sh-h-h-hure they're—uh, uh (he coughed) c-c-car-ried out. Will-yah? Keep—'im there—Elmer—get mon-ey t'all—for now. M-most w-went t'church funds a'ready. Day'll c-come—c-c-con-tents'll—mean m-more—be m-more prec-prec-sh-us—"

The slur in speech and the struggle for breath said time was short.

"Whatever it is, I'll appreciate," Marvel said kindly.

The outside heat had grown more intense now that the blinds were open. Perhaps she should turn the electric fan more his direction. Before she could move or he could explain further about "the box," a firecracker exploded somewhere nearby.

"In cele-bra-tion—"

"Independence Day?" Marvel said as cheerfully as possible although something had exploded within her, too. Not at this pathetic, dying man. More at her own family, her own flesh and blood, having sent her in their place. Why, *why*, WHY? It was unfair—

Silence. Was he gone? Another explosion of fireworks said he was clinging to life, that he had more to say.

"My birthday—and—my death day. 'The wages—of sin...' "

"Happy birthday, Uncle Fred," Marvel whispered and found herself leaning forward to brush a kiss on the parched, colorless forehead. The dying man was unable to open his eyes, but something resembling a sad smile touched the tight lips. Touched deeply by his gratitude, Marvel went on to say, "Yes, you're right. It all goes back to the Garden—man's disobedience. But we believers have a special liberty to celebrate today. Jesus gave us religious liberty just as our ancestors provided our other freedoms—all sacrificed—"

"You—You—wise—don't—leav-v-ve me—for-sake—m-m-me—"

Holding back tears, Marvel clasped her hands over his. "I'll be right here until you step into the world of light."

There was a long silence. The labored breathing gave way to near-nothingness, the sheet covering the wasted body almost still.

"Nev-er re-jec-ted me... nev-er—f-forced... an' knew—h-h-how evil—I—was—"

"That's how Jesus is!" Marvel sang out, feeling a strange joy, all fear washed away.

Washed away, too, was all anger and resentment toward her family. Never mind the *why* of her being here. It was an opportunity to minister, to serve. Had he spoken again? She leaned closer to hear.

"J-J-Jes-us—'n—you—fam-ily—'spec-ial-ly—you—t-t-taught—me h-h-how—t-t-to live—"

"Jesus taught us that—and how to die! And now, you—here, let me moisten that cloth—you are teaching me how the Christian dies. I'll always remember, Uncle Fred. I always will."

It was hard not to cry. But Marvel squeezed back the tears.

Then suddenly the voice was loud and strong. "Praise God! Now I'll not talk more, but ask one question. That young man of yours—did you cry, Marvel—cry when—you said—that sad word 'good-bye'?"

*How on earth—?*

"No, Uncle Fred," she said, wiping his brow, "no, I didn't cry."

"Then—you'll—ap-preciate the—gift. They'll not be—for tears. Tell me—all," he whispered, "all—about—him—"

Haltingly the story began—first, to give one more breath of youth's spring to a man whose winter was rapidly shortening, and then to live again in sweet review those stolen moments so in need of a voice. As the tender romance unfolded like a blossom responding to the kiss of soft rain, Marvel forgot completely the presence of an outsider. She and Titus were alone, safe, secure, and sheltered by the loving arms of the giant oak—a world which knew no crime, poverty, or death...a Garden of Eden—*before the fall.*

The fantasy ended with their sad-sweet good-bye. Somewhere in the ugly world of reality another firecracker violated the quiet of the sultry summer afternoon. And Marvel Harrington stopped, horrified. How could she have shared with the stepuncle she had tried to hate the guarded secret so carefully withheld from those she loved? Oh, the irony—or was this a part of God's plan? What purpose for a dying man?

"Beautiful." And the way Frederick Salsburg said the word was beautiful, too. Of course there was a purpose: the natural desire for a caring relationship! "Beautiful—here—and there. My precious moment—I'm no longer lonely—or afraid. You have—made me—a part of one great family."

Instinctively, Marvel knew these would be his last words. But she had witnessed a miracle. For Frederick Salsburg had demonstrated far more courage, calm, and strength in dying than in living. And in an amazing way she had grown, too, from this blessing. Small wonder then that her next words could be spoken naturally and from the heart.

"Uncle Fred—dear Uncle Fred—I think it would be fitting if you chose to be buried along with us, your family, the Harringtons. I can arrange for a lot—and it would please us all. You're welcome."

There were no words—just a gentle pressure of his fingers around her own and then a faint smile. There was no fear for either of them. Her uncle simply stopped breathing for a moment, then drifted away with the smile still intact. Then he gave a gentle sigh, like a soft breeze...earth's journey ended.

Downstairs, Marvel found the family waiting to comfort her. In the end it was she who would comfort them. All fear was gone, as was the petty irritation of having been thrust into the mysterious moment for which neither she nor they were prepared. It was the dying man's wish and she had honored it—and in so doing had learned so much. There to help her then and here to help her now was the sense of another presence. How could one put it into words, except to say that Uncle Fred's departure had provided for them a holy moment?

"Mrs. Ambrose has prepared a meal for us all," Grandmother said practically. "We'll take it from here. Right, family?"

"Great!" Marvel smiled rapturously. "I'm starved. Let's hope it's not cabbage!"

# 2

# *One Holy Moment*

Grandfather Harrington took over completely, his pleasantly masculine voice barking orders—probably to camouflage whatever emotions he might be feeling. After all, Frederick Salsburg was his stepson, and in that role couldn't he himself have done more, tried harder to establish a warmer relationship between the two. Undoubtedly self-doubt and remorse plagued him now that Uncle Fred was gone.

"There are to be no formalities," Grandfather said now. "No wake, no lying in state—not even a public funeral. Frederick requested only that the Reverend Greer read some appropriate passage with all of us in attendance, with violin music by the Grande Dame—uh, Mrs. Riley—and Snow, if she's been able to replace the broken strings on her violin—and we are to sing hymns. Marvel is to prepare a brief eulogy should she wish to do so—no obligation."

"I will," Marvel said when he hesitated.

Grandfather cleared his throat. "I might have known," he said huskily. "Fred left with me some, uh, documents, a key to his safe, and a few words I shall share after the memorial service. There's more I need to get off my chest—"

The sharp rap of his cane against the uncarpeted area of the boardinghouse lobby expressed frustration, anger, and his self-recrimination. Was there a way to comfort him, to help this beloved man overcome his sense of failure? Marvel wondered what was keeping Brother Greer.

14

But even were he here, she realized suddenly, he was not the one present when peace came at the bedside of the dying man— only she. Could she help mend a broken relationship—comfort Grandfather by imparting the feel of those final moments when denial, fury, desperation, hatred, and envy were washed clean? Could she share with Grandfather how Uncle Fred left a legacy of love which opened far more than the key he had placed in Grandfather's hand? *Help me, Lord*, her heart whispered.

"I'm sure we all understand, Grandfather. We—at least, I— have some regrets. I have to tell myself that's normal and live with it. You did the best you could—circumstances were diffi- cult. And anyway, whatever you did or failed to do was forgiven."

Alexander Jay Harrington's unlined face brightened visibly. "Sure enough? You sure enough believe that, child?"

Marvel smiled. "I sure enough do! He put you in charge, didn't he? You were the only father he knew—please remember that."

Grandmother leaned forward, her rope of pearls swinging with her. "And the rest of us? Tell us, Marvel hon."

"All feelings that made him what he was were put aside. He wanted to be one of us. In life, he failed. But in death, he felt closer—felt a need to be loved. He wanted to be put away in our plot, be buried with our ancestors—and one day with us all—"

"And he will! Be with us, I mean! That settles the interment plans. Thank you, sweetheart. But the real reunion comes later."

Grandmother picked up her musical instrument and, quickly tucking it beneath her round, pink chin, brought the bow trium- phantly across the waiting strings. "Join me the minute you recognize the tune!"

The room filled up with the haunting violin strains, and then with the voices of those in the room and those who gathered to join them:

> When we all—get to heav-en...
> What a day of re-joic-ing that will be!
> When we all—see Je-sus...
> We'll sing and shout the vic-to-ry!"

"Amen!" said Grady Greer from the doorway. "'At thy right hand there are pleasures for evermore.' Psalm 16:11!"

*Forevermore.*

The word was highly significant in view of what happened next. There was a roar resembling the incomparable voice of a tornado. Although the sky was cloudless, the copper sun was blotted out by the blinding dust brought in by a whirlwind such as none of them had witnessed before. Indeed, the two-story boardinghouse might well have been built of broom straws, so fragile and helpless did it feel. Surely it would be swept away.

Billy Joe was crying. The others, white-faced, were huddled together as if there were safety in numbers. Or was there a renewed need to care and nurture one another for the remainder of their earthly days? Yes, Frederick Salsburg's passing had made a difference.

It was sobering, if not frightening. Yet, embedded in the moment—in that entire day—was a striking symbol of what lay in store....

But for the moment, which might be all they had (who knew about life?), Marvel felt a kind of spiritual exhilaration. It was as if all within the building might be caught up in glory.

It was a beautiful thought, but fleeting. With it came the sudden overwhelming desire to see her parents. Grandmother had said they would be coming tonight. Night seemed too far away.

Billy Joe was still crying. Marvel, trying to ignore the fury of the strange trick of the elements, went to the little boy's side and dropped to her knees.

"What's best to do when we're afraid of the dark, sweetie?"

"Whis—whistle," he whimpered, clutching her shoulder.

"Did you like the singing, too?"

The two fat tears on his cheeks rolled down, but there were no more. "Oh Marvel, could we? Could we sing more?"

"You and I can. What shall we sing?" Marvel said, pushing back the curls on his hot forehead, then putting her arms about his middle.

"What we sung—or is it sang—let's sang it."

Marvel laughed outright. Billy Joe joined her, with no idea what prompted the laughter.

When the two of them started, one by one the others joined in. And then they were all singing *songs in the whirlwind....*

\* \* \*

Uncle Worth reported that, although the freak storm had done extensive damage, it didn't really complicate things at all.

Ah, but it did.

True, fallen branches could be removed from the streets, roofs could be repaired, telephone service restored. Even the site for burial could be prepared. But no amount of cooperation could build back two collapsed bridges to allow Captain Bumstead to make his milk route, bringing Mother and Daddy into Pleasant Knoll. And Marvel needed them—needed them with all her heart. As the others made plans, Marvel let the conversation flow around her. Her own heart was elsewhere.

Auntie Rae sensed her unrest and, coming to sit at Marvel's side, said in her own sweet way, "Your concern is for your parents, am I right?"

"Yes," Marvel admitted, "it was."

"Don't be worrying, honey! You know that father of yours. Why, Dale would be here with you if he had two broken legs! And Snow—you know our Snow White—she won't admit that things are a wee bit off-center. Thinks a bad year only happens to wines!"

Sweet—but wrong. Marvel would face things alone, as she had done before.

* * *

The memorial service was simple, in accordance with the late relative's request. Brother Greer spoke briefly, quoting two passages of Scripture which covered death and life eternal more eloquently than human words: John 3:16 and 1 Corinthians 15:51-53.

"'For God so loved the world, that he gave his only begotten Son that whosoever believeth in him should not perish, but have everlasting life.' Fred wanted us to sing together, and what more appropriate hymn could we select than 'Jesus Included Me'?"

Again the only family the deceased had ever known sang together.

Jes-us included me—Yes, He in-cluded me—
When the Lord said *whosoever*
He—in-cluded—me!

When they had finished, the wind had died, too. Sad? No, a cause for rejoicing.

Grady Greer read his next passage of Scripture: "Behold, I shew you a mystery; we shall not all sleep, but we shall be changed, in a moment, in the twinkling of an eye, at the last trump; for the trumpet shall sound, and the dead shall be raised incorruptible, and we shall be changed... and this mortal must put on immortality."

Then, after giving brief vital statistics, he said, "How do we bear up under the circumstances we know existed in this instance? We lean on Jesus, our loving Lord. And then we put our arms about the living and we love them—love them well and tell them so. *Now!*"

Marvel took her place at the graveside and, without tears, said with conviction: "Let us give praise to our blessed Creator that there is no black book, listing what we on earth might call 'failures.' Uncle Fred left to us a sharing of his own inner peace and begged that we put our houses in order before the eleventh hour. 'Store up the sunbeams,' he said, 'then let them light the way when the final steps are shrouded in darkness.' He tried to comfort us by saying that he was stepping from darkness into light. And his countenance shone in a very special way.

"Brother Greer has said we should love one another—*now*! This I believe along with him. And this is what Uncle Fred did in that final moment."

Marvel's voice trembled slightly, but she carried on: "Can't we put our arms about one another around his grave as we hear the benediction? He must have lived a lonely life, but we are together!"

There was love in those arms—a love which cried out for all others who might pass from this earth without God—a love which cried out in Marvel's heart for those she loved so deeply and who were not here: Mother, Daddy, and yes, oh yes, Titus. She had shared her heart, the core of her youth, with her wonderful Titus. How strange that she should long to share death....

The winds had come back and this time the sky had darkened. The cedar trees bent their branches as if weeping, their strange summer fragrance filling the dust-darkened air. As the small group walked away from the family plot in silence, Mary Ann moved to put her arms about Marvel's waist. Leaning her beautiful cascade of black curls against her cousin's shoulder, she whispered, "I love you—I *love* you—"

Marvel put her head against Mary Ann's. "And I love you. Is something troubling you? No secrets, you know!"

"Oh Marvel, was it—uh—horrible?" she shuddered. "Seeing him—you know...?"

"Die?" Marvel said gently. "Don't be afraid. I'm not anymore. What was it like? It was a holy moment."

Mary Ann was comforted. "Oh, thank you—thank you. *A holy moment.* No wonder he loved you. We all do."

The wind groaned and pushed them back as if to force them into the place prepared for Frederick Salsburg. But Marvel was at peace.

# 3

# *A Single Strand of Pearls*

Telling Mother and Daddy about the events of the week was more difficult than Marvel would have supposed. Although each detail was recorded in her memory, facts sounded so black-and-white, so unfeeling. They were not there to sense the warmth, the renewed bond between family members by the passing of an anguished soul, the joy and comfort found in knowing that Frederick Salsburg had moved into a deeper faith. Joy? The idea sounded almost like blasphemy when spoken.

Also, two other matters were of grave concern to her parents. It was obvious from the beginning. Marvel wanted to comfort them, but there was nothing to say until she knew the problems.

Both were silent until she finished. Marvel noticed that Daddy was unusually pale and that his hands shook when he served her plate at the supper table. Mother kept watching him anxiously from the corner of her eye.

He attempted a smile as he said, "You must stop talking, torturing yourself. It has to hurt. Here, have some of the feast we've prepared for your homecoming, sugar. Know what this is? Fanny brought fried squirrel and cream gravy. I heard the bob-whites calling in our pea patch, remember?"

Yes, she remembered. " 'Bob, bob, white—peas quite ripe? No, not quite—will be tomorrow night.' My favorite nursery rhyme. Much better than 'Old Mother Hubbard.' "

Marvel could have bitten her tongue off. To speak of bare

cupboards was to pour salt on an open would. (Was it true Germans shared a bread crust?)

Thankfully, Daddy showed no sign of having heard. Instead, he said, "Let's not dwell on what they put you through. It was unfair. And you were to have a vacation. Daddy's sorry—sorry, too, that we couldn't get in. Oh well, the Works Progress Administration workers came and the neighborhood men pitched in and helped repair damages. It's fine now."

*"Everything's* fine!" Marvel tried to sound reassuring. "What I need is to plunge into the summer's plans: Bible school, community sings, getting Morning Glory Chapel shaped up. Mother, the home demonstrations will continue, won't they? And Daddy, you are going ahead with plans for the baseball games?"

Both nodded. It was Daddy who spoke first.

"Honey, tell us. Didn't you feel just a tiny bit angry?"

"About staying with Uncle Fred? Yes, truthfully, I did at first, but not later. He passed through a crisis in his faith and came out with colors flying. I still don't understand—" Marvel shook her head, sending her short golden hair flying back from her forehead where the curls liked to nestle. "It's incredible that this man should be the one to inspire me to think about good things—you know, such as we want to do while we are alive, well, and happy: giving of ourselves, working with the community and the church, making them come alive again. Even about our own love which makes a home, grows a garden—and Mother's flowers that give off color to colorless lives.

"And Mother—Frederick asked if you and Grandmother would play your violins at the memorial service."

"I'm afraid the flowers will remain colorless this year," Daddy tried to tease.

"Oh Daddy—" Marvel said as she tried equally hard to laugh.

"Oh, what's the use? Let's face it: The well's dry as a bone. Your mother and I are hauling water from the Bumsteads. Thank goodness, they seem to have an underground spring and let all the neighbors haul in barrels—even some for the cows, so far."

The cows might go thirsty? Without water, yes. Then there would be no milk for their use and, worse, none to sell. That meant no income. What would they do? What *could* they do?

The questions went unasked. Marvel knew the answers.

Either to change the subject or to gather more information, Mother asked all about the family. All were well, Marvel reported—

particularly Grandfather Harrington and Grandmother Riley who were well and downright happy. Grandfather was in charge of settling the Salsburg estate, whatever was left. And Grandmother was caught up in a whirl of teaching music and completing decoration of the church, as was Auntie Rae.

Marvel told her parents briefly of the role she herself was to take at Uncle Fred's request. "I don't know why," she said as she spread her hands.

Mother was horrified. "You mean that man—uh, Frederick Salsburg—had the gall to ask *you* to look after his simpleton son? I hope you refused. Why, of all the nerve!"

"No, Mother, I didn't refuse. I'm not sure what I can do or how. My guess is that he only needed consolation. But I said I'd help."

"How *could* you?" Mother cried out. "After all he's done to you—*they've* done, for they're both in on this up to their stiff necks. There's no way *I* could have—would have—played my violin at *his* funeral!"

How could she make Mother understand?

Daddy tried to help. "They're not stiff-necked anymore, Snow dear," he said. "What with Fred gone—humble at the last, I gather—limber-necked would be more like it! And Elmer put away in a padded cell."

"Aren't you scared?" Mother still worried.

Marvel felt suddenly very tired, limp, drained. They didn't understand.

"Not anymore," she said, her tongue thick. "Put your mind at rest. You'll need the energy. Brother Greer told me while helping me prepare the eulogy that he wants to get things going soon. And oh, I borrowed some books from him and brought some more from school."

Mother was still on the subject of Elmer. "Just what's in this for you? I mean, you spoke of a will—"

"Nothing," Marvel spoke a little curtly. "There doesn't always have to be a reward. Charity brings its own." Pausing, she remembered something forgotten. "Oh, there was something—something Elmer's father wanted me to have. I guess Grandfather will know. Daddy, you were going to tell me about the quails?"

"Whole covey in our field," he said with ill-disguised pride, "and your daddy brought down six! So how about quail on toast tomorrow night? We can be fancy-like in the sticks, too, you know."

"The birds are cleaned and let down in a lard bucket in Bumsteads' well for keeping," Mother said brightly, now that she was back on the safe turf of meal-planning. "And I baked bread. Tried out a recipe for soda bread—you know, in case we have no milk later. I'm to demonstrate the method. Look!" *Would the Germans' crust of bread be this fragrant?*

Mother brought out six loaves of sweet-smelling bread, golden-brown on top and, Marvel was sure, soft as a sponge inside. And there would be iced tea, Mother said, even if it took the last dime in the house.

"Let's look at the crops, Daddy. It's still light."

"Not much to look at," Daddy said quietly. "Cover crop failed. Clover wouldn't grow without water, so no nitrogen. You've heard of the so-called nitrogen cycle—you know, putting it back into the soil to cause growth. Animals eat and their waste goes back— Well, there's none and the soil's starving, to put it into the words of the county agent. Oh, even lightning can create nitrogen, too, unless disaster strikes."

"What is it, Daddy? What's wrong?"

"A bolt struck, that's what. The strike burned what cotton looked promising. Even the ground's scorched. Oh well, it's not worth hauling to market."

There was silence—a silence Dale Harrington broke with a carefully casual question. "Did you see Jake?"

Before Marvel could say she had not, Mother interrupted, her voice rising as it always did when the foundation beneath her home was shaken.

"Dale, put the idea out of your mind—about moving, I mean! That *is* what you were going to ask next, wasn't it? Ask if any or all were about to follow out to California to sop up honey?"

"Not exactly."

"We're not going. Do you hear me? *We're not going!* Say it, Dale, say it! I have to hear you *promise*—" Snow Harrington's voice had changed to a pathetic pleading.

Daddy's lips tightened. "I can't. I can't promise, darling."

And for the first time Marvel, too, wondered.

* * *

Chin in cupped hands, Marvel sat on the front doorstep a week later, listening to the outpouring of a Dallas commentator—and thinking.

The winds continue to blow, and "'Tis an ill wind that blows no good." Where will it all lead—if not to destruction for the farmer? And without the benevolent hand of agriculture, where do we look for food? With capitalism collapsed on its own feet, with traditional leaders to whom we have looked for wisdom and guidance wiped out, a big segment of our ailing country is looking for new ways of breaking the trace-chains of tradition. Sources tell us that this quest is reflected in letters and telegrams piling sky-high on the desk of the president.... Financial and political organizations must change, according to their basic premise.... They are clogging the horn of plenty.... Technocracy, supposed to increase wealth by substituting ergs and joules (whatever that may mean!) for good old dollars and cents ... shall we say dollars and common *sense*? Gone, and look what happened to the late Louisiana bayous' Huey P. Long ... sad.... And now Hollywood and New York are coming out with so-called intellectuals... dangerously misguided if well-meaning, who propose the common storehouse not unlike the Communist form of government!

Now, out in sunny southern California, where money grows on bushes, there's a man, an old frontier doctor by the name of Francis Townsend, who thinks the elderly should be protected—maybe even the entire country—by doling out several hundred dollars a month which has to be spent in a 30-day period to put our economy on its feet.... But the decade brings disillusionment as it wears on. We're weaker but wiser. We know now that there are the sly ... oh, so sly, who're apt to open their Christmas packages early and then rewrapping and putting them back under the tree, pretending to be surprised when the grand opening takes place. Beware! We have more to fear than fear! We have reality! Keep your eyes and ears open.... Something has to give.... Too much unrest overseas and we have remained innocent too long. Watch for the false messiahs... for they're closing ranks... Adolph Hitler and his alliances who would spit on our flag, destroy our democracy, and rob us of our freedom. There is no quick panacea...but the winds of war blow on...and on...and on....

The warning voice faded away in a burst of static as the wind tore at what remained of the heartland soil.

\* \* \*

Marvel had been home three days when a sleek, black automobile stopped in front of the shack the Dale Harringtons had called home since the devastating fire swallowed up the lovely old house which had belonged so completely with the endless acres of farmland that it looked as if nature had planted it there. One glance told her that the pretentious vehicle had belonged to Frederick Salsburg; a second, that it was driven by none other than Grandfather Harrington.

"My word, Dale. *Look!*"

Mother pointed a slender, tapering finger to where the Squire was helping Grandmother Riley from the car. Carefully groomed and leaning cozily together as they tripped up the walk (Grandfather was swinging his cane as if it were a yo-yo), the pair beamed conspiratorially.

Daddy laughed outright. "Now what are my father and your mother cooking up between them? Oh, for my second wind!"

Concentrating as they were on the older couple, Marvel and her parents failed to see that Worth Harrington and his family followed in the distance as if to give the spotlight to the driver and his companion. Then Mary Ann, unable to restrain herself another moment, darted ahead and bounded up the steps with such vitality that Marvel feared for the sagging porch.

"Marvel—*Mar-vel*! Come look who we've brought—I mean, who brought us! *Marvel!*"

Marvel laughed as the two of them embraced. "You're panting. You shouldn't run in this sun. Catch your breath before we talk."

There were hugs and kisses and then they all went inside.

They were little more than seated when Grandfather, after consulting the time in a grand gesture of removing the symbolic gold watch from his vest pocket (careful that all saw, and snapping the case shut with a loud click to make double sure) said,

"About time for the milkman's pickup and delivery, wouldn't you say? He does continue to bring ice?"

"Yes, Father. Mr. Bumstead continues the courtesy for those able to afford it," Daddy answered.

"Then flag him down and order! Treat's on me. I'm in need of some iced tea. I feel like I'm wrapped in wool. No fan, huh?"

Grandmother laughed. "Tut, tut, Squire. Just how does one operate an electric fan without electricity?"

"Of course," he murmured and had the grace to appear flustered. Quickly he changed the subject. "Notice the watch? It's still my mascot and a constant reminder of what it represents—all those rewarding years in banking. Sort of an heirloom, this."

Grandfather's voice held no nostalgia. He had a point to make, as was always the case when he spoke. Marvel waited, hardly breathing.

She was right. This was no exception. "Unfortunate, downright unfortunate that none of you would follow my example."

It was Uncle Worth who replied, and his voice was sharp—puckering somewhat like he'd eaten a green persimmon. "About like the electric fan, Father—a little hard to accomplish when banks are shut down!"

"There's another day coming. Give them time, Father," Daddy said quietly. Then he sighed. "As for me, you know I'm no banker."

"You've made that abundantly clear! But at least you've had the backbone to stick with it until it failed."

"It hasn't failed!" Daddy's voice was sharply honed. "Crops have failed. Economy has failed. And the land, like its people, is tired and needs rest, feeding, and restoring—that's all. And someday we'll do it. By jove, we *will*! Wall Street's saying that the economy's come to life and is progressing elsewhere." Marvel saw her mother stiffen.

"What do you mean, Dale? Explain that *elsewhere* business!" she cried.

Oh no, not again! Marvel had known from the sharp words brought on by mention of Jake Brotherton that her parents had had the same clash of wills about "going or staying" before. And it pained Marvel deeply. Mother and Daddy had always been so deeply in love, so deeply that they could weather all storms. Certainly a house (Mother's dream) or the land (Daddy's dream) could not weaken that love. Loving them as she did, Marvel knew their feelings, but she knew with a wisdom beyond her years that the trying times had worn them down. They must strengthen their philosophy of life, enrich their spiritual resources *together*. They were undergoing a crisis in their love. And in living, as in dying (*oh, thank you, Uncle Fred!*) with God's help and hers they could move beyond this crisis into a deeper love and faith. Long ago she had vowed to work her fingers to the bone mentally, achieve, succeed to help them financially. Now she felt responsible for more: their love!

Grandfather interrupted, saving Daddy the ordeal of trying to handle the matter between him and Mother in the presence of others. "I hope you'll believe me," Grandfather said to Marvel's surprise, "when I say that I take no pleasure in all this. You'll hear no I-told-you-so's. As far as I'm concerned, Dale, you've stuck with my teachings."

Daddy nodded. "Did my darnedest—oh, bad word! Okay, gave it my all. How does it go? 'Whatever your hand finds to do,' as I remember you quoted the preacher in Ecclesiastes as writing, 'do it with all your might.' So come on out and see what happens when might's not enough. If I were a builder, a painter, an *anything* tangible, I could point to my creations and say, 'I did this. This I gave my life to!'"

Alexander Jay Harrington cleared his throat. "You can point to Marvel. All these other things fall to ruin or at least fade away like the smell of a rose, the aroma of this morning's coffee—transient, these earthly things, but the human soul lives on. You've nothing to be ashamed of, my son."

Prompted by something greater than herself, Marvel rushed into her father's arms. "Grandfather's right, Daddy. You're a wonderful father—like your father was before you. I love you both!"

Grandfather rapped with his cane. "Come here, young lady!" he commanded. "Don't I get a hug, too?"

Marvel felt a soaring of her spirit. The sun could explode and destroy the planet... earth might fade away... the pyramids, the Alps... did it matter? Love was stronger than death. The Lord said so.

"Hello over there!" Grandmother called out. "What's with you three? One minute somber, the next embracing with heads in the clouds. Talking about war and peace, I wager. Get going, you fellows, if you're foolish enough to brave this sun—"

They were—father and his two sons.

"I guess we'd better prepare to feed them," Mother said, obviously regretting her hasty words.

Auntie Rae laughed. "Why?" she asked with a twinkle.

"We brought some things. Girls, will you bring them in?" Grandmother asked.

"Honestly, Mother, you don't have to unload your larder when you come here. We—we have *some* food left—like leftover quail, soda bread—"

The three women turned to go into the little lean-to kitchen. On the way Grandmother leaned down to whisper in Marvel's ear. "I need to talk to you—hear all about this young man of yours. The Gilbreaths called on Fred when they heard of his illness—you know, Erlene's folks. She is the girl who wanted you to wear her blue dress?"

Marvel nodded quickly, feeling a little uneasy.

Grandmother seemed to understand and kept her voice low. "They were friends—the men grew up together. She—Erlene— is the one who said there was a young man. Now don't be upset with her. Be glad! That young lady's responsible for the gift Frederick left for you. I'd better go—"

Marvel knew by Mary Ann's face that she'd overheard. A little information's a dangerous thing. Her cousin would make too much of this.

Too much? Not really. Nothing could exaggerate the deep feelings in her heart for Titus. It was only that Marvel wasn't ready to share what they had together. Suddenly she felt frightened and insecure. What *did* they have? Just a procession of now-silent ghosts of the past, memories which would fade like the fragrances Grandfather mentioned . . . voices blown away by the wind? The wind, always the wind! It did such cruel, senseless things . . . was so unjust. . . .

Mary Ann surprised her, however. Knowing that their time together was limited, she plunged in to tell about Jake—Jake and Archie! Jake had taken a job with Archie in his repair shop, after all. Wasn't that grand? He insisted that it was only a temporary measure, but who knew? Maybe he's come to his senses and will stay put . . . forget about banking . . . and certainly forget about going to California to make money like their Uncle Alex Jr. and

Jake's Uncle Russ. Not that he ever really planned to go, but there was no real depression there. Things would grow. There was no talk of the Dust Bowl's swallowing up the land like there was here.

Mary Ann stopped suddenly. "You knew Uncle Emory and Uncle Joseph are making sounds about California, I guess? They're as loony as our grandfather about banking. In a way, Daddy is, too—only he wants to shelf his dreams, be realistic, feed us, then one day— Oh, Marvel, he wants to start his own bank. That way Jake could go back to banking, too."

Marvel opened the door for the still-talking Mary Ann. "I understand. That's how Daddy feels about farming, you know. Here, let me take the chocolate cake. Yummy!" Holding the giant layer cake, Marvel saw it as an excuse to get inside, away from probing questions.

"Frosting's melting," she said and turned to hurry away.

Mary Ann stopped her. "Wait! I have a pie—and a question What were you about to say?"

"Just that I want you to finish school. And Mary Ann, tell me if I'm out of order, but I beg you to encourage Jake to finish. Please?"

"I will—oh, I will! The county made some sort of deal with the state and bought a broken-down rig for the bus—gave Jake and Archie a chance to fix it. It's great! I promise, yes, we'll both go on to school now. Daddy'll tell Uncle Dale, but he's not proud—you know, like the other uncles. Daddy's gonna drive the bus! Anything'll help."

Marvel was surprised and pleased, but baking under the merciless sun. "We *must* get inside. They're calling—all ready for iced tea!"

Mary Ann followed her. "Marvel," she whispered at the door, "won't you change your mind and think about Archie? He's crazy about you and—"

"No Mary Ann," Marvel said, opening the screen door. "I'll tell you the rest—you heard some. But after experiencing the real thing, I'd never ever accept a pale imitation. It's serious, truly."

At dinner, talk of Frederick's will dominated the conversation: his bequest to the church, gift of the automobile to Grandfather, and some details they would discuss later—but first, a letter and a gift for Marvel. She accepted both without words. She must wait.

Alone, she saw a breathtakingly lovely single strand of pearls. Titus would love them. Pearls meant so much to the two of them. Erlene's strand had been borrowed for ushering at his graduation—the first jewels Titus had ever seen Marvel wear. They were the first she had ever worn, actually. And what evening could have been more appropriate than for their good-bye? Even the winds took on new meaning, she thought, remembering fragments of Titus' words in treasured moments together:

"I know the winds are sweeping away our soil, but they swept you into my arms—well, not quite, but into my life—"

"A grain of sand can produce a pearl, so my science teacher says. That would be in an oyster, which is a good description for my eyes in this wind. Look at me, Marvel—turn those Harrington-blue eyes toward me and tell me whether you see tears or pearls."

Pearls meant so much to Grandmother, too. The rope she wore was an heirloom, passed from the preceding generation. True virtue was a woman's jewel, she said, and all other ornamentation must have meaning or it is vanity. "Oh!" the Grand Duchess had said, "I love the Mier pearls."

Grandmother Riley was right, of course. Who could afford the price of pearls, even cultured ones (and most certainly not *real* ones)? Imitations? Forget it!

No, pearls would not bring tears....

# 4

# Black Sunday's Aftermath

Mother and Daddy had managed to settle their differences, as far as Marvel could tell. Mother was back to singing or humming as she went about her work, something Marvel had missed greatly but attributed to the heat. She knew differently now that Daddy had called attention to the silver-flute voice coming from the airless kitchen.

"Poor sweetheart," Daddy said in a voice that spelled love, "how can she find the strength to sing in this heat? Had to close and lock that little window to keep this pesky dust out. It's covering everything, including what's left of the crops—precious little left."

"The corn looks good, Daddy, in spite of the stuff. Where on earth is the dust coming from? It's red, actually red—and there's nothing in our soil like it. Daddy, *look!*"

Her father was already looking—looking east. Where the sun had been there was now a looming cloud of strangely mixed colors: red, gray, brown, and near-black. Swirling, writhing as if in pain, the frightening formation commenced to darken the world around them, pen them in, make them prisoners. The winds were suddenly blowing from the four corners of the earth. Surely this was the end of the world!

Mother rushed from the kitchen to be with her family. "We'll be buried alive, Dale. What's happening? *Oh, dear Lord, please—please give us another chance!*" Mother cried in anguish, then dropped to her knees in the middle of the slanting floor of the living room.

Daddy moved quickly to kneel by her side, murmuring a prayer himself while trying to comfort the woman he loved. "Marvel, honey," he said without lifting his head "turn on the radio. See if you can find out what—what this is—what we can do."

Marvel hurried to do his bidding, glancing out the window on her way in time to see the worn canvas over the water barrel ripped apart. Water would be sucked up and replaced by the foreign dirt in no time at all. And oh, was there a cover over the Bumstead well? As she turned the "on" knob, not really expecting to hear anything above the static created by the howl of the wind, it occurred to her for the first time that as this filthy, destructive soil was deposited hazardously to smother all life in this part of the world, their own soil would be stolen away. Then there would be nothing—nothing at all. Oh, how horrible! But if God would only spare human life, not only within this house, but all around them—

There her thinking stopped. Had there been a faint sound on the radio? Pressing her right ear to the cabinet, she lifted a finger in a plea for silence from her parents. And then, closing her eyes, she concentrated with all her might. Again, the sound. Words! Above the crackling static, she heard:

> And so, in the face of this emergency . . . we have with us . . . Doctor . . . (A second voice took over.) The winds have hit . . . after years of drought and predictions . . . Black Sunday has arrived . . . the day which brought them all together . . . which will go down in infamy. . . . Struck Texas . . . those in Panhandle hit first . . . traveling east. . . . Wind blows one way, bringing the dark dust of Oklahoma . . . from another, gray dust . . . from wiped-out Kan-sas . . . still another way . . . brown dust . . . Colorado . . . fourth direction . . . brick-red. . . . New Mexico. East Texas storms'll bury us alive . . . town blackened . . . winds may lay . . . other storms . . . follow. . . . Heartland destroyed . . . gone forever. . . . Concern's with people . . . lights for safety . . . takin' care no fires . . . one smothering storm coattailin' the other.

... I beg ... *plead* ... board windows ... wear masks ...
wet towel'll do ... or die ... suf-fo-cate ... already tragedy! Huddle ... tightest room ... rolling black smoke ...
*deadly*.... Get—in—storm cellar—*now*—if one ... is
... close ... *Now*!

As the warning voice grew weaker and then faded, the station
was silent, leaving them alone, isolated, preparing for burial. The
outside darkness had now crept inside.

"Marvel, Marvel darling!" Daddy screamed hoarsely only to be
caught in a spasm of coughing. "S-st-storm c-c-cel-lar—on-ly
h-h-ho-hope—!"

Marvel ran blindly through the total darkness, feeling her way
toward the voice, and found its owner!

"Daddy—Daddy—" she stopped to cover her face with her
hands, letting the words sift through her fingers. "Mother—is
she?"

"All—right—must—crawl—blinded—"

"The cellar—we must get there. Hurry!" Marvel gasped,
releasing one of her hands to feel for the lantern to the right of
the front door. She found it and, with a silent prayer, felt along the
rough boards for the tin box of stick matches on the wall. There!

Now, if they could only push open the door, link arms for
strength, and remember to turn left, Marvel felt that the three of
them could find the door to the underground cellar. Her parents
had the same idea, and her prayers were answered. Daddy grabbed
the latch, pulled mother behind him, and managed to communicate that she was to put her arms about his waist. Marvel
followed to wind her own arms about Mother. Then with super-
human strength, they began their war against nature. But tug as
they would, they were unable to budge the heavy door.

The wind shrieked like a banshee, tearing at their clothing,
sucking away their very breaths. They were helpless against its
force.

Then came the miracle! Marvel felt two strong arms fold about
her and sensed rather than saw others push past her to help
Daddy. *Oh, praise the Lord. The bottomland folk!*

The wind, seeming to know it was losing the battle (although
it would win the war), grew hoarse in its fury of defeat. The heavy
door yielded to the strength of man in his primitive urge for

survival, and from below came the welcome dank smell of damp earth, its cooling breath whispering a welcome. Hurriedly, they helped one another descend.

It was dangerous to strike a match there underground where gases, in their raw state of combustion, tended to create a hazard in their rush to escape the area of high concentration. Daddy, in more teasing moments than these, called the process "coming up for air." Well, neither the toxic fumes nor the occupants could come up for air now. And so, without complaint, they felt their way to the side benches and sat down.

Casper, too old to whimper now, he said, gripped Marvel's hand—and someone else's she suspected, on his other side. "Couldn' us sang sump'n purty?"

"Of course, we can sing—if the rest of you want to."

Fanny laughed softly in the dark. "Ah—I'm thinkin' the boy's plenty able to talk bettah—better when he goes askin' favors of you white folks."

"How about it, Casper?"

"Yessum, Missy Marvel, I kin—can—ah'm able as can be."

"Something happy—oh *please*, something happy!" Mother's voice, though low, held the sharp edge of impending hysteria.

"I agree," Marvel said hastily. "You choose, Mother—something we all know. You lead and we'll follow!"

"We'll raise the roof!" Daddy said happily.

And, they were to agree later, maybe they did.

> Hap-py day, hap-py day, when Jesus washed—
> My sins away!
> He taught me how—to watch and pray—
> And live re-joic-ing ev-ery day.

Mother had forgotten her fears. She sang out in her angel-sweet voice and the resonant, poignantly beautiful voices of the incurably happy black people joined in what Snow Harrington liked to call her unending song.

Only the song did end.

There was a roar that set the world trembling as if a heavily loaded freight train had lumbered over the mound of earth under which the group had sought refuge. As if unable to make the grade, the object paused, then with renewed fury pried beneath the heavy cellar door, lifted it like a plaything, and hurled the slivered remains high into the layers of evil darkness overhead.

Nobody need be told that the winds had collided, twisting into a funnel cloud. A tornado! And with it came lightning which clawed mulberry streaks from horizon to horizon, striking wherever its deadly arc ended. The tornado roared away with its burden of everything in its path—except the wind. And now came the aftermath, the winds trailing behind their founding father.

"Link arms—*now*. Hold each other *tight—tight*—or we'll all be sucked out—" Dale Harrington ordered.

Arms linked, they dropped to their knees on the bare floor and, with heads tucked, curled themselves into egg shapes and bent low. The wind, finding nothing to take with it, moved on. The crisis was past.

There was a moment of awed silence followed by a chorus of prayers to thank God for their safety. It was then that Mother cried out in sudden anguish, "The *house*! My *violin*!"

*My pearls*, Marvel thought but did not say aloud. Precious as they were to her, she was glad for her silence when Daddy said, "My foot!"

"A-man, a-man, Massy—y'all white bruders dun see de light!" the black preacher of the bottomlands shouted.

Old Ned spoke for the first time. "Ebben ah heered dat, li'l chil'runs—'nudder dem scary marcles de Lawd dun dun!"

Silence ruled again, except for what surely was the centurion scratching his shoulder-length, cotton-lock frizzled hair and Daddy rubbing work-roughened palms against his overalls in concentration. All were breathing deeply in preparation for who knew what.

And still they hesitated. It took Hezzie's back-to-earth take-it-as-it-comes to set the planet back on its course. One had to wince at the bitter truth of the penniless southerner's bitten humor. But his words brought laughter back to a storm-torn world where Daddy had failed.

"Ah's gotta tell y'all ah's mighty grateful t'feel dem bones uv mine, ah is. De Almighty He dun a-gonna keep keerin' sun-time er stawmy wedder. He dun knowed us'ns needs rain. But long as He keeps dem winders shut up, dey's tur'ble sufferin' down heah—'n when us'ns gits down to'rd dat las' bean, dat backbone 'n nable-place dey's gotta roll dem dices t'see which 'un gits hit!"

There was medicine in the burst of laughter, a purging release of tension. Added to it was the sound of a female voice calling from ground level. Fanny! Nobody had known she left.

"Come on, folks! It's all right, Miz Snow, y'hear? Your house—it's there just waitin'. Come on, bein' mighty careful. It's a desert out heah, waves and waves of pure sand—and more blowin'. Hezzie, where are you, man? Give Auntie and Heliotrope bof—both—a hand, hear? Casper's on top here. Stop tossin' sand this minute, else I'm takin' you to th' woodshed, young'un! Sula Mae, where are yah, gal?"

"I's heah—*ahem*—yessum, ah—I knows uh heap bettah, Missy Marvel. I'm here, Fanny," the girl said clearly.

Forming a human chain they moved out, crunching through the shifting sands. the doorsteps were buried beneath a drift. How had Fanny managed to find her way? The miracle was that she had and was now attempting to drag the survivors in with her—and succeeding!

Marvel felt a stir of emotion too deep for human expression. "Fanny?" she whispered and knew by the immediate presence of another beside her on the sand-dune-waved porch that this wonderful servant of the Lord had heard. Handing Daddy the light when he called for the lantern, she took advantage of the darkness—and wound her arms about her ebony friend. It was another holy moment, found in death and life and love.

The telephone was dead, but the radio worked! Marvel, in feeling her way through overturned chairs, by chance laid hand on its big cabinet, still intact, first. She switched on the dial and waited. By then the room was flooded with light, the welcome glow of Daddy's lantern which sent diamond-studded shadows dancing from the ghostly quarters of the living room and what Marvel could see of the bedrooms into the tiny kitchen where the sand must be heaped to the ceiling. For one wild moment Marvel felt like the person of Sir Bedivere, the one knight of the Round Table who witnessed departure of the dying King Arthur for the vale of Avalon....

The fantasy was wiped away by Mother's scream of horror. "It can't be—oh, it *can't* be! Dale, Dale my darling how did it happen? How did this—this covering of H-Hades get inside? You took care, did what the doctor said, boarded up! Then how—oh Dale!"

Dale Harrington put strong arms about his wife. "Sh-h-h-h, the baby's sleeping—see there in Sula Mae's arms? I—I can't ask you to understand. Don't cry, sweetheart. You're breaking my heart!"

But cry she did, her sobs now muffled against his faded shirt. "How?" she whispered.

"I had a choice to make—not easy. I—I opened the front door—"

"You *what*?"

Daddy nodded. "It was either that or lose the house if a tornado struck. And it did, Snow. The pressure's so great, buildings simply blow apart. Sooo," he drew a long, shuddering breath, "I took a chance—a bad one, I guess. But without opening that door, we'd have had no house left. Do you understand, darling—and you, Marvel?"

"Yes, Daddy. And Mother, we'll get this cleaned up."

Maybe she had promised the impossible, Marvel thought, as she looked around at the unbelievable sand—so much it would have to be *shoveled* out. Could they conquer this? Was it worth all the work?

" 'Course we will, Miz Snow, hon. We showed that bermoody— bermuda grass who was boss, didn't we, now? Y'all be remembering back on cotton choppin' time? We—" Fanny, bless her, talked on.

The radio had warmed up and a surprisingly clear voice filled the small house. Marvel lifted a hand, begging for silence.

The storm was bad, very bad...too early to estimate costs...and what's the assessed valuation on human life? That's the sad part, the tragic part... killed in the swarm of tornadoes...others struck by lightning...and so many suffocated we call those of you who managed to survive heroes....But survivors, too, have been scourged, torn by the sword of heartbreak...loss of loved ones...loss of livestock, homes....Even now, we say in shame that names of the poor who perished will be largely lost to posterity. We salute the fidelity of dedicated preachers, reporters, and photographers who, at this very moment, are out there with you, at the risk of their own lives... along with the lawmen who work around the clock to catch looters.... Yes, we salute you in your valiant attempts to bind up bleeding wounds, soothe raw emotions... capture the soul of the Great Depression....

Marvel switched stations, hoping to hear a weather forecast. The men had huddled in the sand-heaped living room to talk in low tones as had the women. She turned the volume down and pressed an ear to the voice box. The voice was fainter, more frightening. There likely would be more storms, all must remain alert. Texas had been declared a disaster area... help was coming.

But in the meantime, folks, you all have to look out for your own! I hold in my hand here a health bulletin... a warnin'! River floods in Loos-ana and Ohio bred mosquitoes... winds now blowin' 'em to us.... Get malaria shots.... Water's bad for fever, so typhoid shots are advised.... But we'll make it.... Oh, I tell you!

# 5

# A Fountain of Gladness

Marvel closed the book of Washington Irving's works and laid it on the dry ground beside her. The chinaberry tree under which she'd sat to study, although having lost two large limbs, had managed to survive the recent storms. Its lacy leaves were twisted into grotesque shapes from the merciless late-July sun and blown away by the relentless wind. Leafless, the tree could no longer live up to its name, "umbrella tree." She looked down to avoid the glare and half-expected her fair-skinned arms to be striped red with sunburn.

"Cap" Bumstead's well had tested bad. Contaminated, health authorities said. Someone would be over to treat it. That meant Daddy must haul water for three miles from Marvel's friend Annie's place. Annie's father had an artesian well drilled and the water was clear and cold—cold when Daddy started home, but the mule-drawn sled sloshed the contents of the barrel, the agitation heating the water. Not the best arrangement in the world. Oh well, on the brighter side, the Bumsteads allowed each family enough of their water to care for livestock and have a weekly tub bath. A sponge bath would have to do between times. Today was "bath day" for the Harringtons. Remembering, Marvel stood up, stretched, and picked up the book, preparing to set the tubful of water in the sun for solar heating and smiled in anticipation. A bath!

Strange, wasn't it, how one learned to be thankful for the small things in life when the large ones were taken away? What was it

Irving had said? Oh yes: "A kind heart is a fountain of gladness, making everything in its vicinity freshen into smiles."

*A fountain of gladness.* What greater goal for a heart? One could be glad about so many things. The winds continued, but the devastating storms were gone. The insects would come (a few scouts had preceded them, buzzing in to collect blood samples and found them rich and red), but the Titus County health doctor had come with his jabbing needles and vials of vaccine for inoculation against malaria and deadly typhoid. The prolonged drought had robbed Mother of her beloved marigolds and climbing roses (even the yellow-rayed sunflowers, sun-worshipers though they were, had drooped and given up), but eventually there would be rain and Mother's flowers would overpower their stalks in their desire to please her. The freak storms had smothered the tired land, but their house was restored to its former coziness (and in the process Marvel had found her precious string of pearls locked away safely in the cedar chest). Mother's violin was a different story, as was Marvel's long, unrewarding wait for the letter which Titus had so faithfully promised. But she and Mother must bear up, carry on, hope, and pray that one day their broken hearts could be healed. Maybe they had cared too much, forgetting that the Lord their God was a jealous God.

Accepting that, Marvel could find gladness in the fact that Mary Ann was coming tomorrow. So were Brother Greer and Mrs. Sutheral. In fact, the home demonstration agent would bring the minister and Marvel's cousin. And there was so much to talk about. Mrs. Sutheral was to bring the first copy of the collected recipes entitled *Stretching to Survive.* Mary Ann would bring a long letter from Clarinda Marlow Thorpe (yes, the home economics teacher, lent to Pleasant Knoll School by a government grant, had gone back to her home in the Deep South to marry her sweetheart). And with Grady Greer would be all the materials needed for organizing and teaching summer school Bible classes and holding prayer meetings for the "clean or the unclean," as Daddy called it—referring, of course, to the bath-night schedule.

Marvel inhaled deeply, coughed a bit (Did the human body, like the soul, ever fully adapt to the dust-laden air?), and continued to the doorsteps—new, thanks to a group of thoughtful neighbors. They had helped the WPA workers repair the telephone lines as well. In fact, most of the farmers had become a part of the maligned group, telling themselves and each other that they might as well since they did all the work anyway. Were they fooling anybody? Oh well, if pride meant that much—Then, allowing her own heart to mount the wings of a butterfly of fantasy, she let herself be swept away with the winds. Destination: the state capital to join Titus Smith.

"Lord, if I were with him now, I would be more bold. I would say what is in my heart, shed my false pride. But the time has gone. I am alone with my true feelings, and You are my only confidant. Is that the way it should be, Lord? Then teach me to carry on with a glad heart, and I will try—try with all my heart, soul, and body to do Your blessed will without uttering a complaint!"

The silent prayer was torn from deep inside her, and the commitment, added to the pressing heat and humidity, left her drained. But at the same time she felt stronger! She now dared look eastward where only the sun-crisped tassels of the once-promising corn were visible above the shifting sands. The government had sent snowplows in from neighboring states with more severe winters than Texas usually had, and the great red monsters had plowed through the sand to open the roads. They should have done the same for the cornfields!

\* \* \*

Mary Ann stared about her in disbelief. "It's horrible!"

"Yes," Marvel agreed as with arms about each other they surveyed the damages of the storm. "We're told the dust will blow out."

"But that won't bring back the corn! I'm remembering how lush it looked—and our grandfather's report. You should have heard him! He sounded so—so *dramatic*. Was it really eight feet tall with eight ears to the stalk? That's mighty big. And look at it now. Is there any way—?"

"I don't know, Mary Ann, about salvaging anything. The county agent's coming. We'll just have to see. And yes, Grandfather may have exaggerated a little—trying to cheer Daddy up. But it was unbelievably tall—tall and promising. Eight ears sounds reasonable."

Mary Ann was not to be put off. "But what happened? All of you prayed—you told me you did. Didn't God hear—care?"

Marvel took one of Mary Ann's sacks before answering. "Let's make haste—get out of this sun. And to answer your question," she said slowly, "yes, we prayed—begged God to spare our lives. And, yes again, He heard. When it's a matter of life and death—well, I guess nobody thought of the corn!"

Her cousin nodded mutely, obviously looking for answers that weren't there. The girls had talked about the unanswerables in life before. Mary Ann reconciled her thinking somehow, but she wasn't through talking.

"Let's not go in yet. It'll be hot in there, too—hotter maybe with all that talk. The sun—I know. I'll settle for the shade, over here under the chinaberry—two chairs, just for us!"

"I'm afraid the poor tree has little shade to offer, but there's the hint of a breeze. We'll try it. You take the green chair."

Seated, Mary Ann got right to the point. "Any minute they'll be calling us—Mrs. Sutheral to talk sewing and Brother Greer more lofty matters."

"*Lofty*—that's a good word. Brushing up on your vocabulary?"

"Oh Marvel, stop teasing. Mrs. Sutheral went home to Dallas and found a bunch of stuff at a fire sale. Lightning strike set the whole block to burn faster than Rome burned," Mary Ann said disjointedly. "And when I told the preacher how long I'd be here—well, he's putting me to work. So what about this knight in shining armor?"

"This *what*?"

"You know—that dream boy. Titus Smith."

Ironically, someone inside the house turned on the radio and caught a fragment of the haunting refrain: "... and stars fell on Ala-bam-a last—night...."

"Oh *Titus*," Marvel breathed almost inaudibly, not sure whether the words were for Mary Ann or for Titus himself, so great was the longing within her. Why hadn't he written, unless he didn't *care*?

"Letters?" Mary Ann pressed.

Marvel shook her head, then found herself defending Titus. He had a demanding schedule. Yes, he had a scholarship, but it didn't cover all costs. And besides, he had to help an older sister at home. That meant he had to work long hours at the State House. His college courses sounded grueling, and there were hours and hours of football practice, plus getting settled in, adjustments to make, all kinds of things.

"Never mind!" Mary Ann waved a white, lace-trimmed hankie in comic surrender. "I'm begging to understand."

"What did I say?" Marvel asked in surprise.

"Nothing. It's what you *didn't* say! Tell me what he looks like."

"I thought I told you—"

"Tell me again!"

Marvel realized suddenly that she *needed* to talk about Titus. Yes, she needed that very much. And with an uncharacteristic burst of words, she said, "Oh, he's wonderful. I wish I could make you see him—see him as *I* see him, I mean. He's tall—'way taller than you and I are. And we're tall, the Harringtons are. And the shape of his face—there's a classic look, good bone structure, nicely shaped nose, sort of patrician, and his mouth is interesting—finely chiseled but something more . . . thoughtful, you know, but with a smile always ready. And then his eyes—oh, his eyes! They just tell you what he's like, what a fine person: high morals, dedicated Christian. One look into those gray eyes that turn dark with feeling and you just *know* what his inner soul is like. Oh Mary Ann!"

Mary Ann was laughing—actually laughing! "Inner soul!" she gasped, holding her sides. "Oh Marvel, you're making him sound like an old shoe!"

Marvel felt violated. She stared at the other girl in dismay. Then from somewhere deep inside her a laugh began and found its way upward to join with her cousin's.

"Oh Mary Ann, you're good for me!"

The taut muscles along the back of her neck relaxed, and once more her heart was a fountain of joy.

Mary Ann rose. "We can go in now. You've told me all I needed to know."

Picking up the sack she had carried for Mary Ann, Marvel puzzled over that statement. The question must have reflected on her face the way Mary Ann spoke.

"You're in love with Titus Smith."

"Yes," she said simply. "Yes, Mary Ann. I am."

Without further conversation, they walked inside.

Mrs. Sutheral was spreading yard goods out on the kitchen table. "Have a look, girls! And you can bet your boots I got the

whole pea-pickin' stock for a song! Now look at this cotton print:
fade-proof—the best. And just this teenie-weenie water circle.
They had to call in the firemen, you know, and you'd better
believe those men are more concerned with saving a building old
as the hills than all its expensive merchandise. Patterns here,
notions— I sound like a peddler just opening his pack, don't I?
Now you three may take what you need, then I have more in the
mother-in-law's seat—"

"The *what*?" It was good to see Mother laughing.

"Sorry about that. The silly word just slipped out. I mean the
rumble seat, of course. And I was fixing to say that the rest of the
wares are to be distributed out here. Certainly, there's a heap of
need—"

"What's wrong?" Mary Ann whispered from the side of her
mouth. "Don't you like it? *I* do!"

Like it? Of course, she liked it. But there was something
wrong. Marvel could sense it. Mrs. Sutheral was talking too much
while holding something back.

"Does she have bad news?" she whispered in reply.

Before Mary Ann could answer, Mrs. Sutheral blurted out her
despair and frustration. "I hope, Snow dear, that you will continue to hold the ladies together out here. They'll need you more
than ever. There'll be no more food. Beef's declared unfit for
human consumption—meat from these parts, anyway. You know
what that means!"

"No more community exchanges—no canning in Culverville?"

"No more *anything*—that is, except for those on the relief
rolls. Believe me, dear, there's no disgrace in that! But you-all
have to decide. Nobody can come up with the perfect answer,
wrap it in tissue, tie it up in ribbons, and lay it at your feet. There
are caseworkers who stand ready to come out, talk confiden-
tially—well, so much for that. My job's finished, too—declared
nonessential."

"But you *are* essential! It's to your guidance we largely owe
our survival. You've been a godsend, an angel in the flesh!"
Mother said.

Mrs. Sutheral was wiping her eyes. "This everlasting dust is
driving me crazy." Then, blowing her nose loudly, she said with
resignation, "See? Even you are using past tense, and that's fine.

The girls here will tell you that the strength of a good teacher reflects in how far beyond her the students can go. Food? There are few surpluses anymore—few shipped out, anyway. Every state's so hard-pressed the governors declared state's rights to keep their food at home. Can't rightly find fault with that. Well, we'll eat *today*. Mary Ann, hon, you and Marvel run right out and bring in the sugar-cured ham the government sent out just before the storm. And your mother sent half-moon pies."

The news came as a blow—a blow that needed more than a bandage. Looking it straight in the face would take time, thought, and prayer. Right now, the girls shied away from the subject. But Mary Ann chose a more deadly one.

As they passed the storm cellar on their left, she said, "Was the storm very awful—as awful as in town? Did—did you go—in that place?"

"Yes, of course. Didn't you use yours?"

"No—and was I glad! I don't think I could have—I mean, after what happened to you down there. We went to Wilbur Benson's store, the strongest building in town. He has that powerful radio—and lightning rods. Uncle Joseph and Uncle Emory brought their families, but Daddy was afraid of the gas. Oh Marvel, weren't you *scared*?"

"Of course!" Marvel said, stretching her neck to tuck her chin against the top package Mary Ann had handed her from Mrs. Sutheral's car. "We all were. No more, I'm loaded."

"Marvel, you know what I mean. Didn't it bring back the nightmare with Elmer—when he caught you alone and—uh, tried to take liberties—then kept threatening—carried out some of those threats, too—"

"No—no, I didn't give that a thought."

"You—you can't have *forgotten*—"

"No, I haven't forgotten. It's just that I'm not afraid anymore."

Mary Ann slammed the lid shut. "Stay down there, you turtle box, rumble seat, mother-in-law's chair—whatever you are! Well, I'm glad to hear it, in a way. In another way, you scare me silly. That thistle will be back. Wait and see. He'll find a way and head for you—you and that string of pearls. You do know their history, don't you?"

"My arms are breaking—come on. But no, Uncle Fred didn't tell me what my gift was to be. The pearls were a surprise, and I love them. He knew that I wore pearls like that when Titus graduated. I—I told him. I wore a dress belonging to the daughter of his friend."

"I know *that* history. I'm talking about the strand that man—"

"Uncle Fred, Mary Ann."

She shrugged. "Have it your way. But the pearls are the magnet that'll cause you tears. He'll be back, Elmer will, to get 'em. They belonged to Fred Salsburg's mother and were for his wife. But you know part of the story. It wasn't a love story between him and Aunt Pauline, so she never got the jewels. Elmer would leave his grave to retaliate—"

"Grave?" Marvel stopped so suddenly that Mary Ann bumped her from behind, causing both of them to drop their loads. As they bent to retrieve the dislodged packages, they bumped heads, causing the cousins to burst out laughing again.

"Oh Marvel, I love you! You're good for me, too—so sober and yet so ready to laugh trouble off. As for *grave*, just a figure of speech. But you *will* be careful?"

"I will."

Mother opened the screen.

Throughout the meal, Mrs. Sutheral kept up a constant flow of conversation as if she feared silence. Marvel suspected the purpose was to postpone the thought of saying good-bye, but was sure the others appreciated the county home demonstration agent's news as much as she did.

Had any of them heard the heartrending story about the Arkansas family who walked 900 miles *(Imagine!)* in search of work?

None of them had.

"Oh me!" Mrs. Sutheral groaned, daintily blotting her lips free of rapidly melting butter. "Even the more fortunate Americans who somehow managed to live out this trying decade in well-heeled comfort have to be shaken. And to think they passed right through our town!"

"They did?" Mother asked, lifting her lovely eyebrows in shock, then spotted the pool of beaded yellow where the butter had done a heat-induced meltdown and murmured an apology. She removed the dish and replaced it with another containing a new mold she'd wrapped in cheesecloth and stored in the cellar.

Politely, Mrs. Sutheral had waited. Now she could go on with her story. "Poor folks," she said, "what chance did they stand what with all those natural disasters—floods, disease, hunger, droughts, and dust storms such as came here—to bury all their efforts? Talk about trying to eke out a living by the 'sweat of the brow'!"

"You were going to tell us about that one family?" Marvel reminded Mrs. Sutheral gently.

"I'm coming to that. Too poor to ride, those brave souls trekked clear through Texas, headin' for the Rio Grande. There was supposed to be work in the cotton fields there, but being tuckered out, they simply had to stop—just bags of bones, all three. The missus was pushing a baby buggy—not a fancy one with a top—and that baby was as red as a lobster's supposed to be, and dirty, whew! And the mister was pushing a wheelbarrow—old iron-wheel rig—with all their earthly belongings. She told me they'd been eating wild greens, violet tops, wild mustard, onions, and lettuce—then took to eating such weeds as the cows would turn up their noses at! He'd shot a jackrabbit and once *stolen* a chicken. But starve or not, his conscience just wouldn't allow that ever again. Guess I shouldn't have told that part, Brother Grady?"

Grady Greer inhaled deeply and shook his head in despair. "Don't you think the Lord would understand—make allowances? Your very story causes shadows to cross my own heart, and God's much more compassionate."

"I'm surprised somebody didn't find out and have the man arrested—probably give him ten years, while the only charges filed against Al Capone are dodging income tax!" Daddy said bitterly. Mother reached for his hand.

"Their clothes—what about them?" Marvel inquired shakily.

Mrs. Sutheral laid her knife, fork, and spoon carefully across her plate before answering. "Filthy, ragged, dirty—and just tops for shoes. Soles had worn out from walking. Why, that was almost a thousand miles! Kept the tops just to avoid sunburn. Poor man tried to find work along the way—something, *anything*. Offered to work free just so his wife and child could eat. And you know what some pompous so-called self-made man had the unmitigated gall to say? 'Get on with it, boy. Bend that back and pull yourself up by your own bootstrings like *I* did!' Well, the man made a pretty good comeback: 'Bootstrings, sir? I ain't got no *boots*!'"

"Yea!" Mary Ann cried loudly.

And they all clapped.

There were other questions about the unfortunate couple—just one of the thousands, Marvel thought sadly. In fact, they *were* fortunate in a way. They had each other and they found people in Pleasant Knoll didn't blame, scold, or look down upon those who were down-and-out and attribute it to their own folly. Everybody had tried to help, Mrs. Sutheral said—saw that they had food, rations to take with them, a chance to take leisurely baths, soak their blistered and bleeding feet, and get a change of clothes. Mr. Benson gave the mister a new straw hat and some of the ladies finished a quilt. And oh, she herself made the wife and baby new sunbonnets. The church was wonderful.

"You'd have been proud of that mother of yours, Snow dear. That's some lady. Almost did the Charleston shaking money from the pockets of the deacons—with *your* father's help, of course, Dale. I find myself thinking of them as a couple and treat them accordingly. Well, no objections so far. Of course, they have a very special granddaughter in common—Marvel here."

"They have more than that," Grady Greer began and then stopped. "Did you ever get that violin you play so beautifully repaired, Snow? *No?*"

Marvel was sorry the well-meaning man had made mention of the violin. It was once upon a time a priceless instrument, a thing of beauty, the pride and joy of her mother's heart—well worth every penny it would cost in repair, if one *had* a penny. And oh, the sounds Snow Harrington's tapering, white fingers could coax from the violin. Each time she brought the bow across the strings, Marvel thought anew that here was a genius who belonged with the New York Symphony Orchestra. So strong was the illusion, that as a small child she could sense the dimming of the lights. Why, Mother's playing could dim the very stars! And then Marvel could catch a vision of the wildflower blur of silks, satins, and priceless gems making up a haughty audience awaiting the signal of the maestro. Then there would be thunderous applause...and Grandfather's ivory-tipped stick keeping time to *Tales of the Vienna Woods....*

The vision faded as talk hummed around her. But Marvel would not soon forget it. It was just another one of the many things she determined to do for her parents. Daddy must have his land, complete with the great colonial house which once looked out on the shimmering croplands and deep-pile velvet of the rolling-hill pastureland dotted with cows too fat and lazy to chew their cuds. And mother must have her violin!

Somewhere Titus fit into the dream—Titus with his high, handsome forehead sometimes half-hidden by wind-tumbled dark hair which escaped its carefully groomed confines and his gray-turned-black eyes which, she realized with a sudden start, just as infrequently betrayed a strange worry. When did it happen? Beneath their private oak—yes, always there when they tried to see beyond the painful present or look back poignantly at their half-remembered past. What a responsibility the speaker at Titus' graduation had placed on their young shoulders. If they wanted the Garden of Eden back, their generation must find a way across the great gulf.

But for now Mary Ann was saying it better: "Sometimes I think it would be easier if we'd never known better—had always lived in squalor."

"Instead of having everything swept away—forced to migrate like the *Tobacco Road* characters, hmmmm? No—no, I think not," Mrs. Sutheral said thoughtfully. "This way you have something to work backward to, you understand? Of course, maybe somehow they'll all get back—those who want to. We like to think that. Who knows where that 'promise of the road' will lead, the world being round? Pretty true-to-life, after all, what those folks in *Tobacco Road* endured. More and more are clearing out, trying to find a place to start over, find a new life."

"How foolish," Mother said with feeling, "leaving familiar surroundings where people care, to become absolute *bums*!"

Mrs. Sutheral, little knowing what lay behind those words, laughed. "Reminds me of what our friends—the people I told you about, you know—said. He was pretty clever at that and said, 'They call us migrants til they're done with us. When we git sick or work plays out we're *bums*.'"

They talked on, fully aware that it was a last-time visit for Mrs. Sutheral, who had come to mean so much in their lives that now they hardly dared face the uncertain future without her sunny ways and help.

Ribbons of iridescent color cross-stitched the gathering twilight sky above the shack the Harringtons had made into a home.

The wind had settled in for a peaceful night, but the house was airless. Daddy and Brother Greer moved the chairs onto the porch for air, and there they watched in fascination as the soft pastels streaking the sky gave way to night's deep purple. The ugliness melted into the softness of the dark of the star-flecked dome above. Somewhere a whippoorwill called softly and his response came from a laughing owl who had somehow mixed his signals. Mockingbirds knew better. A male sang out a gentle love song and his mate responded with a sleepy twitter, but Marvel could sense a certain gladness in the bird's voice, a gladness to match her own.

The men talked then. How could it have happened? The richest nation on earth now accepted poverty as a way of life! Wolf on the doorstep? Few *had* a doorstep. Foreclosed farmers joined a legion of migratory field hands and drifters searching for jobs or breadlines, and bands of ragged youths roaming aimlessly, sleeping in hobo jungles.

But faithfully the stars twinkled on in place in the canopy of sky.

Mrs. Sutheral whispered in parting: "I heard about the pearls— and your young man. I'm glad!"

# 6

# Clarinda's Letter

Miss Marlow's letter—no, Mrs. Thorpe (Marvel would have to get used to that)—set both her own heart and Mary Ann's to dreaming again. Daydreams were more practical than those which came during sleep. Nights were too hot for sleeping and so dreaming was a luxury. Maybe daylight fantasies were better, Marvel told herself, for in this form of escape one could pick and choose the characters.

One couldn't have chosen a more unlikely spot or circumstance for dealing with matters of the heart, the two of them agreed, but did the setting have to be romantic for love to enter?

"We're out of mosquito repellent," Daddy said uncertainly, "but I need to haul drinking water. Do I hear any volunteers?"

"Here are two able-bodied young ladies!" Marvel said with mock formality. "At your service, sir."

"Those boogers have hit the bottomlands, according to Hezzie—said they came in swarms last night, so we'd better double up on the ammunition. They'll lie low until nightfall. Thanks, honey. Oh, the parson's going with me and we'll speak to neighbors along the way about getting on with the prayer meetings. You three girls," he looked significantly at Mother and grinned impishly, "will get a chance to earn your keep. Me? I'm going to spend my leisure hours playing baseball!"

Marvel's heart gave a jog of joy. So Daddy was going ahead with his baseball plans? Good! Marvel's heart gave another leap when her father took her mother in his arms tenderly to say a good-bye worthy of his departure on a lengthy journey. And he was on his way to a neighbor's to haul water.

She shook her head in fascination. "They're still lovers," she whispered to Mary Ann. "Wonderful. If ever I *do* marry—"

*If?* It was such a big word. Mary Ann grinned, seeing her hesitation, and Marvel felt the telltale blood rush to her cheeks.

Outside, the heat waves were shimmering across the foreign sands, searching out hidden particles to create a momentary illusion of sparkling-gem beauty. But the breath of the wind was feverish, warning of deadly heat later in the day. Wordlessly, the girls donned wide-brimmed straw hats and secured them against the hot breeze by pulling provided elastic beneath their chins. Then Marvel bravely picked up a burlap bag.

Mary Ann eyed it suspiciously as they turned toward the cow lot. "Just what is it we're looking for?"

"Cow chips. The doctor told us to burn them as a repellent."

Mary Ann stopped to look at her in disbelief. "You don't mean—you *can't* mean *dung*! How archaic! Mercy me, Marvel, we're back in the pioneer days when they burned that stinking stuff for warmth. And who on this scorched earth could lay claim to chilling?"

"Our friends down there a piece." Marvel nodded to the bottomlands. "They'd be suffering chills, fevers, maybe death if the caring doctor hadn't listened to their pleas. Even he said it was a first—and poor man. Would you believe his job's in jeopardy, too? Doctors have it rough like the rest of us. Nobody can pay, and this one works without paying patients anyway and gets paid by small monies collected from a government grant and a little from the county. He said it was best if we made no mention—"

"Of their color? How inhuman—not that he's at fault. *I'm hot!*"

"Everybody is, so get going and we'll talk as we collect."

"Now Marvel, I want to do my part, but I'm not following any cow around until she—well, dumps that stuff into your sack!"

Marvel whooped with laughter. "Oh, you *are* good for me. It won't be so bad. Head for the grove. The cows usually gather around the salt lick Daddy has down there for them and lie down and rest. Their waste dries out in short order in this kind of weather. There by your feet—that's a cow chip. I'll hold the bag open."

Mary Ann hesitated, then stooped to eye the chip before gingerly picking it up between her right thumb and forefinger to deposit it as one would let go of a fire coal.

"See? That wasn't so bad," Marvel said, hiding her amusement.

Her cousin glanced at the bag in repugnance. "Poor mosquitoes," she said, "no wonder they're repelled! You were going to say more. Did you mean the doctor vaccinated them? How on earth did you pull that one off? Leave it to you. Anybody who can get me into *this*—"

They walked on, talking and collecting chips, pausing to look up at the persimmon trees from which most of the leaves had been stripped. The few remaining, instead of their usual rich yellow, had succumbed to a dirty ochre. Marvel explained that here was where the black children sought safety from the doctor's fearful needle, but the trees, which ordinarily would have concealed their whereabouts, were of no help this year. The poor dears had no other refuge, and it was she who had to betray them. Then Daddy had to literally drag the men out, reason with them, and appeal to their manhood—say that there were times when "we men, who *know* we're tougher, have to prove it by setting an example." Did it work? Well, yes. The children actually saw it as funny until it was their turn.

"Then we needed a couple of bloodhounds to sniff them out, a block-and-tackle to bring them in, and six well-trained sailors to hold them for the doctor. They'd rather die of chills than by needle!"

"Poor darlings. Who helped: just you, Auntie Snow, and Uncle Dale?"

"Then those big, strong men who'd endured the terrible ordeal," Marvel laughed. "You should have heard them and seen them—screaming, scratching, kicking! The doctor said he'd need first aid when it was all over. But they're proud of themselves now—just as wild as quail when strangers come near. But Mary Ann, I feel so relieved, so happy, and in a way triumphant, you know? Like we may have taken a small step forward—"

"Oh, I agree, I agree! They got shots for malaria and typhoid?"

"Plus quinine which I see that they take daily. Wonderful?"

"Wonderful. And now, although I'm sure we'll both have heat strokes, I insist that we share Miss Marlow's letter. It needs privacy. Can you stand it?"

Marvel could. And there, squatting and fanning, wet with a downpour of sweat and red-faced from the burning heat, between a sun-reflecting sandpile and a sack of cow dung, Mary Ann pulled their former home economics teacher's letter from the pocket of her cotton dress.

My dear Mary Ann:

You and Marvel wanted to hear all about my wedding. But I could never tell all because either it was the most beautiful, wonderful, romantic wedding this world has ever known or both my heart and my eyes lie! I was married in that cloud of white, that breathtaking satin you and I made, Mary Ann, and my Jim said I looked like an angel taking a recess from heaven. Could be he's right, because the two of us made the trip back to heaven together and we'll never, ever come down—just do our business in the cloud-bank 'round the corner from our house. *Our* house, did I say? You-all have to understand things are a whole lot different than what they used to be. I mean, I guess it's the same everywhere; leastwise, here in Kentucky where us mountaineers live (some pretty smart ones, if folks knew history, but we're hillbillies to all you-all). Since we got so poor, young couples just keep staying at home—just build on another room and be a part of the happy Marlow clan. Makes no difference where we are or where we go as long as we're together—and that will be forever and ever and ever. (Have you guessed this hillbilly bride is one happy woman?)

Mary Ann paused to wipe a stream of sweat from her eyes. "I never would have guessed," she smiled, "would you?"

"Well, I'd have suspected. Let's be glad for her. Is there more?" Marvel asked eagerly.

There was. Lots more, Mary Ann said. Clarinda Marlow Thorpe wrote then just how desperate the economy was "down home." People were moving out, and there was a whisper of a chance she and Jim would join them one day. Could it be possible that this man Jim had known called Russell Brotherton could be related to Mary Ann's Jake, names being the same? Well, *this* Mr. Brotherton had bought a hops farm (Did they know what hops were? She didn't—sounded like steps in hopscotch to her), but the thrilling news was that he wondered if Jim would like to bring his new wife and come to the great Pacific Northwest where there was rain and gardens sky-high!

"Can you beat that?" Mary Ann asked. "But Jake said it was true. He scared me stiff doing all that silly research on hops. Do you know what they're about, those hop things?"

"Kind of. I think they ferment juices, malt beverages—and are used for certain types of medicine. We'll look it up. But why were you scared? Oh—that Jake would go? I think they depend on migratory labor. Seems to me the season's short. I doubt that Jake would be interested."

Nope, still wanted banking. Still, she'd just as soon he wasn't tempted with some get-rich-quick scheme. She still wanted that special wedding right here! Even Miss—*Mrs.* Thorpe—said to stay put...get their education...*share* that dress with loved ones. But then she wrote:

Oh girls, when you find him—that one God's saving just for you—don't ever let him go! Give him your heart and say, "Oh, my darling 'whither thou goest, I go'!" Meanwhile, *dream....*

# 7

# *Like a Field of Grain*

Summer passed quickly, but not uneventfully.

The mosquitoes came in great black swarms not unlike storm clouds—and with equal threat of disaster. So great was their number that their drone could be detected by the human ear for miles before they descended. The weary residents of the plagued area had already endured five long, grueling years of drought and despair. But the poisonous insects found few human beings as victims for siphoning red blood and injecting their lethal venom. People took cover, and the mosquitoes, finding the fumes from the burning cow chips unsavory, buzzed away to pester the livestock.

"Holy smoke!" Mary Ann said the first night of burning, then clapped a quick hand over her mouth at sight of Brother Greer.

But Grady Greer laughed with her. "Seems to me," he commented, "those pests are about as fond of cow chips as our city lady, judging by reports. Think we had better rub our skins with that stuff or carry a chip on our shoulders when we hold our prayer meetings and the summer revival?"

"Heaven forbid! Oh, there I go again. I think *I* need instruction more than the ones I volunteered to teach. I do want to get down to my friends in the bottom. But wait! That won't interfere with my helping with Sunday school. Then I want to sing in the choir. My land! I do believe some of Marvel's rubbing off on me."

Marvel felt a surge of affection. "Nothing's rubbing off on you, Mary Ann. It's just that thin protective coating you've hidden

56

behind rubbing off, exposing the real you. I told you God wasn't finished with you yet."

Her prophecy was to reach greater heights than anyone possibly could have foreseen....

The winds were as persistent as the mosquitoes and as damaging. However, in a strange way, they proved helpful. Having done all the damage possible, they howled remorsefully and gradually, ever so gradually, swept away the dust they had brought and deposited it elsewhere. Marvel hoped that "elsewhere" was some wasteland it was unlikely to harm. The winds swept the mosquitoes away, too—hopefully de-winging them.

When Mr. Inman, the county agent came, he showed the men how to salvage the parched ears of corn. No food value remained in the stalks, so why not burn them in the field, then turn them under by plow. Then they could smooth the land with a harrow and pray for rain.

"I can just see another field of grain—bigger, better—and the whole world looking to *us* for food," Mr. Inman said, a part of his job being to help boost morale. But that would do little to satisfy hunger right now, Marvel thought, remembering last night's supper of dried black-eyed peas at a time when green vines should be boasting fresh, green vegetables. But nobody had complained. Mother had said how much the sugar-cured ham Mrs. Sutheral brought enriched the peas' natural goodness. And Mary Ann had opened the treasury of recipes to the few the budget allowed and said, "Oh, looky—pea sausage! Remember those? Couldn't we have some tomorrow night with the left-overs?"

Oh yes, poverty was a way of life....

The corn was turned under throughout the neighborhood except at the Harringtons'. Daddy had volunteered to help Mr. Inman, saying he would organize his baseball team recruits as they worked and remind the other farm families when Bible studies would begin.

Now, with the cornstalks exposed, a frightening phenomenon occurred. The steady rhythm of the wind changed to sharp huffs and puffs, a pattern changing at intervals to whirlwinds which uprooted the exposed stalks and lifted them—twisting and writhing as if in pain—to great heights. The force sharpened the stalks into facsimiles of swords—weapons which darted with full force at all within their path. Fiercely, the sharpened stalks beat against the house and across the porch where Marvel and Mary Ann were watching in horror until Mother grabbed them each by an arm and jerked them to safety.

There, letting herself go, Mother whispered through tight lips, "Not only are these hungry years, they're dangerous ones. How long, how long, oh Lord?"

The three of them sat in silence, all thinking directed at the men working in the fields—especially Dale Harrington and Grady Greer. That silence was broken only when the men entered the front door. The three awaiting their safe return bounded to meet and embrace them. Only then did the women take note that the wind had lost its punch. And that meant their own fields could be burned that night. Thank goodness.

It occurred to nobody that the burning itself would create another storm—a storm much different, but much more pathetic. The flames leaped skyward in the airless dark and then, when a little lost wind blew in, the entire field burst into flame. When the wind picked up unexpected speed, showers of sparks flew all directions. Since there was no water, the entire family rushed out, grabbed shovels, and scooped dirt, setting up a fireguard against the spreading flames.

Faces blackened, hands blistered, and breath coming in short gasps, they leaned on their implements in exhaustion.

In that still position, they heard the terrified screams of the bottomland folk, mingled with hysterical prayers. "Take keer uv us po', he'pless sinners, sweet Jesus. Save dese bones an dis soul. Hab mercy, sweet Jesus—hab mercy!" And then the piteous moanings and groanings, followed by, "Pre-shush Je-sus, don' rain down no mo' fi-re fum heben. Don' burn up dis ole world. Save us, sweet Jes-us ... or iffen hit's dat debil whut burns thangs—us'ns *skeered*...."

Mary Ann was weeping. "Oh Brother Greer," she sobbed, "see why I must help them? See?"

"I always did," the kindly preacher said.

\* \* \*

Grady Greer had stayed with neighbors at their invitation since coming to the rural community. The Harringtons had offered to make room for him. They'd manage, they promised. Marvel had wondered how, but never questioned. One of her parents' endearing qualities was their ability to make rash promises and want them so much that they could believe they could keep them, never wasting time on just how they were to be accomplished—as if wishing would make it so. College for her was a prime example. "Marvel must *not* be taken out of school . . . never . . . no matter what the sacrifice. Marvel *must* be prepared for college."

Marvel had sighed, inwardly remembering that when they invited Brother Greer. She had been relieved when he had refused. "I truly need to get to know these other folks better. Nothing like an overnight stay. It'll pay off for them and me, too—make us feel a part of each other before we begin the task before us. Not an easy one, getting church going again."

Well, the time had come now. And, feeling welcome without discussion, the wonderful friend simply said, "I'll take you up on that invitation now, Dale. We'll all have to take the lead, and that means a need to prepare together to keep ahead, be able to put them to work, too. I have Marvel's challenging questions, have researched them, and have come up with some satisfying answers. Then there's a wagon-load of printed material Mrs. Riley and Squire Harrington collected—all new. They're so excited over this, as well as other matters—"

Again he looked vague and let the subject taper off. It was as if he knew something about Grandmother Riley and Grandfather Harrington that the rest of them didn't know. Marvel decided not to pursue the matter. There was too much else scuffling for her attention—like where on earth were they to put their newest guest?

It was Mary Ann who came up with an answer—a good one in Marvel's mind. And her parents would go along, forgetting that it would never have occurred to them. Didn't they always keep their promises?

"You and I can sleep in Gran'mere's house—you know, where she kept the piano? Nobody's living there. Right, Marvel?"

"Right," Marvel told her while trying to remember what was in the sharecroppers' shack. An old bed, she believed, a table, some chairs—furnished about like the three bears' house. But the place was in fair repair in preparation for Grandmother Riley who elected instead to live with her son during her short time out here. The day of sharecropping was over, almost forgotten, since the crash on Wall Street which left this part of the world reeling, and melding the population into one class: the class of the poor. Yes, the house would be vacant.

"Well?" Mary Ann reminded her.

"Sounds like fun. We could study, talk, have some privacy— and still be with the family, go about the work we plan. Let's do it!"

Only later did it cross her mind that the place would be layered with hateful dust inside and out. And by that time Fanny had learned the plans—Marvel never knew how—and, with the help of the younger children, put it in near-perfect order, complete with a few pots and pans in case the girls wanted a snack for themselves. Would they be afraid? Fanny asked with concern when they tried to thank her. No, they were not afraid, situated as they were halfway between Marvel's family and Fanny's people. And what was there to fear anyway? Fanny's answer was expressed by a roll of her dark eyes which made the whites of her eyes stand out so much they appeared to bulge. Having lived in town and associated so closely with all the Harringtons, she was much more enlightened than the rest of her family. But old superstitions die hard....

The organizational meeting for resuming church services was well-attended and the crowd was bursting with enthusiasm. Someone had cleaned the old building and, although Mother's heavenly-blue morning glories had died of thirst, not to worry! The lovely vines would reseed themselves with the first rain. And meantime, of *course* they would retain the original name. It *had* to be Morning Glory Chapel! Mr. Bumstead passed out the hymnals with pride. The donors were the Stamps Quartet, of course, he said—them gentlemen what sung like a heavenly choir. And they'd be comin' back, by jove! Keep 'em all happy 'til them rains come—and better be soon, since his well got lower by th' day. "But le's sing—good fer th' soul!"

They sang—sang to the very rafters that their sister church (with a bit of urging from the Squire) and the sponsoring church in Culverville had paid to have secured before replacing broken windows and the like.

Afterward, Brother Greer outlined the program, asked for volunteers (and got them!), and then addressed the congregation with a brief but graphic message, first allowing grain to sift from his one hand to the other:

> See these seeds? Sowed, they will sprout and emerge in a new image—a field of green which will whiten for harvest, a time for us to reap what we have sowed! Now these seeds can be likened to mankind—for out there lies our challenge. Like a field of green grain, the seeds will ripen with our prayers for rain which only God can provide. Only with the rain—our help—and God's love can they be ready for His mighty harvest. Our God is faithful. Our God is true. He made a promise and He will keep that promise. We, too, shall spring up prepared for life eternal—like a field of grain....

# 8

# *The Sound of Music, The Silences Between*

Suddenly the winds stopped. They would be back, everyone said. But they were wrong. And the silence the winds left behind was awesome. People had become accustomed to the winds' incessant roar, their keeping everything in motion. Nobody liked the devastating results. But neither did they like the sudden still, the lack of movement, their seeming inability to breathe without the constant fanning, even though the wind-pushed air was furnace-heated. The stillness was unnatural.

"Now you'll be able to go ahead with your game, Daddy," Marvel said hopefully. "It was almost impossible to control a baseball when it was pushed around by the wind."

Daddy nodded. "We'll start this afternoon—unless any of you feel we'd all be too tuckered out for prayer meeting tonight?"

"This outfielder'll be tough enough for both—and I must be the senior man on the team," outfielder Greer volunteered. "We'll stick to the schedule. Let's see, girls, which question are we on? Remember?"

Yes, they remembered. Mary Ann had brought her notes from the place the two cousins shared. She was on the way to work with Fanny's family and wanted Brother Greer's help on the final question. Quickly she spread her sheets of notes on the kitchen table and shuffled through them for the list. "You read the questions, Marvel. I've got a mess to put in order here. I started to say before the wind blows 'em."

62

"No wind," Marvel said, still wondering what had happened. "Here is the list: What makes the Bible special? Why is Jesus the only way to get to God? What is Christian conversion? What is the 'plan of salvation'? How do I become a Christian...Gift? Grace? Don't high morals count...and what of my good works? We've tried to review for believers and figure out answers for the unchurched and the doubters—and then there are the scoffers, I—I guess I'm not the one to help *them*—"

"God will take care of them in His own way. Our job, my dear, is to introduce Jesus to them as best we know how. Then, if they laugh in our faces, they're laughing in the face of the Almighty! What does He tell us to do?"

"Shake the dust off our feet. Well, that's an easy one!" Mary Ann said, as, papers in order, she placed them in her loose-leaf notebook. "This thing reminds me of school—ugh! Summer's nearly over, and much as I want to see my family and Jake, I can't say I look forward to that new school." She looked up uncertainly at Marvel. "You did promise to help me? I—I'll *have* to have you. I know I promised Jake I'd go, but I'm plain scared. Me and math just don't like each other. Math simply doesn't add up—"

Marvel glanced at the minister and laughed. "My cousin is saying that dollars don't make *sense*!"

He caught the play on words and cleverly tossed them right back. "She's right, you know. *Cents* make dollars!"

"Go ahead, share your little joke, you two! But stop talking about me like I'm not here—well, not *all* here. Now you've got *me* doing it! Where were we? Down to the bottom, aren't we, about morals and works?"

"Right on schedule," Brother Greer said. "I planned on summarizing (Oh-ho! *Summerizing*?) in review tonight. Stamps Quartet's due out here tomorrow night, then the next day I have to be on hand for the dedication of Pleasant Knoll First Baptist Church. It's not finished yet, but the Squire can't wait. They plan a *real* jubilee when it's all done, some of it secret. You'll all be on hand for the announcements and program."

Marvel and Mary Ann looked at each other questioningly, but he obviously planned to say no more on that subject. Instead, Brother Greer expertly shifted back to his original question.

"So, that's fine—and I'm looking on down at your notes, Mary Ann. Looks to me as if you're well-armed. Let's see," and he mumbled references to himself, "Hebrew 9:22...Ephesians 2:8,9 ...Titus 2:11...ummm-hmmm...and you'll want to go over the reasons people are lost: rejection of the Word, their stubborn refusal to give up relationship with the world and their own sinful ways, their deafness to His tender calling and refusal to enter into a love-relationship with our Father. All these other things come later. I see here that you've taken notes, have all the Scripture references to support your claims...."

And that evening, true to his promise, Grady Greer summed up the summer's learnings by posing questions and receiving answers which satisfied him. His voice was loud and clear without competition from the wind, and the words seemed to wing their way straight to the star-studded sky.

What was repentance? *Turning from sin!* Faith? *Turning to the Savior!* Reconciliation? *Holy togetherness!* Remission of sins? *Rubbing them out, forgiveness!* Regeneration? *Born again, receiving a new nature.* Redemption? *Saved by the sacrifice of Jesus!* Justification? *Man's repentance and having God declare him righteous through his faith.* Predestination? *God's eternal plan whereby all believing sinners are conformed to the image of Christ who purchased them with His blood!* (Holy? Nope, only God was that, but they'd learnt right smart!)

Amen...*Amen*...AMEN!

"And now can we sing?"

"Tonight, brother, tomorrow night, and forevermore. The wind's hot breath shall not carry our songs away, except to deposit them in the heart of some scoffer whom our words have not seemed to touch!"

\* \* \*

A new foursome made up the Stamps Quartet when they paid Morning Glory Chapel their second visit. An improvement, Marvel and Mary Ann agreed, when improvement had seemed impossible. Was it because of the short, chunky, dusky-skinned bass? Oh, how he could sing! When he sang of heaven, a listener was transported to that heavenly realm, saw its wonders, and heard the saints who had gone on before as they surrounded the throne.

And in sharp contrast, Solomon Cruze of the quartet could revert a person back to the flesh (as Mrs. Bumstead was to express it, turn a body's tickle box over) with that comical roll of his big brown eyes and a winning flash of his dazzlingly white teeth. "From pearly gates to pearly teeth," Mary Ann whispered. "I've got an idea."

Mother and Daddy had completed their Wednesday evening Bible studies and now members were reminding them from time to time of their promise of an ice-cream social as a finishing touch. They had worked hard and certainly were deserving. Some would go on to be very effective Sunday school teachers. But how did one keep such a promise when there was no longer an ice delivery, and no longer milk or cream? At the close of the concert that evening all were trying to work out a solution. *Another promise—and I can't help,* Marvel thought to herself, feeling the usual surge of responsibility—and yes, guilt.

She was relieved when Mary Ann tugged at her arm and said, "I want to get to that group—tell 'em how great they are. *Oh, yoo-hoo, Brother Greer, wait!* I need help. Hang onto our guests' coattails!"

The men waited, all of them smiling graciously. Breathlessly but boldly, Mary Ann said, "You were wonderful, just wonderful! Brother Greer here can introduce us later—tell you about our mission, whatever formalities it takes. But gentlemen, I have an unusual request—maybe the most important and urgent request you'll ever get. Will you come with us down into the bottomlands and sing for the people the way you sang for us? *Please*, oh please say you will—"

"Mary Ann! We can't ask that. I mean their schedule's so busy—"

"Yes!" boomed the dusky-skinned bass singer. "I was one of 13 children born and bred in the bottomlands. You-all don't hafta beg, missy. It's all right, reverend suh. I understand mah black brothers."

Grady Greer's mouth had gaped open. Recovering quickly, he made the introductions and asked if tomorrow night would be all right.

It would. In fact, the group was scheduled for Pleasant Knoll tomorrow morning, Culverville tomorrow afternoon, then back to Dallas the day following. Night travel? No problem, 'twould be cooler.

The date conflicted with the great compromise party the Bible study group planned. They decided a fresh grape juice and cookie party would be fine. They would meet at the Bumstead home (it was the biggest around since fire took the Harrington home), play some parlor games, then have a musical...you know, ever'body bring plain ole instruments: Slim Hibbard played th' banjo, Curly Blackstone, the git-tar, and maybe Miz Snow'd bring her fiddle?

Snow Harrington was every inch a lady, her husband always said. And her reaction underscored his claim. "I'd be more than happy to fiddle, boys," she smiled with only a hint of a quiver in her soft voice, "but—my vio—fiddle—needs repair. The winds, you know."

People were sympathetic, but Marvel was sure they had no idea what the violin meant to her mother. Now the instrument was stored in what her parents referred to as their "attic." Actually, it was a small section between the roof and the rafters of the poorly built house which had been boarded up. It was probably the beginnings of a ceiling, as the rest was unfinished with the rough rafters left bare. That put them right next to nature, Daddy had grinned. He made no attempt to finish the job. The place wasn't worth the effort—and who had money to buy boards anyway? When they needed something from the "attic," he willingly brought in the pole ladder, and dreamed aloud that one of these days he would bring Mother's instrument tucked beneath one arm as he climbed down. They would have it repaired by some reliable expert. And once again she would serenade the house, the community—the *world*!

When he talked like that, Mother's eyes sparkled with new light and unconsciously her long, artistic fingers moved as if she were hearing the music of the spheres and playing along with the symphony. Tchaikovsky's "Waltz of the Flowers," Strauss' "Blue Danube," Offenbach's "Barcarolle," Brahms' "Lullaby," Beethoven's "Moonlight Sonata," Schubert's "Ave Maria"...oh, the memories mention of the ravaged instrument must conjure up in the mind of Snow Riley Harrington!

They had floated away, leaving no clues to follow. Where were those beautiful vibrations which once strummed the hearts of all who heard? Where were those melodies now, other than in her memory? Must everything one loved break into fragments, linger momentarily to tantalize, then fade and die? Was all beauty so transitory: great music...beautiful landscape...the smiles of loved ones? Oh *Titus*...

Marvel forced her mind back to the present. Each day was sufficient unto itself. The Bible said so. She knew then that she would be going with Mary Ann to hear the quartet sing for their friends in the bottomlands. This was a big step for both performers and audience.

It was a beautiful time together. Solomon Cruze took over completely, setting the large crowd at ease immediately. "Greetings, yeah suh, yeah suh, we're bound on making the good Lord proud of us tonight. Can't y'all catch a vision of His black and white angels gathering 'round that great, shining throne? Y'all that see, signify by saying, 'Aye, brother!'"

There was an ear-splitting "Aye, brothah!" response. And the mood was set.

Brother Greer had joined the chorus. And it was hard telling who was weeping harder: Mary Ann or Fanny! Marvel dropped her head and whispered, *Thank You, Lord—thank You for this miracle!*

All were enthralled as the visiting quartet entertained. Not a sound came from the listeners. Were they so much as breathing? Oh, yes! When the foursome skillfully drew them in to sing along on the old hymns they knew and loved, they were carried away with the eternal enthusiasm and optimism, so much a part of their culture. At points they were out of control, some crooning in soft, mellow tones, while with eyes closed they swayed to and fro. Heliotrope toppled over completely and rolled back and forth on the dirt floor. Fanny, knowing that things could get out of hand, quietly moved to help the plushy-bodied woman back to the log where she had been sitting. At that precise moment, Casper came double-shuffling through the remnants of the sand. Overalls pulled mid-calf above his dark, bare feet, the boy danced in wild abandon in a real showstopper. He was the center of attention and he knew it. Grinning from ear to ear, he rolled his eyes comically.

"Get y'sef set down this minute, y'hear?" Fanny whispered fiercely into his ear. "Whatcha think yore doin'?"

In her embarrassment, Fanny had slipped back to her native tongue. Casper observed that, too. "Why, ah'm doin' uh holy dance, ah am!"

"Holy dance, mah foot! Showin' out, thet's whut. Gonna git dat black bottom switched. Yore whole hide needs uh tannin'!"

Sullenly, the boy plopped down, crossed his scrawny arms, and glared at his oldest sister in defiance.

Solomon, true to his claim, knew the ways of the bottomland folk. "Hey, small fry, get yourself up here and give us some help. Here's a song for the birds—birds like you 'n me. Come on, boy, y'hear?"

Casper's pout was over! He was center stage again. Solomon Cruze, shortest member of the group, stood no more than a head taller than the boy.

"Here are the words. Just once—Casper, I believe? Yeah suree—y'all listen. You look smart enough to remember. Here goes!"

> La-zy Bones—sleepin' in de sun—
> How yo' gonna git—yo' day's work done?
> Eber git yo' day's work done—
> Sleepin' in dat noon-day sun?
> La-zy Bones, sleepin' in de shade
> How yo' gonna git—day co'n meal made?
> Eber git dat co'n meal made—
> Sleepin' in de noon-day shade?

The two of them burst into song, the bass singer bending his legs to squat on the low notes and standing on tiptoe on the high ones. One by one other members of the quartet joined in. Then, at the signal, the entire audience picked up the sliding-note croon, slapping their thighs on the offbeat, minstrel-show style, their voices filling the night.

"I guess," Mary Ann said thoughtfully as she and Marvel walked toward their quarters in the moon-bathed night, "I'll never accomplish *any*thing great. I just jump into things—do not think, not being smart like you. You and Jake—you two are patient. Me, I see things as cruel, senseless, unjust. I—I don't have the words—words or the courage—to—to even help—you know, like you did—when he, Frederick—all right, *Uncle* Fred—passed from life to the grave."

"From darkness to life," Marvel whispered, ignoring the rest.

"All I can do is some small thing like tonight. And where is it now? Blown away—like the winds took the mosquitoes."

"That sums it up right there. Solomon told us that there's a purpose for all things. I've wrestled with that question—Mother's silent violin. It's not silent—not really. I mean, the wind stole away its silver tongue, but no power on earth can rob me of the memories stored up in my heart. I guess what I'm trying to say is that eventually the bad's swept away, maybe even some of the good—I just don't know. But I do think that nothing can sweep away all the good—"

There was silence, and Marvel liked its sound. It told her that her disturbed cousin was thinking—not about herself . . . leaving tomorrow . . . school . . . Jake. No, she was thinking about life—an exercise new to the other girl. Mary Ann was experiencing a kind of depression, but it would pass. In its stead would be a new insight.

Mary Ann suddenly lashed out at herself, as if giving one last gasp before surrendering herself as her own brand of instrument, an instrument to be used according to His will. "I'm not a good student. I'm not talented at anything—can't write pretty words. I—I'm not even anything to look at! Not drop-dead gorgeous like *you!*"

Marvel bit her lower lip to keep from laughing at that one— Mary Ann, the person she would most love to look like with that wealth of raven curls. Compared to her, Marvel felt her image fade into the woodwork—with one great difference. She no longer felt unacceptable. Beauty was in the eye of the beholder— and talk about transitory passions. Beauty came from inside. That kind of beauty lived forever.

Someday she would tell Mary Ann that the answers were as new to herself as to her—that some of them, in fact, had come this very night because of what Mary Ann had had the courage to undertake. But not now. She must see that we are *not* all equal or forever—*except with God.*

"It doesn't matter, does it, Marvel?" Mary Ann asked, and her voice spelled peace.

"No. And if you're through berating yourself, I'll say you left a legacy in the hearts of all who gave and received tonight. Love never fails."

"And doesn't the Bible say love's stronger than death?"

"It does indeed!"

Mary Ann inhaled audibly. "Oh Marvel, I understand, only it's hard to explain."

"It needs no explaining—just acceptance."

There was another silence and Marvel felt talked-out and grateful for the moment to ponder earthly love, put it into that context. Then Mary Ann spoke again. "We're almost there. Auntie Snow and Uncle Dale'll be talking about their evening. I can just hear the hobo songs and all that yodeling—a part of the scene, I guess?"

"I don't claim to know all the answers, but I'd say it *can* be. Fellowship's important—all a part of the broad word called 'love.'"

Mary Ann stopped suddenly. "Marvel, I know there are no marriages in heaven, but I keep thinking Jake and I—well, we have something lasting—that we'll be together. We're *so* in love—"

"I know you are. And who thought up the honorable state of matrimony anyway? Where did it all begin?"

"In the beginning, with God as the author, just like He's the author and the finisher of our faith. Only faith won't end."

"Neither will love, Mary Ann. It'll be increased. There! Daddy lighted the lamp for us—"

But Mary Ann wasn't ready—not quite. "Wait—I have to know. Not the answer, but how you *feel*. I'll come right out with it. What—what about Titus? Any word?"

"No word. Don't push it. Please don't. I told you not to make too much of him—us. Oh Mary Ann—" Marvel's voice broke.

"But I don't understand. Don't build up defenses. Say it meant nothing. I *know* you loved him. So, 'Better to have loved and lost'?"

"'Than not to have loved at all'?" Marvel finished the quote. "*Lost?* Nothing's lost. It's here—in the silence of my heart." Yes, forever. . . .

# 9

# *Good-bye—and Hello*

Marvel slept fitfully. Strangers stalked through her slumber and all the while she kept searching the crowd for a familiar face, finally admitting that it was no use. A sputtering noise followed by the howl of protest from car brakes jolted her rudely awake. Her eyes flew open, but her brain took its time. What... who... at this hour of the morning? It was still dark. Even the birds and the speckled rooster knew better, she thought, in drowsy confusion. Then, pushing a strand of hair stiffened by last night's sweat from her brow, she felt for Mary Ann.

"Over here—here by the window. Get up—hurry! Oh Marvel, it's Jake! And the best I can make out, that's Archie with him!" Her cousin's words were hyphenated with excitement.

Of course—Mary Ann was going home today.

The boys were apologetic. "We should have called—told you the plans. Only we didn't know until late last night—" Jake began to explain.

"It's all right. Nobody would've been home. It's all right!" Mary Ann insisted, her hand still caught in Jake's hand. Everything in the world was all right, Marvel thought in near envy, as long as Mary Ann was with Jake. Her mood suited the bright promise in the pink fingers heralding the sunrise.

Jake smiled down affectionately at Mary Ann. "I've missed you. We'll have a lot of talking to catch up on—in time. As to why we're such early birds, you tell 'em, Archie," he said, with a conspiratorial wink at the girls.

Archie shifted his weight from one foot to the other, sat down, and then stood up again. "Well, I—we—all us been busy as bees: me, Jake, 'n our daddies. Put us in uh gas pump, so we've got uh fillin' station, too—and business, mankind!" he said with ill-concealed pride. "Yep, I always said we'd do it—'n we done it! Folks ain't speculatin' on new-model cars. Up t'their necks in debt a'ready. So everbody's brangin' us their ole buckets fer fixin'—'n sump'n else! Sometimes they jest dump 'em 'n we gut 'em fer th' parts. Y'all git it? Me'n my daddy can jest about make up uh new car—fact is, can! Done it a'ready t'tell th' truth! Yore old man—I mean Mr. Worth, Mary Ann—Mr. Worth he's fixin' t'git th' new bus ready. Y'all know th' county 'n state's gonna furnish them buses, but they ain't painted—I mean with th' right letterin': Culverville High School, Titus County, Texas. Gee whiz! That man can paint! Anyways, we gotta git back and hep out. Right grand, ain't it?"

"Right grand is right, Archie! We're proud of all of you. Come on in for coffee," Marvel smiled.

They came inside, but Archie hesitated, rolling and unrolling the brim of his straw hat. "Not sure th' time, Jake—I dunno—"

"I insist," Marvel smiled. "You have to eat somewhere, and Jake should see this young lady of his in the kitchen, sort of test her out for service, you know. Anyway, Archie, the way I hear it, you'll want to see Annie—or is it Ruth?"

Jake, busy laying a fire in the little potbellied stove in the kitchen, answered for his friend. "Probably both—both are giving him a run for his money. He'd be a full-time lover if it weren't for that rushing business the man's built up!"

"Aw, cut it out, Jake!" Archie said in embarrassment. His face was crimson. "Don't pay no 'tention to 'im, Marvel." The look of longing in his eyes reminded her of the hungry hounds slinking around the shacks of the bottomland people. Her heart ached deeply for him, because now she knew how he felt.

Over steaming amber coffee and buttery French toast, the girls caught the fellows up on their activities. Marvel and Mary Ann had hungered for news of the family, but Jake and Archie teasingly coaxed them into talking first—while they ate!

Archie drowned his toast in sorghum syrup and asked for more. There was no more. Even the sorghum had failed, Marvel told him regretfully. "And as for honey," she said to Jake who was spooning out the last from a container the girls had found in the cellar, "I guess the bees have called it quits, too. They've nested somewhere else, I guess, left our hives vacant when some zigzagging scout buzzed in to announce he'd found the land flowing with milk and pollen."

Jake nodded. "Kind of like us, hmmmm?" he mused, blotting his lips with a cross-stitched napkin Grandmother had made. "You know how things are going. It's the vogue to follow the promise of the road."

"Don't!" Mary Ann burst out, her face pale. "I hate it when you talk like that."

Marvel understood. Archie had no idea what Mary Ann was talking about. But it was Jake's face she was looking into pleadingly.

"It's a hard pill to swallow, Mary Ann. None of us like facing facts when they hurt. But what are people to do—sit around and wait for a government dole from our already overburdened president? The migrants are streaming through Pleasant Knoll now— haggard women trying to beg milk to fill Coca Cola bottles they've found along the way, while their men ask for handouts and prayers—saying grimly that even a piece of baling wire to hold the junky car doors shut would help. 'Yessir, we're drove outta Oklahomey, tryin' for Californey, but I'm guessin' there ain't no hope makin' it. We're stalled, starved . . . 'n now stranded.'"

"Oh Jake!" Mary Ann gasped, tears sparkling in her eyes. "W-what happened to them?"

"Folks helped—or tried to. Arch there did the best he could with the wreck of car, but it had died of old age. They were proud—accepted a square meal and a 'grub stake' as they called what Marvel's grandmother led the ladies' aid group of the church to fix, then hitchhiked on, saying they'd find a boxcar on the tracks and sleep there."

"Jus' hafta look on th' bright side, my pa says. Them Oakies left th' ole flivver with its leaky radiator, busted winders, sawed-off top—'n would you-all believe no tars, jes' a-runnin' on them wooden spokes?"

Archie shook his head in sympathy, then gave his mouth a swipe with the napkin before going on. "Uh gift, he said—'n we used them spare parts. Like I say, just hafta look on th' bright side."

Mary Ann cried then, and Jake put a comforting arm about her thin shoulders. "Don't cry, honey—sh-h-h-h. You see, this migrating has nothing to do with you and me. Nothing—at—all."

Jake helped with the cleanup job after their simple meal, having suggested that they save family news until they were with Marvel's parents. Tactfully he'd suggested that Archie might have other business, to which a red-faced Archie had mumbled something about the day's being "a-nother scorcher," so he'd take care of that business quick-like.

"By the way, Marvel," Jake said as they walked the short distance to the Harrington house, "did your call come through?"

"My call—telephone call? No—no, I guess not. Mother talks with Grandmother, and Mary Ann with Auntie Rae. Now and then, one or the other talks to me, but—"

"No, this one was for you."

"Oh who? Who *was* it, Jake?" Mary Ann, a hopeless romantic, was unable to restrain herself.

"The call was for Marvel, hon," he reminded her gently. "And yes, it *was* especially for you, Marvel—some lady none of us knew."

*"None?* You—you mean this person called others, too? Did she leave her name or number? Could have been one of the teachers," Marvel speculated.

Mother had spotted them and was waving from the porch. But Jake took time to answer. "No, not a teacher. This lady didn't know you and was trying to locate you. I gave her your number so she'll be calling, I imagine. She didn't leave her name, no— But let's see, I remember it was Lucille, I think. Yep, that's right— Lucille something— Ring a bell?"

Marvel lost her breath. And worse, her entire body stiffened with a sort of delirium that translated into shock and robbed her of the power of speech and the power to so much as nod.

*Lucille?* Yes, she knew. Yes, oh yes. But why—what? Oh, could there be something wrong with Titus? *Oh dear God, please*, her heart pleaded. *Don't take him away, now that I'm so close to finding him....*

The trio started on. Mother was already talking and Daddy had come out on the porch. But Marvel's legs were leaden. She *had* to know more, any little tidbit, just as the migrants begged for a crust of bread. "Did she say—anything else?" she managed to ask thickly.

"No—well yes, she did say it had something to do with someone else. What was that name? Her brother, I believe. Sorry, I've drawn a blank. Marvel—Marvel, are you all right?"

"Yes—oh yes, I'm fine—just need some shade. Uh, Jake, did I hear right? Did you say the caller asked—others—other members of the family—and told them what you told me?"

"You heard right. Let's get you out of this sun."

Mary Ann had picked up the signal. "Marvel, is it—could it be? Then Titus doesn't have another playmate, after all?"

"Playmate?" Marvel said dully. "Titus—I never thought that—"

"Titus—that was the name. Come on, girls!"

Marvel's heart gave a jog, then seemed to stop, happiness overcoming her apprehension. So the whole family knew! Who cared? Oh *Titus, Titus*! For some reason Titus was trying to get in touch. . . .

Mother hardly waited for an exchange of pleasantries before showering Jake with questions. "I know I'm in constant contact by phone," she apologized, "but somehow that's not the same. I—well, can never be sure they'd tell me if there were problems— I mean real trouble."

"They're fit—believe me, Mrs. Harrington." He paused to chuckle with something akin to satisfaction. "Honestly, your mother's learned the secret of turning the calendar backward. Look young enough to belong to junior league—bright enough, too."

"I believe there are some other qualifications," Daddy put in as if angry, "like a New York address close to Wall Street somewhere, and having the leisure time of the rich!"

Jake looked uncertain. "Right, sir. But they'd miss out on a lot we have here. I'm right proud of my own community—well, aren't we all? I was going to say that the Squire's just as frisky. They're good for each other. They seem to share a secret, but it'll *stay* secret until they think the time's right. But there's some news about your brothers, Mr. Harrington, and their families— part speculation, other part fact. Or maybe it isn't news, maybe you know?"

"I know about Worth and his plans to drive the bus. He and I talk. As for Emory and Joseph," Daddy pressed his lips together so hard that his eyes disappeared, "I'd be the *last* to know."

Jake's face reflected confusion, and he stumbled on, obviously regretting that he'd brought up the matter. "At least you know what banking means to them—their life. I live with that, too—almost like the desire's inherited. But they—we—those of us of that mind—we'll make a comeback one day, if rumors are true. Only it's too bad it takes a war—"

"War!" Mother leaped from her chair. "You don't . . . you can't mean that! Our president promised—you *know* he did—our boys would *not*—"

When she stopped, too horrified to go on, Jake finished for her. "Yes ma'am, he did, but that doesn't mean boys can't volunteer. I'll just outright say it. Your nephews likely will be going."

"Duke and Thomas?" Marvel gasped, then felt silly. What other nephews *were* there?

"They can't! They're not old enough, and—there's—no—war—" Mary Ann's words, spaced apart wildly and without inflection, told of shock. "What—how— It's impossible!"

"R.A.F."

"Royal Air Force," Marvel translated, "Great Britain. But what about age and other qualifications?"

Jake explained as best he was able. The news was bad. They'd been listening? Admittedly, they had failed to follow it as in the past. The summer had been too demanding. They would need to tune in then. It *was* bad, and undoubtedly our country would get caught up in the conflict. At least his father thought so. He'd been in the world war. It seemed that the British trained young boys, educated them, *welcomed* them. There would be compensation, prestige—and preparation, just in case. . . .

Mother had covered her ears. The conversation was unpleasant.

If that signaled silence, Daddy ignored it. "Their father?"

"I don't know, sir. I guess you mean how's he taking it? I think his time's taken up with decisions for himself and your brother Joseph. They're talking about the big defense plants: high pay, their chance to set the records straight financially."

"Building planes, ships, and so on? But that means California—"

"That's what I meant by the threat of war. The plants are getting big contracts, training men. My father even talks about it, what with Uncle Russ buying that hop farm on up in Oregon—"

When he stopped uncertainly and cast a cautious glance at Mary Ann, she managed a small laugh. "I suppose *I'm* the one to shut out the world now, huh? Surprise! I'm not going to. You said none of this affected us, and I'm taking your word. You'll be staying right here—with me and," she smiled coyly, "my wedding dress!"

Did Jake notice the change in her? Apparently, judging by the look of pride in his face. He was proud of her and proud of himself.

"I'll never let you down," he whispered as if they were alone.

Not intentionally, Marvel thought a little sadly. Deep down there was a strange, new feeling. The serpent of war had invaded their garden. Were they able to look Satan in the eye and conquer?

\* \* \*

Marvel tripped over a rug Mother had braided as she rushed to answer the telephone. Her hands beneath the table where she sat making notes for tomorrow's new-school-year schedule, she had counted on white knuckles: one long shrill ring...two... three, then three successive buzzes.

"Hello? This is Marvel Harrington."

Her heart pounded with such fury it was difficult to hear the soft voice of the caller: "Marvel, this is Lucille Smith Taylor. My brother, Titus, wants to contact you. He failed to ask for your address, wrote to you once here, then asked for the letter back. Do you want to hear?"

War clouds dissipated...stars fell...and Marvel whispered, "I do."

# 10

# *Lilacs*
# *in the Fall*

Marvel stood alone at the bus stop. While disappointed that last year's line of students was missing—and that included Ruth and Annie, it was good to be alone with her thoughts in the still of the gray-pink early dawn. She wanted to savor the memory and the promise of last night's telephone call from Lucille Smith Taylor, taste the words, feel them tingle in the tips of her fingers, and sense the full joy she experienced when, carried by a rush of warm blood, they completed the journey to her heart. Oh, the joy—the incomparable joy of it all! Titus was alive and well. Titus had not forgotten her and what they had together. Titus would be in touch. All the sublimated fears, misgivings, and doubts which she could never bring herself to talk about, admit even to herself, faded away. Heaven and earth had become one.

Unbridled joy flooded her being. Marvel felt herself swaying with the song in her heart—a song to which nobody knew the words because it was as yet unwritten. With eyes closed, she let the music carry her away as if riding the wings of a butterfly...up...up...up and away beyond the planet's gravitational pull the melody lifted. At the rude sound of the bus' distant rumble, she opened her eyes, half-expecting to see the unsung notes hanging in the leafless trees overhead. There were no notes, of course, but the bright, happy twitter of the waking birds carried the echo of the song. And her heart carried its glory.

It was a surprise to see "Cap" Bumstead at the wheel of the bright lemon-yellow bus. Marvel had given no thought to who would replace Mr. Newland now that he was working with Archie, but her guess would not have been Mr. Bumstead. It made sense, of course. Now that he had discontinued hauling milk and cream to the dairy, he would look for employment elsewhere. Experience with the heavy truck qualified him for the long, tedious drive, and he was familiar with the route.

In her frame of mind, it was easy for Marvel to greet the driver warmly and offer to check roll as she had done for Archie's father. The offer was welcomed as Mr. Bumstead would need both hands for the wheel and both eyes for the road, he said. "Lucky feller, yore Uncle Worth," he grumbled, "havin' that graveled road. One of these bright days we're bound on havin' same done out here. Folks've got plum used to lookin' up when there's nary a cloud 'n askin', 'Thank it's gonna rain?' And I says, 'Y'all know it's gonna be one mighty long dry spell if she don't.'"

A 40-mile trip, winding back and forth and doubling back several times in order to be sure all students were accounted for, could be wearying. Had a wee bit of her reason for offering to help been from the remembered ennui? If so, she was doing penance, Marvel smiled to herself, by listening to the constant flow of chatter from the normally silent man. Of course he'd had his pipe then and, lighted or unlighted, kept it clenched between stained teeth, mumbling only an occasional word.

"I'm keepin' that truck all fine-tuned, ready fer startin' on a minute's notice. Guess all us is used to quick doles—never know. Just you wait 'n see. Them heifers'll freshen 'n that'll cause all th' 'Bossies' 'n 'Daisy Maes' t'give down their milk. Government'll dole feed t'go 'round. They gotta keep them cheese factories goin'—cheese 'n paster'ized milk, whatever that is, fer city kids. Shure thang, huh?"

The man drove on, little dreaming of the job lying in waiting for his "fine-tuned" truck—one which would jolt the countryside awake . . . make them see just how desperate the situation had become . . . open their eyes to gore such as they had never in their darkest hour dreamed possible. But for now—

Having had a year's experience in Culverville High School, Marvel found that registration and working out her schedule were an easy matter. She would take the same heavy load while reserving time to help her cousins—especially Mary Ann—and Erlene Gilbreath, whose lovely blue dress Marvel had borrowed for ushering during last June's graduation exercises. Thought of the older girl and the priceless favor she had turned to a stranger reminded Marvel of the pearls she had borrowed from Erlene, also—never dreaming, of course, that she would fall heir to an even more precious strand of the lovely gems. Did she prize them more because of the dying man's wish for her happiness— Frederick Salsburg, who never seemed to care about *anybody's* happiness, until the end? Or—and with the alternate thought, her heart began to beat against her rib cage like a bird trying to escape from captivity—could it be because she had worn Erlene's necklace the night she and Titus parted on the steps of the church? Marvel only knew that she loved the pearls, treasured them, and guarded them. She had found herself unable to wear the pearls since that night. When she and Titus met again, she dreamed, she would wear the blue he loved—and the pearls.

Uncle Frederick was right. The pearls would become more and more precious. Each day was another gem to be added to the string. The final two would be when she and Titus were reunited. Only then would their love come full circle.

Meantime, she must discipline herself to meet the demands of the day. Where *was* Erlene? Her name was not on the list Marvel had checked for Mr. Bumstead. She must check on her, find out what happened.

When the bus came in from Pleasant Knoll, Marvel was there to greet it. There were greetings galore from lifelong friends made there, but all the while, her eyes were searching the crowd for the cousins. Uncle Worth had alighted first, opened the door, and now stood behind it talking with Mr. Bumstead. Duke and Thomas came her direction, happy to see her and excited about school—or was it something else? There was no time to ask as Mary Ann and Jake were pushing through the line to where Marvel stood.

"Oh Marvel, I'm scared out of my wits. Even sight of that building scares me spitless—"

"*Beautifully* put, Mary Ann," Jake grinned, with just the right amount of gentle scolding to remind her that there were better words. "She'll be fine, Marvel," he said, directing his attention to her. "I'll let the two of you talk—in a hurry anyway to find this Mr. Angelo. Some problems in arranging a proper schedule—you know, one to accommodate my regular courses—college prep, required subjects—yet allowing time for his trades and industry class. More about it later. Arch is a no-show, but I can understand." He waved over his shoulder and hurried away.

Yes, Marvel could understand, too. But what did *Jake* have in mind? Surely not mechanics—not with his future plans, his aptitude?

"He's looking into accounting, that kind of thing. But I wonder—classes are crowded. Most students are feeling a need to make a living—same for agriculture. Then the girls helping me register—"

"Girls? That's a teacher's job—" Marvel said in surprise.

Mary Ann waved the matter aside, then pulled Marvel away from the lines of traffic. "Yeah-uh, yes—usually. Something new this year, I guess. Big Sister, you know? Oh, there go Cousin Erin and Cousin Lucinda—" she rolled her eyes and put just enough emphasis on the new title to tuck a giggle behind it.

"*Lucinda?* Since when... You mean our Cindy? And *cousin* yet!"

"Yep, I mean! Always a little uppity, those two—three really. But I guess Monica doesn't count—too young. When? You know, Marvel, Uncle Joseph and Aunt Dorthea both have illusions of grandeur—just plain snooty. You *do* know?"

"Proud—the Harringtons. *We* Harringtons, try to live up to our heritage."

"Come off it, Marvel! There's a difference, and you know it. Uncle Dale and Auntie Snow and my parents are so *human*—commoners, hmmm? There! See who's meeting said cousins? Their Big Sister, somebody important—and, mark my words, their folks said cultivate. There, I make 'em sound like dirt. And so my name's mud—so?"

Somebody important? *Amanda Cohane!* Yes, Marvel recalled very well.

"The daughter of that banker Grandfather had it out with—remember?"

"Oh, somebody Cohane, when the bank was going to foreclose—that figures. Look! There, waving at you. Opalene—hi, Angie—Clara Lynn!"

Marvel returned their wave with a broad smile. How nice to see longtime friends, even when they were on the run. "We'd better trot, too," she said to Mary Ann. "Classes will run late, but even so—"

Mary Ann grabbed her arm. "Wait! I have to know. Did she call?"

"Lucille—that's her name, Lucille Smith Taylor. Yes, oh yes. But we have no time now—" Marvel tried to pull free and failed.

"Smith? *His* relation—*Titus*? It was. I can tell by your face! Oh Marvel, how—*how* romantic!"

Romantic? There was no need to pretend. "Isn't it? Oh Mary Ann!"

They did run then, and for the remainder of the day Marvel was able to keep on schedule. All the teachers greeted her happily. It was going to be a wonderful, exciting, and challenging year—in *every* way!

On her way to the bus at the end of the day, Marvel slipped into Mr. Phillips' office long enough to exchange greetings and for her to explain her mission, which was twofold.

"Mr. Phillips, it seems that I'm forever asking favors."

"You're entitled to them. You're a credit to this school, my dear."

"Thank you, sir," Marvel said, a little embarrassed. "My cousin, Mary Ann Harrington, is here this year. Several of my cousins are here, in fact. But I'm wondering if I might act as Big Sister to Mary Ann? Are relatives eligible?"

The principal's brown eyes flashed with interest. "I see no reason why not. Actually, it's an excellent idea. Just don't over-schedule yourself in this, your senior year. You'll be kept busy!"

Marvel thanked him, promised not to overwork, and then asked in an offhand manner if Erlene Gilbreath had registered today. "Gilbreath . . . let's see, there was a boy who graduated last year. His sister perhaps? I see no Erlene Gilbreath. I'm sorry. I do remember the name—"

"Yes," Marvel said hopefully. "Yes, sir, Erlene was here two years ago and failed to finish. She promised—that is, planned to return."

Mr. Phillips shuffled some more papers. "Oh, here we are—preregistered yesterday. Yes, the young lady was here before and didn't do too well. Miss Gilbreath's mind was somewhere other than on learning. She was in my geometry class and lost no time in letting me know her distaste."

So that was it—Erlene had dared dislike math. That was the unpardonable sin. Oh, Erlene must be warned or history would repeat itself.

The buses were late. Jake explained that he knew in advance that the vehicles must be checked for safety after their trial run—new safety code. He was too excited to care if he had to *walk* home. He'd been successful in wedging into Mr. Angelo's class, and yes, there was every reason to hope that, after some preparation, considering his experience and grade point average, the teacher could place him in a part-time job. Mary Ann was all but jumping up and popping her heels together with excitement when Duke and Thomas sauntered (*strutted*, Mary Ann phrased their walk) over to engage Jake in conversation, obviously not intended for Marvel and Mary Ann.

"That makes me mad," said Mary Ann, her eyes showing it. "You know very well they know I'm opposed to that business: jumping into something as big and awful as *war*—something our president has promised we won't get into!"

"Mr. Roosevelt didn't say that, Mary Ann. Nobody could guarantee that. He only vowed that our boys will not be *sent*. Why are Duke and Thomas doing this? Has Jake told you details?"

"Enough! And they're *our* cousins, Marvel. We know their parents, too . . . just as ambitious as Uncle Joseph. Uncle Emory and Aunt Eleanore are social climbers, too. Oh, they give me a cramp in my brain!"

"Don't take it too seriously, Mary Ann. Let them go their own way. Aren't you taking it personally—seeing all those who leave for whatever reason as a threat? Trust Jake. He has a good head."

Mary Ann dropped her head. "You make me ashamed," she said remorsefully. She ran shaking fingers through her black curls, then, lifting her chin, looked long and hard at Marvel. "I should be gagged. I talk too much—but only to *you*," she said defensively. "Just as bad in God's sight, I guess. I—I feel like a hypocrite through and through."

"Because of your feelings? There's a difference in being critical and being a hypocrite. You weren't pretending piety out on the farm when you worked with Fanny's family, had the quartet out. You had a spiritual blessing. Don't deny the change!" When her cousin did not correct her, Marvel suddenly realized that they weren't talking about the cousins at all, true though the accusations might be. "What's bothering you, Mary Ann? It's something else, isn't it?"

"Well, yes. I'm *thinking* more these days—about everything I do. And Marvel, try to understand. I can't always tell what's right."

"Example?"

Mary Ann shook her crown of curls. "I can't— Oh, I wish I'd kept my mixed-up feeling to myself. I can't tell you—especially *you*."

Marvel had to be satisfied with that. Both of them had caught sight of Erlene Gilbreath. Mary Ann had met her when the Gilbreaths came in to see Uncle Fred, talked with her as the families visited, and knew about the lovely blue dress—and the pearls.

Now she was talking fast—too fast. Had the day gone well? No? Oh, oh yes, Mary Ann understood about dreading math. Marvel was going to help her. No, she wasn't afraid of Mr. Phillips—just math.

"You'd better be!" Erlene said gruffly. "I tried for another class—thumbs down! There's another teacher, yep, but Marvel can tell you I'm telling the truth. Anytime you fail in this place, you're doomed—no chance of favors. Nope! You don't just flunk. You're going to pay for it—take the same course 'til the building burns—*with the same teacher*! I'll turn my books in tomorrow. He hates me!"

Mary Ann laughed heartily. "Oh Erlene! You sound like Billy Joe when he wanted me to come home this summer. Kept calling to say he thought Mother had dropsy—she kept dropping everything! Daddy looked 'dross,' and he'd heard a man-eating rhino was wandering around. They could all be swallowed up. Gran' mere? Close to death—no, not sick, but wouldn't make it if she dropped dead, would she? If I wanted to see them alive—"

The three of them were laughing when the buses pulled up to the curb. Erlene would be back, but what about Mary Ann? Something troubled her *deeply*. As she rode home, Marvel was still disturbed. When Marvel walked in the door, Mother told her there was a package for her. A package? That was strange, but it served to rechannel her thoughts.

Without looking at the return address, Marvel tore off the wrapping with Mother and Daddy leaning over her shoulder. And when the exquisite stationery fluttered from beneath its satin ribbon like thistledown, they gasped in admiration with her. Oh, how beautiful! And when she pressed a near-transparent sheet to her face, there came a faint scent of lilacs—lilacs in the fall! The stationery came from the newspaper, Daddy said. To Marvel, it was a paper bridge to springtime—and Titus.

# 11

# *Life's Deeper Meaning*

The next two weeks were trying. Marvel adjusted quickly to her schedule, but there were so many other demands. Having promised both Mary Ann and Erlene that she would help them through geometry, they must head her priority list. Right away she saw that the other two girls depended on her completely. And she must set up a program with proper study habits or they would find themselves too far behind to meet Mr. Phillips' expectations. Checking her schedule, she found a ten-minute module of time during their common noon hour and alerted them. Mary Ann fumed. She had planned on a sack lunch with Jake. Oh well, she could spare *one* day, she conceded. Erlene, still too frightened to believe in herself, said this whole thing was ridiculous. Why, she didn't even know her multiplication tables. "Then *learn* them!" Marvel had ordered. "I warned you that we'd have to do this by rote."

"You're sounding more and more like a *teacher*," Erlene said gruffly, but with a hint of admiration.

"I'm *feeling* like one," Marvel said, realizing suddenly that it was true—and liking the feel of it.

Then teachers closed in around her. Marvel must remember that she would be in the senior division in all county meet events, starting early.... Marvel would please help Miss Ingersoll in judging and evaluating class projects, plus "some other matters." And there was the school newspaper.

Marvel had been delighted when she learned at registration that Miss Robertson, the red-haired spinster who taught junior English, had chosen to teach seniors this year. It was Miss Robertson who spoke to her about the school newspaper (Marvel *would* serve as editor?). Last year Marvel would have jumped at the chance. This year she was a bit more cautious, remembering her other commitments. The teacher, noticing her hesitation, did a good job of salesmanship.

In the end, Marvel bought it all, bought it willingly, wondering why Miss Robertson would thank *her*, when it should be the other way.

"We'll enlarge the paper this year, Marvel, make it into a mini-version of our daily paper. Which reminds me, I have a letter with me from our city editor. It's addressed to you here but marked PERSONAL."

Marvel accepted the brief, professional note, hesitated, and at the nod of her teacher, scanned it quickly. Mr. A. Thomas Corey would like to request Marvel's assistance again this year. Her responsibilities would be similar to, but much farther-reaching than last year's... if she would consent to write a community news column telling of rural life, its problems, and their solutions. People...they wanted *names*...needed to increase circulation, else they, too, must close up shop! Mr. Corey went on to express hope that the package of personal stationery had pleased her, that she would put it to use, and he would like to suggest that perhaps that promising young man, Titus Smith, would contribute from the capital... the two of them working together.

Miss Robertson saw Marvel's face light up and hurried to extract a promise. "Mr. Corey has told me, Marvel. *Please* say yes!"

"Yes," Marvel breathed, her heart returning to its unwritten song.

Work came easy then. Out of the morass of her jumbled thinking, one thought emerged. Life had taken on a deeper meaning than she would have dreamed possible. And nothing, with God's help, could take that from her!

\* \* \*

Titus' letter to Marvel came as more of a surprise to Mother and Daddy than to her. She had expected it. What she had not expected was the overwhelming surge of joy inside her. The entire world exploded in a galaxy of stars. The stars which once "fell in Alabama" in remembered song now fell at her feet. She wanted to walk in the upsweep of stardust...run...escape the world. Anywhere would do, just as long as she could be alone to read her first love letter.

But there was no opportunity. Mother and Daddy hovered close, their eyes wide with interest and curiosity. What could it mean? Who would be writing to her in a franked envelope, with a return address stamped in gold saying State Capitol Building, and officially bearing the state seal? "Oh hurry, Marvel—open it! We've waited all day. What business could the government have with *you*?"

And for the first time in her young life, Marvel Harrington resented the intrusion on her privacy.

"Please—please give me a minute. It's so hot, and I'm so tired—"

The words sounded feeble even in her own ears, and the hurt in her parents' eyes was more than she could bear. "I need a drink of water," she managed through stiff lips. "Then I'll read the letter—and share. We *do* have water?"

Did they see through her stalling? Marvel hoped not. But the two of them shared sacred moments in which a daughter had no part. Shouldn't they realize that she must have the same opportunity—that it was a natural part of maturity? Nothing could take her from them or destroy her plans for the three of them. But she must have a bit of breathing space, a chance to expand that love, draw others in.

"Water we have, Miss Marvelous!" Daddy said, but his attempt at lightness failed. Because of the letter? No, Marvel realized with concern that he had been less jovial for some time now. He was more—what was the word?—*resigned*. Didn't Mother notice? No she didn't, the next few moments told Marvel.

Daddy handed her the water. "I'm sorry, honey. I guess we were prying. But it wasn't intentional. It's just that the news is so upsetting, I guess we're too concerned—too jumpy."

"Oh, it's not so bad, Dale," Mother put in brightly. "Just yesterday I heard talk of the plan—whatever it's called. But Marvel, it would mean *electricity*. We'd have lights again thanks to—uh—" she cast a questioning look at her husband.

"R.E.A.—Rural Electricity Act." He did not explain further, and Marvel noticed that his voice sounded hollow and unnatural, as if he were speaking in an empty room. She almost wished that the letter carried good news for *him*. No! That would mean no letter from Titus. . . .

Trying to regain control of her emotions, Marvel turned to another matter, one she perhaps would have made no mention of had the situation been different. "I wish some of these government funds could go for bettering education, making it compulsory—or maybe it is suppose to be, so I'll say enforcing the law if there is one. I guess we've learned there's no pill we can swallow and watch the world get well—that it'll take time and we'd better be starting at the bottom."

"Which is where we are," Daddy said with a quiet sigh.

"Oh Dale—"

But Marvel interrupted. Her father needed no meaningless words. "I was thinking," she continued, "about the need for education among the Negro people. Even in better times, you both know that they're the last to be hired and the first to be fired, and that'll be the story until we change things for them. It's important even in wee-small things—you know, like Mr. Bumstead's calling out to a young black boy who ran after a ball dangerously close to the bus, 'Be careful there, Snowball!' "

"Oh, I'm sure he meant no harm!" Mother protested quickly.

"But it was thoughtless, and the name had to hurt."

"He probably didn't know the difference, honey—that black boy, I mean. You didn't *say* anything, did you, Marvel?" Why was she so anxious?

"Oh, but I did! It has to begin in our hearts—spread out."

Mother's face paled. "Not the Bumsteads," she whispered. "Oh no—"

There was a pause, a pause which spelled trouble. Then Daddy sighed more deeply before saying, "Their well's playing out, and that means some of us will be without water for the cows—completely out."

Marvel's heart swelled within her, just as—horrible as the thought was—the cows' tongues in some pastures they had passed had appeared to be swelling. They were going to—*oh dear God, no!*—die of thirst!

Her hand tightened its grip on the envelope holding the long-awaited message from Titus. Had Mother and Daddy forgotten? Each buried in private thought, they looked out the window. Each, Marvel thought, seeing a personal vision. Two human beings wanting to share, *needing* to share, and not knowing how. She sighed deeply, ambiguous thoughts overcrowding her overloaded mind. In some way she was unable to express or even pretend to understand came a pinpoint of light—an understanding that mankind was better able to tolerate strains and stresses, trials and tribulations if only one other person knew. And that was the only way they could handle today's challenges and tomorrow's uncertainty. "Communicate!" she longed to cry out in frustration.

Instead she noiselessly tore the end from the envelope and let her unsteady eyes scan the contents. There was so much—so very much she wanted to think through and share as promised. But, and her heart commenced its wild beating again, there were other lines that were too personal, including terms of endearment which were meant for her alone—words she would cherish forever. Memorizing them would be far easier than the geometrical Pythagorean Theorem. Numbers were matters of the mind, words, a matter of the heart.

Tomorrow she would read the letter through, savoring each word, in the proper setting—in the shade of their private oak. . . .

Marvel cleared her throat, causing her parents to jump. "The letter," she said, clearing her throat again, "the letter is from a friend. I worked with him last year."

"Him?" Daddy said. "Someone we know?"

"I doubt it—but the family maybe. Smith . . . some of them owned the old Smith Hotel in Culverville."

But Mother and Daddy seemed to have lost interest. Marvel was relieved.

My darling: (Marvel paused to let the beautiful term course through her body to lodge in her heart before proceeding as she sat alone beneath the old oak tree in the schoolyard before reading on)

You will never know how many letters I've written, only to discard them all. I managed to complete one, only to realize that I was too torn apart to ask for your address that last night. Sis tells me you two have talked, so I'm sure you know that I sent it in her care. And then I asked her to return it and tell me how to reach you instead. I said too much in that letter, Marvel—some things I had no right to say. Not now anyway. So, until such time, will you settle for our sharing other things? Our activities, our victories and defeats—praying all the while that life's answers will come in time and accepting that we, you and I, and hopefully others in our generation will help make this world right again? Need I say how busy I've been? You know about the football practice, the G.P.A. (as they call it, patterned after our government alphabet programs, I guess—meaning Grade Point Average) requirements. Classes are different, instructors less caring. We're on our own. But I need an understanding friend like you, Miss Marvelous—only there will never be another *you*. My work is more demanding than I expected, too. But I "press toward the mark," neither asking for nor expecting perfection on this earth, but if you were here— Well, you might be unable to change the situation. But you always made me feel better than I am, just by saying I did an admirable job. However, you and I understand one another, accept that we are *driven* to serve in this world before it's too late. . . . Antichrist's knock at our door . . . even in the high places . . . what with such dictators as Adolph Hitler trying to rule the world. War? God forbid! But He knows my longings, my fears . . . is there to comfort me. Memories of you and our bonding experiences keep me going. Your Titus.

## 12

# *As Innocence Fades*

Marvel took far less time in preparing her letter than he had spent on hers. There beneath the protective arms of the giant oak it took no effort to imagine him sitting cross-legged, releasing his deepest feelings, knowing that each word would fall upon a sensitive heart. There he could be Titus and she could be Marvel. There in the nonjudgmental atmosphere each could reveal an inner self others had never known. Watching his expressive gray eyes turn black with emotion, Marvel had grown closer and closer to him—so close that he was a part of herself. And now his letter had told her that she was equally essential to him. Here in this leafy bower then was where the idea she had applied to her parents had originated. Yes, oh yes indeed! One *could* meet life's enemies—the evils of stress and frustration—head-on and conquer, if one other person knew and understood! And that was lacking in her life this year, Marvel realized. Her confidant was gone.

Her pen flew across the lilac-scented paper and, as if talking to him in person, she felt herself grow transparent in revealing her doings and her thinkings. Yes to everything—ditto, ditto, ditto! And more. She went on to tell of her own activities briefly, underplaying them somewhat as was her simple, humble nature. She reserved until last the exciting question regarding the possibility of his writing the columns as the editor had outlined the need to her. "And, oh Titus, you know it would mean something special! We'd be working together again...."

Titus responded immediately. Yes, of *course* he would prepare the wanted column. He had spoken with the senator ("He insists that I call him Cliff now, but I can't bring myself to do that," Titus explained) who was all for the idea. Senator Norton would cooperate fully, furnishing more information than one man could hope to boil down for the newspaper. "He'll get the needed recognition. He aims on being governor one of these days. Me? Oh Marvel, I'm finding it easy to praise God today! Remember that hymn 'Rescue the Perishing'? There's a line that promises, 'Strength for thy labor the Lord will provide,' and I belief that. I depend on Him for *everything*, and look what He has provided: this golden opportunity for me to gain experience—and *you*! Now, that's love at its greatest! As Miss Robertson would say, 'in the superlative degree'! What else matters?" Titus had written in conclusion, and again signed the letter "Your Titus."

Letters winged back and forth regularly after that. Their work for the newspaper made the frequent exchange possible. Mr. Corey had provided another reward: stamps! Three cents a letter was beyond their reach. But now, now anything was possible.

\* \* \*

Marvel made a part of her day listening to the news. The outlook was dismal, frightening—more threatening than the terrible drought. Losing all life's material things could not compare with the loss of human life, the awfulness of taking away today's youth who were the hope of tomorrow—its *only* hope. *Would Titus be among them?*

"Oh honey, war won't happen! It's going on overseas, but it won't come *here*. You worry me, spending so much time listening to those rumors. *Propaganda*, that's what it is," Mother said brightly.

Marvel shook her head in despair. It was no use, so why answer?

Daddy saw. And on his face was a look of sadness. So that accounted for his look of resignation. Daddy had discovered a long time ago that his beloved Snow would close out all unpleasantries. And who knew but what she had a point? It was not one Marvel could accept. Unlike her father, she could never become resigned to their lot, or to the terrible plight of the world. Someone must care.

"I'll listen with you, sweetie," Daddy had said. "Who knows but what those guys'll come up with something cheerful, and I want to be on hand. Besides, I want to talk one day about your uncles, the boys, and some other things. But not now! Let's listen."

Marvel was surprised to find that news was available at almost any hour as it dominated the airwaves. She realized how much she had missed from the very first broadcast the two of them heard:

"Capitalism has collapsed about our feet!" the announcer boomed. Marvel felt herself shudder, a dark memory closing in around her. "We are finished! At the end of our string. . . . There is nothing more we can do." Those had been the mournful words of a defeated president by the name of Herbert Hoover. That had been the spirit of the nation, a tired nation rudely jolted away before its Roaring Twenties nap was finished—and forcing a little girl with flyaway short hair to grow up too fast and too soon. How long had it been then since the big crash? Almost four years, she believed now. But Mother had waved it all away, told an upset little girl—no, *two* little girls, because Mary Ann had been with her—that Wall Street was a long, long way off.

And it had been, but its tentacles had reached out farther and farther, squeezing, squeezing . . . never letting go. Not even now. And the wars, so very far away, could come closer, too. Wars came from need—and greed.

The announcer's excited voice brought her back to the present:

Yes, it is gone—that capitalism we once thought was indestructible has proven Americans to be wrong again. Gone are our Psalm singers out there, those traditional leaders with snake-oil fix—their foolish formulas wiped out, all of them—and with them our horn of plenty! Their shallow schemes traveled from the East Coast to the West. Remember the Greenwich Village leather-coated gentleman who hoodwinked a gullible public into falling for technocracy? That social scheme would increase wealth tenfold . . . neighbors could quit sharing . . . fathers could quit farming. Oh, would that they had! No longer was there a need for the almighty dollar to be the medium of exchange.

We'd have energy units, Engineer Scott promised—and a whole new vocabulary crept on its hands and knees right into our parlors: *ergs* and *joules* instead of dollars and cents! People got scared after a time. Could this be the mark of the beast? But now, a preacher, that's different—Reverend Coughlin had another way of plumping out our faltering economy: silver-backed currency. Then wading out of the bayous came Huey Long with his "share your wealth" nostrum which smacked of communism. Not only was capitalism dying a slow death, we were losing our democratic way of life as well! And mark my word someday we're going to lose it. "The wages of sin is death" the Good Book says. Can't those words apply to a nation? The West? Out in the sunshine state of California where money grows on bushes, there was the old frontier doctor—you remember Dr. Townsend and his program for the elderly.... Well, we're wiser now. Faith dwindles as hope fades....

At that point Mother had hurried into the living room, still heated like an oven from the day's setting sun, and switched the radio off as if it were responsible for the world's ills.

"Enough!" she'd said in a sharper voice than usual. "And does anybody mind if we use leftovers? It's too hot to build a fire."

Marvel was not interested in food. She wanted to hear the rest of the news broadcast. Her behavior, too, departed from its accepted pattern. Rising quickly, she switched the radio back on. The announcer's voice filled the room again as the machine was still warmed up and there was not the usual waiting period.

...so some of the long-awaited Messiahs are appearing in different guises—more dangerous really, as the new thinking aligns itself with the age-old problem of "hate the Jews."...They hold the purse strings...money without power. As the scene shifts, we see dreams dying.... Coughlin, for one, has slid so far to the political right that his loaded speeches deal less with our nation's economy than the Jew-baiting! And don't you know Adolf Hitler, declared by too many to be the Messiah, has contacts here—double agents who carry back our woes and the danger signs of a weakening economy? He's closing ranks this very minute with the Berlin-directed Bund...and the disillusioned Soviets. Americans—weary of unkept promises, facing goodness-knows-what in the face of the Great Depression, the great state of Texas being among the hardest hit, as we're victims of the Great Drought in addition—are seeking answers. Will there be an ideological turnabout? There are those who claim the economy's alive and flourishing— as indeed is the case in some areas, where lands produce and defense plants hire on new men and even some women in order to meet the foreign demands for the vehicles of war! Smell danger? We do from here—here where the winds have laid bare our fields and swept away our hopes. Leave it to the politicians, the more affluent tell us. And there our problems go again...back into the hands of the Democrats and the Republicans. And maybe they *are* our salvation....

Static blurred the announcer's speech while he was in the process of signing off. But Marvel had a feeling that he said something more before giving his name and his Dallas radio station's call number. It made no great difference. She had leaped to her feet, taking issue with the godless thinking he had hinted to be rampant in this, the United States of America.

"Nobody, absolutely nobody is our salvation except God!" she cried passionately. "That's blasphemy."

Daddy's head was in his hands. "And even He seems to have forsaken us."

Marvel walked the two steps to him, knelt beside him, and whispered reassuringly, "He'll never forsake us, Daddy. Remember His beautiful promise, 'Lo, I am with you always, even unto the end of the world'? Remember, Daddy?"

"Yes," he said, lifting his head and putting an affectionate arm around her. "Thank you for reminding me. You're special!"

Throughout the meal, Mother was silent that evening. Was Marvel expected to apologize for what she might have thought was done in defiance? If she'd wounded her mother, she was sorry—but not for her behavior. There would be other evenings and other news.

Life went on in school hurriedly, but with no great changes. Something still troubled Mary Ann, but Marvel decided not to push her. The entire world was troubled, the news told her, and school was such a small part of it. Her own world was enlarging, and she was exploring new horizons and sharing discoveries with Titus as he shared his widening views with her. But their sharing remained unaffected, open, and natural. Innocence was fading, the announcer had said, but an outsider would have said that was untrue of the relationship between Marvel Harrington and Titus Smith—Titus Smith who was now an aide to the senator. Once an "office boy," then a page, Titus was still climbing the political ladder rung by rung as Senator Cliff Norton had done before him. Once representative Norton, now *Senator* Norton had his eye on the gubernatorial race. Titus must be prepared to serve as his personal aide—wonderful . . . challenging . . . but sobering.

Would Titus reach his political aspirations or would his dreams be interrupted by war? Marvel listened to the news faithfully, knowing that he was listening, too. Everything, colored by conditions, was changing.

And now the complexion of the local newspaper was changing, too. Readers, in their disillusionment, had donned political blinders, saying them wine-bibbers in Washington didn't give a flip for the ordinary man. Look at that red-blooded bunch on Wall Street—leastwise, in New York somewheres—calling theirselves Daughters of the Revolution, and proud as peacocks of their heritage. They had stopped celebratin' Paul Revere's ride. Could it be they'd decided them redcoats was nigh onto right, after all, about us colonists? Nope, it was a heap worse! Take that deep-dish-faced ole woman calling herself "Mother Bloor" and all the evils *she* stood for! Misleading all them young folks to go marchin' down Broadway totin' a zany sign claiming' "The DAR forgets but the YCL remembers!" Anybody hereabouts know what them letters stood for? Sure 'nuf wasn't a part of Mr. Roosevelt's alphabet programs! No sirree! *Young Communist League*, that's what! And working like a hive of bees, they was, and gettin' by with it. Had the wool pulled over the eyes of our leaders. And come to think on it, it was plain as the nose on yore face, didn't take no head-scratching idee to come up with their conclusions here at home. Why, them politicians probably sicked 'em on when they oughta be squashin' 'em like a bug! Need some clean politickin'.

This, then, had been their thinking—until Titus Smith's column began to appear. Now here was a hometown boy making good, just what they needed—an unbiased report straight from the capital of Texas: homespun, cheerful, hopeful. Let those traitors organize all the new "fronts" as they called them (and with a snicker the men said among themselves that the only "front" they could see was on the bosoms of those half-naked gals parading around in skimpy bathing suits!). Well, young men like Smith held hope. The lad couldn't clean the mess up by himself, but he could expose it all! A *few* politicians around here couldn't be hoodwinked and cat-hauled around. A new interest developed in reading. Those who could afford newspapers bought them and others shared. Barbershops posted the black-and-white newspapers in their windows. But rural dwellers couldn't afford to be scissored. Out in the Morning Glory Chapel area, as it had come to be called, the male population gathered at "Linc" Denney's house. Young Linc had no training, but he owned a pair of clippers. They pinched a little, but being rednecked was better than wearing a dog-shag in this heat.

Another of Linc's services was furnishing a copy of the weekend newspaper. It passed from hand to hand of the waiting customers on Saturday afternoon. And from time to time one of them could dig up a dime to help pay for the printed pages. That led to gathering at the homes of those who owned radios to listen to commentators.

And then Marvel's columns made their bow. People began to take notice when their own Marvel Harrington appeared with her name right there in black-and-white to show that the writing was her own. And then, one by one, they spotted their own names. Imagine! It was, Marvel supposed by their unexpected enthusiasm, the first time ever to see their names in print. Just ordinary things made special: Mr. and Mrs. So-and-so did this, and that turned them into overnight celebrities. Grandmother called to congratulate Marvel and report that more and more people were reworking their ironbound budgets in an effort to subscribe. Would Marvel believe that some of the few remaining merchants were toying with placing "ads"?

"But how are other things, honey?" she asked a little anxiously. "I talk with Snow, but you know your mother—how she sort of glosses over the rough spots in life. And it can't be easy out there."

"We're all right, Grandmother dear. We're managing. And no, it's not what you might call Easy Street here. But then, where *is* that mythical place?" Then, with a smile in her voice, Marvel said, "If anything happens, you'll read about it in my columns!"

Something more hung unsaid. There was a pause before Grandmother Riley murmured, "There's sickness. Typhoid's broken out—"

Marvel reminded her that they'd had their shots, but forgot completely to ask if all had been vaccinated there. But she was sure they had. The subject inspired a special medical report based on surveys and interviews. She sent a copy of the report to Titus, and it inspired him to look into the possibility of a state-wide health program, especially for those who could not afford a doctor. His column took on the name Ears of Austin—Marvel's, Eyes of East Texas. They editorialized freely. And then they were named as coauthors of Heartbeats of America, U.S.A.

In their Heartbeat column, Marvel and Titus covered the world news as best they were able. Drawing from news they digested through news broadcasts and materials which crossed Senator Norton's desk, the two of them summarized it and presented it in a warm, chatty style which the average reader could understand and appreciate, little dreaming that the Smith-Harrington columns were setting them apart. Neither of them was inclined toward egotism or self-importance, and so they remained blissfully unaware of the far-reaching appeal and attraction of their work. True, Titus was the Ears and Marvel the Eyes. But editors were both—all three, in fact, as they not only looked and listened. They kept fingers on the pulse of America....

Mary Ann was enthralled. "Oh, it's superwonderful! The two of you together like this—sooooo romantic. Now tell me, *please* tell me: Has he—uh, Titus—said anything? You know—declared himself? I mean, is there an understanding?"

Marvel didn't want to discuss that—not even think about it. It was too soon. They had work to do. And marriage? It was all confusing.

"We understand each other—*without* an understanding."

Mary Ann was confused, too. "That makes no sense. Okay, so I'll come right out and ask: *Has Titus Smith proposed?*"

"Has Jake Brotherton?" Marvel shot back, afraid to face the issue.

"There's a difference and you know it, Miss Pris!"

Yes, there was a difference. Did that account for her keeping Titus secret?

Marvel spun on her heel and left hurriedly—and then regretted her huff. Her cousin looked pale, and now she was holding her middle as if there were pains in her stomach. But she was boarding her bus....

The local editor was impressed with Marvel and Titus' columns and notified them they would receive complimentary copies of the paper. Now Mother could share at her clubs; Daddy, with his baseball team. All would read. And the Age of Innocence *had* ended—or so they thought....

# 13

# "Water, Water Everywhere—and Not a Drop to Drink"

Jake stopped Marvel in the hall between classes the day after she and Mary Ann had talked. There was a revealing brightness in his eyes which spoke of success. But his face was chalky. Immediately she felt that something was wrong.

To her surprise, Jake spoke of neither—not at first.

"Mr. Angelo wants to see you as soon as you can find a minute to spare. Something to do with your writing, I think. Interested?"

"Hi, Jake! I'll make a point of seeing him. But interested?" Marvel attempted a small laugh. "I'm up to my neck in writing. How are *you* doing in his class? Enjoying it?"

"I wish I had time to tell you everything, but Marvel, I—I have something else on my mind—"

"I thought so. Mary Ann? She hasn't been herself. What's wrong?"

"I don't know," he said miserably. "I just know Mary Ann's sick, real sick. And either the doctor doesn't know the problem or won't tell us yet. He won't let any of us see her, but we can hear her rambling, sometimes almost screaming about something— somebody—who's coming back to harm her, you, all of us. She's delirious and burning up with fever. Her dad knows Dr. Porter— Kate Lynn's father. You know her—the friend of the Cohane girl. Trouble brewing there again, too—between Mr. Harrington and Mr. Cohane, I think. But never mind that. Dr. Porter came and has been with Mary Ann for the past 24 hours—alone."

"Oh Jake! I had no idea! Well, maybe I did. I knew *something* was wrong. I'll call Mother and Daddy, and you make arrangements for me to ride home with Uncle Worth so I can be with her."

Jake shook his head. "No use, Marvel. They won't let you in. Mary Ann's not to be disturbed. And the scary thing is there's a *quarantine* sign on the door! It could be contagious. Oh Marvel, what if I never see her again? What if—"

The boy was going to cry. Strong and courageous as Jake Brotherton was, his soft spot was Mary Ann. She was his reason for living.

Quickly, Marvel said, "Jake—Jake, listen to me! Don't even think such things! We don't know anything yet. And fevers cause people to say strange things. I think she's remembering Elmer and, in her feverish condition, seeing him as a threat. Now the best thing we can do for our patient is to go about our business. She'd want that. So draw a deep breath and tell me your *good* news. You have some. I saw it in your eyes!"

Jake's voice broke several times, but he managed to share that he had gotten the big break both he and Mr. Angelo had hoped for. The teacher had been *so* good to him, taken such an interest, and—although it had looked hopeless—Jake had landed a little job at the bank! Not much—just a little work with accounting. But if that worked out, the bank had promised a little on-the-job experience in the teller's cage! It was hard to tell who was proudest: Jake himself, his father, or the teacher. If only— No! he wouldn't say it, not even think it, Jake promised. He would go ahead, get through the day, make good—yeah, make good, be a real success for Mary Ann. But Marvel *would* pray?

"Of course I will, Jake," she whispered softly and brushed his cheek with a light kiss, tasting the salt of his drying tears....

And pray she did—all night, it seemed. "Lord, just tell me what to do—which direction I should take. Anything, *anything*, Lord, to help Mary Ann!" she begged over and over, humbly, without berating herself. All had sinned before God, fallen short of His glory. The Bible said so. What the Bible did *not* say was that sinners couldn't be forgiven and start a new life. She and Mary Ann had decided a long time ago that they would avoid the destructive pitfall of calling themselves *worms* (Marvel smiled, remembering). Jesus did not come down from heaven to give His life for worms! He needed followers who could stand upright, walk proudly, and serve whatever the need.

It was during one of those agonizing prayers that answers began to emerge. Once release came, those answers bombarded her heart. Just because she was not allowed to see Mary Ann did not mean she was shut off from serving her—any more than her inability to see the Lord kept her from serving Him! But first she herself needed some answers from others.

"Mother?" Marvel whispered at the door separating the two small bedrooms. "Are you awake? I—"

"Marvel—*honey*!" Mother sounded warm, soothing, as she had so many years ago when Marvel had had a bad dream. Her mother was glad, actually glad—even though her own voice reflected anxiety—to be needed. With a lump in her throat, Marvel realized that, unintentionally, she'd taken that away. Somehow Mother must have that feeling restored.

And then they were all together, fighting fear with love and faith. Fear lost out, leaving them able to think and talk clearly. They were awake, Daddy told her—awake and praying just as she was. And Mother kept saying that she understood. She understood, too, how Rae and Worth would be taking all this—it was in her voice. Yes, they'd talked and Mother's own little girl mustn't worry anymore. Oh, how they loved her, appreciated her, and had they ever said how *proud* they were of her?

Marvel cuddled close to her mother, allowed herself to be comforted and felt better inside. Daddy put his arms about them both. It was a sacred moment—one Marvel regretted she must interrupt.

"I love you both *so* much—even when I seem to be too busy to tell you," she whispered, meaning the words with all her heart. And then she asked, "Mother, did Auntie Rae tell you whether they've had their shots—against typhoid, I mean?"

"*Typhoid!*" her parents gasped in unison. Then Mother regained her composure. "Oh, I'm sure they did—well, not really sure. I mean, I *guess*. We never talked about it. Didn't Mary Ann tell you?"

"No. We talked about our neighbors. I guess all of them had—"

"Not all," Daddy said shakily. "Not all—some refused. And Father told me that—oh mercy, why didn't I *do* something—there were some cases reported. I—I just neglected checking on Worth's family!"

Marvel forgot whatever the three of them may have said next. Her mind was on her next newspaper column....

She had learned the skill of researching, interviewing, and (by use of the inverted-pyramid style of journalism), putting it all together quickly. There was no time for outlines and rough drafts when a story broke. And the possible outbreak of typhoid fever was *news*! Longhand was just that: long and time-consuming. So she had mastered the skill of typing on her own, her schedule not allowing for another class. Mr. Angelo had agreed quickly to her request to use one of his two typewriters anytime a class was not in session. With the aid of a manual, she had mastered the aging, manually operated machine and found it an invaluable tool. The county health doctor would have had supporting information, but there was too little time for statistics as to how many had received the serum. Dr. Porter was in charge of Mary Ann's case anyway, and by now should be able to give a diagnosis.

Dr. Porter was cooperative. "Yes," he said from his office, his voice hollow with fatigue, "Worth Harrington's daughter has typhoid fever. It's a highly infectious disease—not contagious, but might as well be. We have to keep the patient isolated, for both the patient's sake and those closely associated."

"I understand, doctor: soft diet, lots of rest, something to reduce the fever. Typhoid's related somewhat to typhus, isn't it?"

The doctor chuckled in spite of his exhaustion. "You sound well-informed, young lady. My daughter has said you were very intelligent—Marvel, isn't it? Are you doing a story on this?"

"Yes sir, with your permission and help. Thank you for the compliment, and I hope I can do justice to the column. I feel we owe it to Titus County residents. They need to be informed and take precautions."

"You'll be doing us a service, Marvel," Dr. Potter said, and then went on to describe the terrible illness, part of which she knew.

Typhoid fever, a febrile disease caused by typhoid bacillus, invaded the human body through food or drink—usually but not always by drinking impure water. Before them lay the difficult job of running down the source. First it was necessary to see what relationship existed between treated and reported victims.... There was Mary Ann, a preacher by the name of Grady Greer (*Brother Greer—oh no!* Marvel's heart protested, but her lips were still), the county agent (again she gasped)—a lady by the name of—what was it? Suther? No, Sutheral. That was it. If they'd been in the same area...

A terrible suspicion was forming like a dark cloud overhead and then descending to smother Marvel's vision, her hearing, and thinking. All of them—*all*—had been in her own area. Morning Glory Chapel people were in terrible danger!

What had been the answer to her prayers last night? That God needed followers who could stand upright, walk proudly, and serve wherever needed. With an effort, Marvel pushed away the darkness surrounding her. "Symptoms, doctor—and advice?" she asked calmly.

"Sometimes no symptoms until it's too late. Best advice is to be on guard against overfatigue and stomach pains. It's a sort of intestinal catarrh, you know, usually accompanied by diarrhea, sometimes vomiting. And there can be red splotches or eruptions on the abdomen or chest, and then a soaring fever that triggers a stupor. A combination of dysentery and vomiting can dehydrate the body quickly, which can lead to death. Helpers must—absolutely *must*—wear gauze masks until we know more than medical science has uncovered. Fluids are essential. And we'll try to outline a program for disposing of body wastes. Watch for difficulty in breathing because of pneumonia—"

"We'll need help from the county health department—and whatever I can dig up from the state," Marvel spoke her thoughts. "And will there be shots available for those who missed them?"

The doctor would look into that, he promised. Marvel would get the word out through her column. They thanked each other and went to work....

*The Drought Kills More Than Land and Cattle—It Kills People!* Marvel's headline read, and her column made the lead story on the front page of the newspaper. Exhausted, she deposited it on the editor's desk and hurried to the waiting bus. Mr. Bumstead understood and cooperated, concern written on his face. She remembered that look later, but not his words—if he spoke. Later there was regret as the Captain was to play the leading role in a tragic drama played out on the Morning Glory Chapel stage. The story was to reach out to the county, the state, and eventually to the entire United States, so factual and yet so emotional was its appeal.

But tonight she was tired, so tired. And for the first time she was unable to write to Titus. *Avoid exhaustion.* Yes, she must.

That marked the beginning of the slowdown in their exchange of letters. In their zeal to reach out to others, Marvel realized later, both forgot their hearts' personal needs. But their mutual pursuits kept them in touch. Titus reviewed Marvel's incredible exposé and renewed his campaign for a health-aid program. Senator Norton included the matter on his platform, hoping for voters' support. He telephoned the Titus County Board of Supervisors, alerted his colleagues to the danger of typhoid and other possible diseases within their own districts, and warned that even now these diseases might be "coiled and ready to strike." Then he boldly addressed President Franklin Delano Roosevelt himself.

Results were immediate at the county level. The county health officer found there was adequate vaccine on hand to inoculate a number of county residents on a first-come-first-served basis. But the announcement frightened more than it soothed when he made the mistake of cautioning that some of the protective medication could be contaminated since it was derived from cows, some of which were afflicted. He ordered all cattle tested and destroyed should tests show positive. Overstrained nerves snapped. *"Could be"* translated as *is*. And far too many refused to subject themselves to risks. "No cowpox!" they said firmly. Marvel put out another emotional appeal in her column. Other doctors supported her. And in the end they won most of the people over.

Meantime, *all* water must be considered a possible source of the deadly typhoid germs and was condemned until tested—the one exception being an artesian well, usually considered safe. Other water—even for domestic use, including baths—must be boiled, preferably treated.

Mr. Bumstead paid the Harringtons a visit. "'Water, water everywhere, and not a drop to drink'—don't th' pome say? Gotta git rid of this stuff, still—" And then Marvel knew. It was—it had to be—the Bumstead well.

# 14

# "There Is a Way Which Seemeth Right Unto Man..."

In sudden reversal, the wind roared in fiercely from the north. That was just before Thanksgiving. Marvel, feeling their little house shudder in the storm, hurried to look out her bedroom window. Her first impression was that snow had powdered the ground too early. But a closer look said it was sand, and some of it was sifting through the ill-fitting window frames. In the early-morning light Marvel made her way to the corner where a sheeted-off space served as a closet and located a three-year-old red turtleneck sweater and matching wool skirt which hung with it.

A crack of light appeared beneath her door followed by the welcome scent of perking coffee. Dressing hurriedly, she wondered just how much coffee—how much *anything*—remained in Mother's skimpy larder.

Still cold, Marvel wrapped a quilt around herself before hurrying into the kitchen to rub her hands over the smoking woodstove.

"Hog-killing weather, as we used to call these northers," she said between chattering teeth, then paused, "back when we had hogs."

"'Morning, Sunshine!" Daddy said, squinting against the smoke that tumbled out as he tried to push more wood into the stove's firebox. "No hogs—not that it matters. Porkers are on hold, too." He reached hard to be amusing: "Soooo, if we had the ham, we'd have ham and eggs, if we had the eggs! Well, no ham, no eggs—and how many out here can afford Armour's breakfast bacon, hmmm?"

"Sit down, you two. Breakfast is served!" Mother said with a practiced smile. "You'll need something to warm your insides today," she added, giving the cornmeal mush a final stir, dishing the steaming substance into bowls, and sprinkling the tops with brown sugar.

The three of them sat down, nobody commenting on the lack of cream. The gruel was lumpy, and Marvel had trouble swallowing—both because it stuck to the roof of her mouth and because her heart felt as heavy as the food. "Your father's helping test wells today. The health official needed volunteers, and nobody knew the wind would be like this. You'll have to be out in it, too, Marvel. In fact, we all will."

When Mother pushed back from the table to pour the coffee, Daddy explained. "Your mother's trying to alert families to the importance of having the typhoid shots. This kind of emergency can't wait for a change in the weather. Uh—Marvel, honey, did you—did you know—?"

Was he having trouble with the mush, too? No, he was drinking his scalding coffee with the urgency of a man dying of thirst. Marvel, too, finished her coffee and allowed the bracing contents to warm her body enough to toss the quilt aside before asking, "What's wrong, Daddy? Are—are other cases reported?"

"It's your friend Annie. Like the rest of us, her family uses artesian water. But everybody drank water at church, prayer meeting, at our house—and it came from one well until it played out."

"Bumsteads'," Marvel said, feeling dead inside.

Daddy nodded. And the Harringtons went their separate ways.

It was a trying day—cruelly cold, and everywhere there was the silence of a tomb. Mr. Bumstead was unduly quiet, undoubtedly condemning himself. Marvel longed to offer words of reassurance but could think of nothing to say. The students, who usually chattered like magpies to and from school, sat blue-lipped with cold without uttering a word.

Bracing herself against the bitter wind, Marvel drew her thin cloth coat about her and waited until the bus came in from Pleasant Knoll. But Uncle Worth wasn't driving. "Tummy" Tucker had taken his place, qualifying because of his experience with delivering ice in his small truck. That might mean Mary Ann was worse. Frantically, she watched for Jake—so relieved when she caught sight of him that she ran to meet him.

"Mary Ann?" she cried, raising her voice against the wind.

Jake's voice was choppy, and it was hard to hear him at first, even when he shouted. "No change," Marvel thought she heard. "Sick—*so* sick—and nobody allowed in." Her parents took precautions—sat by her bed day and night—almost crazy with worry. Mary Ann was still hallucinating—talked about a thistle like something was sticking her, but no signs.

"And she keeps talking about a dress—and, of all things, *hops*. Oh, and orange blossoms. Oh Marvel, if they'd just let me see her—"

"They will one of these days, Jake. Believe that! I understand about it all: thistle, the dress, orange blossoms. She's remembering—even the hops—"

"But they're in California! And she's vowed never, *ever* to go there. I have to be ready if she pulls through. What can I do—or say?"

They were at the door of the school, but Jake grabbed at Marvel's arm desperately. She paused, looked into his ashen face, and said, "Yes, you must see her—and the sooner the better. Talk with the doctor, make him understand. There have been many cases—you know that—telling us that sometimes one person's love can bring an unconscious person back—*your* kind of love. What can you say? Tell her you love her!"

Jake clung. "She knows. We've always planned on marriage." Marvel looked him in the eye. "Have you ever proposed?"

"Why—well, no. It wasn't necessary—I mean, *was* it?"

"Was and is! Women like to be asked."

\* \* \*

One look at her father's face that night told Marvel the verdict. "Contaminated?" she asked of the Bumstead well.

"Beyond a reasonable doubt. The water discolored the solution Dr. Bronson used for testing—preliminary testing, he called it. Seems the true results depend on a culture, taking several days. Meantime, no water from that source. No other source from around here either, except the one artesian, so drinking water's all we have."

"No baths?" Mother looked horrified.

But Marvel's mind went other-directional. "The cows?"

His silence was worse than not knowing. "Daddy?" she whispered.

"They—they'll have to—to go," Dale Harrington said unsteadily, his speech as thick as that of a drunken man. "Oh honey, I don't know how to tell you—"

"Then don't !" Mother said quickly. "Don't think about it."

"We have to know, Mother," Marvel said gently. "No matter how much it hurts, we have to know. It's unpleasant, but go ahead, Daddy."

Marvel bit her lip so hard she felt the salty tang of blood sting her tongue in the gallant effort to hold back tears as the death knell sounded for the cows: theirs, their neighbors', the whole county's. All would have to be destroyed. They were dying from thirst and lack of proper feed, and there was no hope for help. Grain-producing states were equally hard-pressed. Even nutritious hay from California wouldn't help. It was too late to save the cattle—and who could pay the price? So there were no winners, just losers! Aid from the government? Yes, in an emergency grant, but too late... too late....

"We—we'll manage," Mother gulped, sickened. "There's the meat—"

"No meat, Snow. The cows are diseased. Meat's inedible, dangerous. The state's going to help, as well as the government. It's illegal for us to take meat for table use."

"But we own them—" Mother began.

"Not anymore, we don't," Daddy said fiercely. "The government's buying them—a forced sale—"

"Buying" I don't understand," Marvel said quickly, more to take her mind off the awfulness lying ahead than actual interest.

"Their hides—nothing more."

"How much?" she asked, trying to push away the pictures flashing before her eyes. The velvet-eyed cows, lowing softly at milking time, trusting them, knowing they would be fed and watered... and then their being hauled away live and returned dead—without *skins*...

A little moan escaped her lips. Quickly she faked a cough and murmured an apology in an effort to regain her composure.

Her parents did not seem to notice. "How much?" Daddy repeated her question, as if he were unable to believe the answer.

"Thirty-five cents," he said bitterly. "Thirty-five lousy cents for our prize cattle—the remnant from which we'd start again. How much more can a man be expected to take?"

Nobody was able to answer. And in view of what lay ahead, Marvel was glad....

Escape—she must escape. The wind was too sharp to allow for a long walk, and darkness was closing in. The radio—yes, that would help. How long had it been since she had listened to the news? Marvel turned the knob to on and waited, unable in the silence to close out memories that came trooping back: babyhood in the big house which once sat commandingly, a queen on her throne, centered on the endless green of rolling pastures ...living in Pleasant Knoll, laughing, loving, dining from faultlessly white linen...her Mother's singing and then playing the violin, how it came alive in her hands, filling the hearts of all who heard. And now? Gone...all gone...even, she remembered, the last detail of the past: the little cleft in Mother's cheek which showed where her precious instrument once rested. Shining moments as transient as sands sifting through the fingers of time...compressed into poignant memories. *Titus, oh Titus, do you hear? Do you understand?* her heart agonized. How long, oh how very long it seemed since she had seen him, heard his voice and his deep soft-bass laughter, felt the single touch of his hand—or even had a letter. So this was the price of relentless love for mankind, the radical sacrifice in the currency of broken hearts. Well, Marvel thought miserably (yet strangely uplifted), God never promised it would be easy when He chose the two of them. It just reminded them that He, too, had sacrificed His all, His Son—and who better understood two broken hearts? If they loved Him, they must love His children—His *other* children (so few did in this self-pitying world)—and be radical, foolhardy, risk all. Easy? No, God never promised that. But He *did* promise that one day tears would be blotted away by joy...one day... *one day*!

Marvel's heavenly thoughts faded as the harsh voice of a radio announcer filled the small room. She hurried to turn the volume down. There was a special guest in the studio, he said, a state health official whose name she failed to catch. In a monotone the guest opened the wound of the catastrophic circumstances in which several east Texas counties were caught (making special mention of Titus County).

"The symbolic four horsemen of the Apocalypse have stampeded in—four riders on white, red, black, and pale horses, symbolizing pestilence, war, famine, and *death*, respectively—and found us unprepared! For all have struck at once. We are compelled to take drastic measures. Medicine will arrive, but it will take time, even after the injections, for it to be effective.... Water must be preserved...most condemned...cattle destroyed...homes quarantined...foods flushed down toilets of city dwellers, buried in case of rural dwellers...."

Shuddering, Marvel switched to another station, feeling unable to bear hearing a reminder. Death, the man had said. *Death!* First the cows, then the people—unless help hurried. Otherwise it would be too late, just as it was too late to save the cows. But war? Was there a real threat? Oh surely the man was wrong. But he wasn't.

And so it is possible that we've been too busy with our do-gooding—sending the makings of the wars we claim to abhor to our very own enemies. "Save China!" we cried in good faith, sending aid, allowing our own youth to volunteer—for high pay, sure, but where is our loudly proclaimed value on human life? Yes, blindly we continued our scrap metal under the sacred terms of "foreign trade," closing our political eyes to what their enemies, the Japanese, were forging into weapons of war! And now, as those of you who follow the fast breaking news knew, we've found out the awful truth. We're trying to back away from what should have been as plain all along as the nose that centers your face. It's too late! They've got a good toehold.... We've been tried and convicted.... And, mark my word! We'll be punished. "No more!" we declare like the scared little boy who'd had a dozen eggs smashed against his head and sees the basket's empty...too late...too late!

At this very minute there's a Jap freighter waitin' in an American harbor ready to unload and reload with scrap metal. We balk. Where will it lead? And is that the only front? Not by any means...not when Communist newspapers are asking for funds right here in our own country ...when Germany's Messiah Adolf Hitler's become a bedfellow of Joseph Stalin—while within our own borders are young American groups saluting "das el Fuehrer." They're as misguided as the fine young Germans so pitifully misled....New fronts springing up everywhere. Contradictory, all of it—trotting out such utensils as Italy's Mussolini and Spain's Fascist General Franco as heroes...while we, like mindless canaries, chirp in our cages of isolationism our emotional songs of pity for the long-suffering leaders....

*Wake up, America!* You send your boys to Europe— preparing the mother country for war—yet continue to lay claim to being conscientious objectors—opposing military training. "No more conscriptions" like *the* world war. Want it to be called World War I—huh, do ya? With another world war breathing down its neck? Let the R.O.T.C. continue in college...train the reserves...equip our Navy... let our defense plants build for their own country! Of course, this is only one man's opinion, but prepare for a draft!

*One man's opinion.* How many did it take? Quickly Marvel turned off the radio and hurried outside, finding her parents as she had expected. Mother was stroking the bony backbones of the cows, and Daddy's arm was about her shoulders. There were no words. "There is a way which seemeth right unto man, but the end thereof are the ways of death." *Proverbs 14:12*, Marvel thought with a shudder.

# 15

# *The Strength to Go On*

The day before Thanksgiving Marvel awoke with an alien sense of depression. The wind wailed fiercely as it whipped around her corner of the house, paused as if to inhale, and then tried again with a humanlike moan as if to echo her mother's stifled groans. All night Mother had cried, parting with the tears she'd held pent-up inside for so long. Her pillow, so recently soaked with the sweat born of summer heat, must be wringing wet with tears in the premature onslaught of winter. Daddy was helpless. What hope could he offer? And Marvel herself, almost choking with her own unshed tears, decided that there was only one course of action for her: She must play the little girl. And that took practice—practice and self-discipline.

So thinking, she made believe that she, like Alice in Wonderland, had shrunk in size. She was tiny . . . tiny . . . *tiny*, and the fat feather bed was much too large. Snuggling down, she tried to feel Mother's lovely hands tucking the quilt beneath her chin and hear the sleep-inducing drone of Daddy's voice telling her favorite bedtime stories. But the illusion would not come. Instead came the awfulness of reality: the agonized pleadings of dying cattle . . . the cemeteries where dark-coated men lowered coffin after coffin, until at last it became necessary to hang out a No Vacancy sign. The wind songs becoming dirges, mercifully covering the horror of it all with a film of dust, only to change personalities and blow in clouds—black clouds growing ever blacker. The clouds of war! And then came the most awful visions of all she'd imagined and sounds she had never heard but recognized immediately: pilots wearing helmets and goggles climbing into cockpits, then waiting for the word "Contact!" as a mechanic spun wooden propellers to send antiquated airplanes of world war vintage reeling drunkenly through the wind-shredded clouds ... the blinding flash of lightning.... No! It was not lightning that threatened the helplessly rocking planes spiraling downward. ... Worse! The explosion of bombs, some in midair, sent showers of live coals rocketing like the fireworks of Christmas in their arch downward, others more successful ... down ... down ... *down* to strike live targets, masses huddled together screaming out in terror, their voices lost in the madness of the storm. And then the sound of harsh, guttural laughter ... and the sharp, military click of Nazi boots ...

"Oh no, dear God, no!" Marvel protested against the relentless whine of the wind. She tried to pray then, but the prayers sounded empty and meaningless even to her own ears—like dry blades of grass lifted by a whirlwind, striking the unfinished rafters overhead, and falling lifelessly to the cold bare floor. Dry bones to rise and haunt her—"the four horsemen"—*pestilence, war, famine,* and *death*!

Wet with sweat, Marvel leaped from her bed and, although shivering with cold, splashed cold water on her face in an effort to drive away the satanic images that threatened her very soul. Her nerveless fingers felt for something warm to wear—warm and bright—anything to help dispel this mood. No, not the red—not *bloodred*! Oh, the blue wool Grandmother had made. *Could* that have been five years ago? But she and Mary Ann had reached their full height at 13, and now at 16—*Oh Mary Ann*, her heart cried out as she pulled the simple princess-line garment over her head. Such a pretty color.

In view of all else, Marvel felt it was almost a sacrilege to ask what any caring person would ask at breakfast on an ordinary day. But her parents (bless them!) understood—welcomed her question, in fact, because they, too, needed a release which tears had failed to bring.

"How is everybody? Grandfather? Grandmother? *Everybody?*" she repeated, finding herself unable to mention Mary Ann's name.

"Oh, fine. I mean, my mother—busy, of course—but fine. You know, she's an amazing woman. She calls. I call. They're fine—"

"Under the circumstances, yes—yes, you could say that," Daddy said a little uncertainly, as if trying to reach a decision. Then his face brightened as one corner of his mouth turned upward in a first-phase smile. "I guess Billy Joe's keeping her on the run. Oh, maybe you didn't know Mother Riley's keeping Worth's boy until—until Mary Ann gets back on her feet. She— your grandmother, I mean—had to show the lad who ruled the roost." He looked at Mother questioningly and, seeing something only a loving husband would be able to discern, chuckled and went on, "And the showdown was a riot! That young sprout got sassy, didn't like what Mother Riley said, and proceeded to cut a dido—and with a *guest*. Announced he wanted roasting ears, black-eyed peas, something else—oh yeah, butterbeans cooked with okra. Ummmm, sounds good! and a little-bitsy piece of cake so he could hold all the watermelon in the world because that's how much he wanted... *right* now! Seems his Gran'mere told him to be seated and prepare for spaghetti—and be thankful for that! Well, he sat. But be thankful? He crossed those arms, grabbed the platter from the lady next to him, and said, 'Don't take so long. When stuff's *that* slippery, just do like this. My hands are clean, so here, just eat what you're given—and be thankful!' Your mother's laughing—see, Marvel, *laughing*—because she knows the rest."

He stopped to wipe his eyes, his laughter matching Mother's, and she managed to take the story from there, laughing her way through it. It really wasn't *that* funny, but her parents were sharing their common grief and frustration. And Marvel felt a lift of her own sagging spirits even though some of the fragmented report was less than spirit-lifting. Slowly—slowly—the Dale Harringtons were learning the bitter lesson of facing the unthinkable, not liking it—maybe hating it—but living with it without raging at their surroundings... being strong, hopeful, resilient. Could they continue to grow? Could *she*?

"...and of course Mother marched over and grabbed the plate, handed the guest a clean one and—oh, this is funny!— said, 'So your hands are clean, young man? Well, mine are not!' and scooped the stuff into Billy Joe's plate and ordered, '*You* eat it. Sop that plate clean—and be thankful'! Can't you just see his eyes?"

Mother broke into laughter again. She was still laughing as Daddy told about Grandmother's disappointment at being unable to have the Thanksgiving reunion. The cousins needed memories like her own unimaginable childhood...cousins by the dozens, aunts, uncles, grandparents swapping stories. Never mind the barren hillbilly miles of dusty oaks...just storing memories of songs and music, swapping stories of remembered smokehouse-cured hams, squabbling over who got the wishbone from heaped-up platters of fried chicken and more pies than you could shake a stick at...especially the pound cakes made from the yolks left over from meringue pies sweating with beads of sugared amber. Remember? 'Course that was back when meat was safe and before the hens quit cackling! But memories brought dreams—dreams of days when it would all happen again. And by then everybody would've learned to get by on less. Oh no, they wouldn't! They'd stuff 'til they were sick, then roll on the floor....

It was late. But her parents talked on, even as she brushed her teeth over the washbasin, gave her hair a quick fluff-up, and collected her school supplies. They, too, were remembering and dreaming, hardly aware of another's presence, although the conversation supposedly was for her benefit. Grasping at straws of strength to go on...

Grandmother had saved some special news for Thanksgiving....Grandfather was part of it, but everything depended on Mary Ann's progress. Thank goodness, that spunky young thing was holding her own, begging to see Jake, Billy Joe, and Marvel—out of the question, of course. Both the older people had their hands full. Mercy sakes alive, did they ever! What with Brother Grady there with nobody to wait on him—but yes, he was pulling through...same for Mrs. Sutheral, poor dear. It would have seemed wiser to stay in Dallas like she'd planned, only she got right homesick for Pleasant Knoll folks. Like as not, she'd have come down with this thing anyway, doctors said. Oh yes, a whole team of them, mostly strangers, responding to the all-points alert. Fanny was a lifesaver: everywhere at once, even caring for Mrs. Ambrose who had given up trying to run the boardinghouse—just too much for her arthritis, all bent-over like she was. And Fanny brought her sister Prissy, younger than Sula Mae—what a little worker! That worked out real well, too. The arrangement put Sula Mae and Casper in charge back home—good for them. And now, surprise!

"Now that Billy Joe knows what's good for him, he's right handy—doing his homework, too. But the best part is that he's helping Prissy and the two of them read the Bible to boarders here whose vision is playing out. The Squire wants to see his sons. You can bet he's got something tucked up those starched shirtsleeves!"

Marvel had left with a hurried good-bye and wondered if her parents knew when she left. So began the day before Thanksgiving. . . .

# 16

# Part of a
# Painted Dream

Riders on the school bus, huddled together for warmth, had little to say as the Model A Ford engine choked and coughed when billows of dust rose up to shut out the sky ahead of and behind them. The driver's teeth were clenched as if his pipe were between them as he squinted to see the dirt road and keep watch for the narrow plank bridges. Gone, like everything else they had all known and loved in the past, was the wild abandon of rules and regulations which used to mark the day preceding a holiday. Where was the exultation, the joy? Would each be remembering a special holiday, no longer observed, now stored hopefully for—for *when*? Next year ... the next generation?

Marvel sighed and rubbed her palms together, wishing she had a pair of warm gloves. Her fingers felt too numb to check names off as other students boarded. Cap Bumstead saw her effort to increase circulation and grunted. "Some Thanksgivin'," he grunted again.

The smile she tried for felt unnatural, frozen. "Not like the roast pig and blackberry cobbler days, served from those expandable tables," she conceded, hoping her words carried over the asthmatic combination of bus and wind. Marvel smiled, remembering how Daddy and Uncle Worth searched high and low for more and more boards to lay over sawhorses as the big white house of her Pleasant Knoll childhood filled up with relatives and then overflowed with neighbors. And oh, the incomparable line-dried smell of Mother and Auntie Rae's starched, white linen

tablecloths! Grandmother was right. There must be memories—
not all white linen ones—bright, colorful too, a heritage of
beauty.

Mr. Bumstead was in no mood for nostalgia. "No time t'be
revertin' t'childhood," he said, sounding downright edgy. "I'm
lookin' tomorror in th' eye and ain't likin' what I see—no stuff
t'be makin' memories out uv: sickness, wind, death. Gray 'n
gloomy—ever'thing's plum *black*."

*Even your mood and your face*, Marvel thought but said instead, "We all feel discouraged—gray, if you will. But we can be
thankful for friends who understand, and find it within ourselves
to thank God for them—"

She planned to say that such wonderful friends didn't just
happen, that they, like the land, had been cultivated (wondering
if this man would understand if she added, "for, like the land,
they can be swept away—so we dared not neglect the great
harvest of friendship which trying circumstances had yielded").
He gave her no opportunity.

"Hard tellin' 'em from enemies these days! Come fetchin'
water from my well 'n turnin' into robbers."

The harsh words were shocking. "What do you mean?" Marvel
asked cautiously, pausing to smile at two girls, one of whom was
Erlene.

"We're gonna run short on medicine, that's what! An' folks'll
die off like our cows. Guess y'all know I'll be haulin' carcuses uv
them pore critters. Next, it'll be people. Ain't it wailsome?"

"There must be some mistake, Mr. Bumstead. There's no
shortage as far as I know. Oh *please*, let's not make it worse than
it is!"

"That's right. I keep forgittin' you Harringtons are nigger-
lovers!"

A white-hot arrow of anger pierced Marvel's heart.

"I'm going to try to forget you said that, but right now, sir, I'll
go on record as saying I take offense with that—your remark
about my family and about our black neighbors! *Wailsome*, you
say? Your attitude's the most deplorable of all. We're Christian,
Mr. Bumstead—God-filled, love-filled. Oh, how *dare* you take
such liberties!"

She paused in an effort to regain composure, but instead she
took on more fuel. "And just who are you calling *thieves*?"

"Betcha think I'm about t'say them niggers!" He took a curve too fast in his fury and all but overturned the bus, a move which set the riders to screaming. Marvel took a fierce satisfaction in his having to call out a begrudging apology to reassure them. "Nope!" he went on after righting the vehicle. "I got suspicious-like when none of them—well, I was gonna use a colored word for colored people since it fits—squatters down yonder come down with typhoid. So I asked around, found out from yore friend Annie's papa that blasted health doctor comin' out th' first time up 'n taken care uv them 'stead uv his gal—an' she's on her death bed. I got him fired all right, but I ain't got her blood on *my* hands. Th' guilty one's whoever talked th' weaklin' into doin' such!"

They were nearing the school. Marvel checked off the last name and calmly closed her notebook before answering with deadly calm.

"*I* am responsible, so you need not look farther. Furthermore, I feel no remorse. None! I question that Annie's on her deathbed, but if you must place blame on someone, place it on her father. Did he tell you that he refused to allow his family to be inoculated? I wish I could tell you what those 'niggers' are doing for the sick in Pleasant Knoll, all because they're immune. Once they get all on their feet, they'll be back here to act as your servants in case *you* become ill."

Mr. Bumstead's hand was trembling as he opened the door, and his face was deathly pale. "I—I don't know what to say. What can I *do*?"

"Pray," Marvel Harrington said.

\* \* \*

Marvel walked away from the bus with a heavy heart. Mr. Bumstead undoubtedly regretted his words once he found himself wrong, but the Civil War still raged inside. And he saw no quarrel with Christian principles and his prejudice. She sighed, wishing herself stronger, above letting such narrowness bring back the heaviness to her heart and lay the world's ills about her shoulders like a too-tight scarf. A quote from Forbes Robinson came back to her as she waved to friends and entered the building: "The great triumph of Christianity is to produce a few saints. They make us discontent with our own lives." Well, she was no saint! So why did she go on acting as if she were superior? A saint never knew she was one—and pretending was just as bad. That made her a sinner—a sinner of the worst order! Suddenly Marvel loathed herself. She felt all mixed-up, uncertain, afraid.

Oh, if only Titus were here, she could stop this silly game of make-believe, self-sacrificing only to hide her own tears. She could be herself: unaffected, unpretentious Marvel Harrington, letting herself lean on the protective arm of another's strength. Everything seemed so different when he was around—Titus, wonderful Titus who, just by being himself, filled her dark days with prisms of light. Each moment became a kaleidoscope of shifting emotions, colorful and music-filled. His mood was contagious and she was a willing victim—no yesterdays and no tomorrows...just this golden day...*together*.

Sometimes that togetherness was only for a moment, but in that moment the universe became wholesome, beautiful, and filled with total happiness. Just remembering such a moment got her through the day.

Miss Ingersoll, bright-eyed with plans of her own, wished the girls a "Happy Thanksgiving!" and dismissed them 15 minutes early. Marvel, busy collecting her assignments, did not look up when a tall shadow filled the French-paned front door of the domestic science cottage.

The other girls tittered, which must mean they knew the caller's identity. Miss Ingersoll's attorney-fiancé? Marvel was curious, too, but she'd dropped her pencil. She was on hands and knees in an effort to recover it before the class trooped out, when the teacher came to stand before her. Feeling foolish, Marvel scrambled to her feet, her face red from bending over. She needn't have been embarrassed.

Miss Ingersoll bent from the waist comically while the other girls looked on knowingly. It was as if they thought the two of them were harboring some secret they knew already. How strange!

And stranger yet was Miss Ingersoll's beaming expression and formal manner. "A gentleman to see you, miss," she announced grandly, as if she were a maid-in-waiting. And then she *winked*.

Marvel's fingers tingled as if she were feeling a fine piece of silk? Why? And who could explain the 50-fold increase of her heartbeat? There was no accounting for her sudden entry into a painted dream, a beautiful painting she had viewed in awe, little dreaming she could step inside. But it had happened. God had heard her unsaid prayer.

She was at the door, and *he* was smiling down at her.

"Titus," she whispered, hardly daring to say his name.

"Marvel," he whispered back, closing the door behind her.

Knowing they had an audience, they walked down the path in a proper manner, their shoulders not so much as brushing. "There—that old rattletrap, the one that honked us apart—last June?"

Marvel nodded. "A million years ago," she said, scarcely able to breathe, and stepped on the running board when Titus opened the door.

He entered the old car from the opposite side and, without looking her direction, pressed his foot on the self-starter on the worn floorboard. When there was a response, it happened suddenly, causing the car to backfire as it jerked forward, causing them both to laugh.

Neither of them tried to speak above the complaints of the aging car. When Titus steered to the curb to park alongside their tree, Marvel was not surprised. She had known he would. Hurriedly, he turned off the ignition before releasing the clutch and brake.

"Let's run for it!" he said, as if daring the wind.

And they ran, hands laced tightly, and laughing in sheer joy.

Titus tossed a worn blanket at the base of the giant oak on the side opposite the wind, and they sat cross-ankled, backs against the rough bark of the great tree trunk. Here they were protected: away from prying eyes, out of reach of the wind's long arm, and beyond the cares of the world around them.

"My dear Miss Harrington, I just happened to be in your city and was, uh, hoping— Oh Marvel, I can't play games! *Please* say you're happy to see me."

"You *know* I am," she managed to whisper.

He gripped her hands until his knuckles were white. "Surprised?"

"That, too. No, not really. I mean I should be, but I'm not."

"Because we were never apart. Look at me, Marvel."

She raised her eyes, aware that her heart was in them—and not caring. Under the spell of their togetherness, anything was possible. She was looking into the very soul of the most wonderful man she would ever meet. It would be easy to take too much for granted, decide the deep emotion reflected in the depth of those gray-eyes-turned-black was reserved for her alone. But no, here was a person driven to seek new worlds to conquer. He must have the freedom his sister begged.

If she blinked she would cry, so with eyes open wide, Marvel met his gaze unflinchingly and reached for the banter he'd failed to manage. "Sooo what brings you to these parts, Mr. Smith— business or pleasure? Few get home for the holidays anymore."

"So few do. *Oh, those eyes!*" The words were torn from his lips. "What color are they? I've never seen eyes so—so *beautiful.*"

"We—we call it Harrington-blue." Marvel, too, found words difficult. She wanted to laugh, to sing, to cry with sheer joy.

"I prefer *Marvel*-blue," he said as if talking to himself. "No— Marvelous. That's it, Marvelous-blue!" The words were almost triumphant—as if, momentarily, her eyes were the only thing that mattered.

The golden minutes were slipping away. "Titus?" Marvel's voice trembled. He was stroking her hands, then rubbing them both between his palms.

"Yes darling? (*Darling*, Titus had called her *darling*.) Your hands are like ice. You should have warm gloves. What were you going to say?"

"How *did* you happen to—to come? You—didn't tell me—"

Part business—and the thought of seeing her, Titus explained quickly. Lucille needed him, something to do with restoring the old Smith Hotel, making it into a historical landmark. But who could afford that? Then she had lost her husband and wasn't strong herself.

Marvel expressed sympathy, but Titus only shook his head. It wasn't unexpected. And besides, life had been difficult together. Marvel tried to recall how Miss Ingersoll had put it. The sister's husband was much older. And wasn't he an alcoholic? A veteran and they lived on his disability check. And yet she was determined that her brother should have every chance to use his fine mind. Nothing, absolutely *nothing* must stand in his way. His future was her only goal.

"Were there children?" Marvel asked woodenly. *She* must be no obstacle.

Titus inhaled deeply as if the subject were painful. "Fortunately, no. That would have complicated matters even more. Poor sis—she's crippled from—from trying to give birth. And I've told you—told you that our mother died, be—because of me."

"Oh Titus!" Marvel longed to reach up and touch his face, draw his head to her shoulder, anything to take away his misery because she understood his feelings of guilt.

"I know. But I missed knowing her, and it put such a burden on my sister—one I can never repay. But there's something else—something I've never put into words—" Titus said haltingly.

"Go ahead, you'll feel better to say it. And I *want* to share."

His words tumbled out, releasing deepest feelings, his remorse, and his fears. There was no medical evidence that he knew of to support his thinking—he'd looked for it. But could this be an inherited thing, this inability to give birth? Titus could never give thought to having a family of his own—not even marriage—without resolving the issue in his own mind. It made no sense to others, but—

"I understand, Titus. I honestly do."

He was gripping her hands again—gripping so hard they hurt. But she needed to hurt because life was making her hurt inside.

"Only you would—only you. Oh Marvel!"

"I understand because memories are powerful things. Some are ugly and leave scars, but others are beautiful and blot out all ugliness."

"Don't I know—don't I? The memory of *you* kept me going." His voice was suddenly light as if the sun were breaking through the dark clouds around them. "I knew you'd be wearing blue, the way I remembered. I half-expected the pearls, too. I memorized every detail of you standing on the church steps alone. Do you remember, too?"

*Remember?* A lump rose to Marvel's throat. Was she trying to rub the lump away, or was she feeling for the pearls Titus mentioned, half-expecting them to be there? The thought startled her. Not the absence of the necklace—she never wore it to school—but the sudden realization that she hadn't seen it for so long. But had she looked? Probably not, so what was there to concern herself with?

Titus moved closer and studied her profile.

"Marvel? A penny for your thoughts."

"They aren't worth it," she said dreamily. "Oh yes, they are! My thoughts are worth more money than Wall Street has. A million dollars wouldn't do in down payment. I was dreaming— I—"

Marvel gulped and stopped, feeling she had said far too much.

"Dream aloud," Titus encouraged gently. "Why, you're blushing!"

"I—I'm not accustomed to conversations that are so—so personal. Sometimes I wish I were older, more experienced—"

"Older?" His voice was low and intimate. Touching her hair, he whispered, "Age has nothing to do with feelings, trust me."

"Oh, I do, I do!" she said without guile. "I was thinking of the things money won't buy—like our being here together, dreaming of when our missions are finished. I never talk about this to anybody else—never—"

Reaching out, he cupped her chin in the hand which so recently had stroked her hair. Then, slowly, he lifted her chin, forcing her gaze to meet his. "I'm not anybody else—I'm Titus, remember? Go ahead and dream, my dear—and know I'm dreaming, too. Maybe I *do* wish we were older," Titus said miserably. "And that education and all this we're going through were over— and I could offer you the world."

"I don't want the world—just—"

He bent forward, causing Marvel to withdraw quickly. "Don't be afraid. You want just *what*?"

*Just you!* she wanted to sing out. But there they were, those commitments, promises to keep. "J-just the simple things. I told you money can't buy them: sunrises, sweet clover, lilacs, poetry—"

Titus squeezed her hands again. "And *me*, Marvel. Say it!"

The words were fresh, sweet, and boyish. "And you, Titus," Marvel said simply. Silence . . . and then a mutual sigh.

"I wish I could take you home. I said that then, too, didn't I? Same car, gas tank still rusty above the one-gallon mark. We'd have to back up the hills anyway, the gearshift's so cranky. Someday—"

"Someday," Marvel repeated, dreamingly tasting the promise.

She was back on her mountaintop where the air was clean, pure, and unclogged by evil. There nothing could disturb her tranquility. And so she was unbothered by the next question Titus asked.

"Oh, I almost forgot. I promised Lucille to ask about a man my brother-in-law knew, a Salsburg. Someone you know?"

"*Knew*, yes—Frederick Salsburg, my father's stepbrother. I was with him when he died. Not easy when he hadn't been a very nice man, but he left with me a reminder to store up bright moments—like we're doing—for the dark ones. I watched a weak man grow strong, and he left me another gift—oddly enough, because of *you*. Someday I'll tell you."

"There's no need. I'd rather talk about you and me. You're *my* bright moment. I wish we could be together more. That's why—I mean *one* of the whys—I'm here. I had a chance to come with Bill Johnson. You remember my cocaptain. He's with me in college."

"Yes, I remember him. But I never saw you play—never so much as saw a game of football in my life, Titus. I had to leave on the bus for the 40-mile ride home."

His groan came from deep inside. "Oh Marvel, you've missed so much. *We've* missed so much together. I have a lot to make up to *you*, too."

Marvel shook her head mutely, but her heart cried out: *Just love me.*

"The trip home was sudden. The old boy's budget won't allow it, but his sanity's involved. He and Amanda Cohane went steady and now—well, it's all off. She found herself somebody more exciting. Bill was fine when he was in the limelight, making touchdowns—a star."

"How cruel. I wish he could say 'good riddance' and forget it."

"Bill's not like that. But I wanted to tell you about the offer I have to start a newspaper office in Greenville. I'd be closer to here. Of course it would mean giving up school, but there would be money to take care of my sister. Only," he hesitated, "she's against it. What do you think?"

*I think I would like to wail like a spoiled child* from *disappointment.* But aloud she said calmly, "That only *you* can decide. A dream is not for sale, and you'll know no peace without following yours."

"I know, darling, I know," Titus whispered raggedly. "I feel so helpless sometimes, like I'm trying to cross that gulf the speaker spoke of at graduation. I feel trapped, stuck with a calling I'm unable to fulfill or resist. I—I guess I'm looking for a secure place."

"How well I know. I'm there with you—wanting that land of perfect balance where all things beautiful grow, another Garden of Eden. Adam and Eve had it and wanted more. So we go on paying."

"When we don't have to. Jesus paid the price!" Titus was alive and exuberant again. "Oh Marvel, what would I do without you?"

"Don't try!" she sang out without restraint. "You've reached your decision, and I'm with you there, too. We have to get the Word out!" Their private world was invaded then by the blast of horns announcing the arrival of the school buses. "With a little help I could hate horns!"

"No pun intended?" Titus laughed. "Don't *hate*. I want to remember you happy!" Then with a sudden release of her hands, he cupped his own into a megaphone and crooned Rudy Vallee fashion: "Oh, the beautiful lady in blue, we met just like two shadows dooooo. Not one word was said—she kissed me then fled. And our little romance was through. No, *never!*"

*"Never!"* she repeated his vow and, blowing him a fingertip kiss, hurried away to leave them both smiling radiantly. The wind had found their hiding place, carried away their light song. But it could not steal the memory—the little whisper of beauty stored in the gray arches of her heart....

# 17

# *The Darkest Hour*

Marvel attacked her work with renewed vigor, sending column after column for the ever-widening reading audience of *The News Review*. Her own reviews covered the spectrum of fast-breaking news objectively: the weather, the continued drought, the increasing illnesses and their treatment. She had learned to make use of "cause and effect," and that allowed all columns to end on an upbeat note. Cause gave an opportunity to point out gently the misuse of cultivated lands and overtaming the natural grasslands which resulted in the unreserved slashing away at the native stand of timber. The natural blanket of grass was gone. Gone, too, were the trees nature had lined up so perfectly, fencing out the winds. And now gone, sadly, was the once-productive soil—gone with the wind which had stripped earth from thousands of square miles of rich farmland and pasture. Texas, indeed, had become a part of the Dust Bowl. The "dusted out" areas which once stretched from the panhandle north to the Dakotas and parts of West Virginia, now included the entire heartland. The drought struck most severely in Wyoming, Colorado, New Mexico, Nebraska, Kansas, Oklahoma, and the very heart of Texas . . . beautiful, beautiful Texas, land where the bluebonnets once grew.

That, then, was the devastating effect. First to go was the soil, and close on its heels went water. The result was the dusting out, the drying out—and now, the *dying out. . . .*

The writing, squeezed from the young writer's heart, hit home. Local residents saw themselves and their plight reflected in the newspaper as the wind grew stronger, developing gully-like trenches called blowouts. And rightly so, for following the paths where dry-farming practices had allowed the powdery-fine topsoil to be stripped away, the wind plowed deeper and deeper, until at last the fields were but the barren clay of hopelessness. For how could one hope when it would take years, maybe a lifetime, or another generation to repair the damage—or maybe *never*?

Marvel's researched "Thirteen Million Acres of Wasteland" reached far beyond Titus County, far beyond the state. True, some of the dust was spread too finely to benefit other states, but some, the young journalist wrote, had heaped up to become *loess*—another word for their increasing vocabulary, but well worth looking into. A loess made excellent soil wherever it was formed, according to that agricultural expert Senator Cliff Norton. He was a good man for the job, and he'd likely find support if ever he tossed his hat in the ring for governor. The expert, of course, was his young aide, for Marvel and Titus were burning midnight oil to keep alive their joint "Heartbeats of America, U.S.A." series in addition to his "Ears of Austin" and her "Eyes of East Texas" columns. Of course that meant sacrificing time for more personal letters, but then, it was all worth it. Well, wasn't it?

It was financial panic, their elders told them, which set off the Great Depression. The two of them must form a sort of windbreak—similar to trees against the winds—in their efforts to hold back a similar panic in the face of the drought. They must keep hope alive even as the plants and animals became corpses, dry bones in the white sepulcher of mankind's folly.

So Marvel's pen duplicated the contour plowing the county agent had recommended—differing only in that Mr. Inman's efforts were to preserve the land; hers, to preserve its people. Her hand had faltered slightly, however, at the thought of the congenial man's services. She was remembering that he, too, had been stricken with typhoid. Had anyone heard more? Maybe Daddy had inquired. Meantime, she must warn the people again.

Marvel's next column was devoted to the help people were receiving and would continue to receive: replenishment of the serum against typhoid, and the urgency of making a point to take advantage as well of quinine, for malaria remained a distinct possibility. And yes, it too was plentiful. Doctors? More were on the way as new illnesses continued to add to the problem. Many of the diseases were difficult to diagnose, but research was underway. In short, the situation would be controlled, providing there was full cooperation from everybody. One person did make a difference because there were "carriers." She repeated the instructions Dr. Porter and Dr. Bronson had left with them all: Boil water, have all wells treated, drink fluids (a problem, of course, with the scarcity of water and milk, but they did have home-canned tomato juice, kraut juice, grape juice. *Any* fluids would help), make cleanliness a way of life, and *work together*! Think of each other. Be every man's keeper. And here Marvel was able to work in her essay on friendship.

The article was well-received and her reward was learning that more and more of their own neighbors were getting their shots and checking on one another, although all public meetings—including church services—had been suspended until the emergency was past. All fatigue faded when her parents reported that the neighborhood was drawing closer, caring even more because of the dire need of each other in the great crisis.

That freed her to make use of the bulletins Titus had sent regarding more financial aid at a later date and the great strides made in combating drought. *There need never be another one!*

Even now measures were underway to avoid a similar catastrophe. One included the development of drought-resistant food plants—plants which could be grown with reasonable safety in areas where rainfall might be insufficient. Expeditions went as far as the bone-dry plateaus of Tibet. And the outcome? Kanred and durum wheat were among them—wheat for bread . . . the staff of life.

Hungry people were warring people, and war must be avoided at any cost!

The newspaper featuring that story carried an obituary which shook the very foundation of every household in the community: County Agricultural Agent Dead, Victim of the Typhoid Epidemic! Mother's voice trembled when she read the headline aloud, but she could never have imagined Daddy's reaction. Without reading details, he dropped his head into his hands as his knees buckled beneath him. It was so unexpected that Marvel wondered if he so much as checked to make sure there was a chair to break his fall. She sprang forward, strewing books behind her in the rush to reach him, comfort him. There was no opportunity.

Cap Bumstead was at the door, peering through the screen with cupped hands. "Dale—Snow—did you read—?" His breath came in little gasps as if he'd been running. "I—we—it cain't be true. It cain't."

But it was. And suddenly the house was filled with men, some from close by and others from neighboring communities, all talking at once, finding different means of expressing their shock and grief.

"Such a fine feller . . . real square-dealer thet Mr. Inman . . . real *white!*"

This time it was Mr. Bumstead who took issue. "Don't say that word. Right fine he wuz, no doubt 'bout it, but color don't make th' man. We all bleed th' same—an' we gonna need each other!"

The talk went on, but for the moment Marvel heard none of it. Mr. Bumstead said *that*? She had witnessed a miracle. He *had* prayed. . . .

Words began to take shape again. "No, fun'ral ain't here. He warn't from these parts . . . jest visitin' . . . sent by th' state like as not . . . or th' gov'ment maybe? Hit's too late t'tell 'im how we 'preciated all he done. Best foller them rules 'bout with th' disk 'no plow . . . not git in debt dependin' on cash crops t'pull 'em out. Yeah, like Marvel here said, he'ps comin' but folks could'n' 'spect a gov'ment dole when three-qua'ters wuz on relief a'ready."

"You're all right," Mother said hurriedly. "We must be prepared to dig new wells, make room for—for progress—maybe a boom! Here—how about grape juice, everybody? The bottom-land neighbors found wild vines. Those who missed the Captain's words needn't hesitate. I squeezed!"

How thoughtful. Marvel moved to help immediately, while keeping an ear tuned to the ongoing conversation. Those who had not had their injections must do so—except for the Smiths. (Ruth's parents? How strange that they would hold out after seeing how ill Annie Pruitt next door was. But one of the men was to explain the question in Marvel's mind.) Will and Mercy Smith had submitted to the inoculations and precious little good it did, he said, when both were down now, too. (Marvel felt an electrical shock travel down her spine. The Smiths? If only she'd gone to them in person. But no, she must not feel guilty, for doctors had warned that the medication took time.)

"This sad news plays havoc with—with our other plans, too," a man Marvel didn't know said quietly. "You know—the slaughtering. Mr. Inman was to help out—help us get shut of the cattle—"

Marvel, in her emotional state, felt a wild desire to laugh. *Shut*, shut as in "rid, to dispose of." She was remembering the satisfaction Mary Ann took in pointing out to Marvel that *she* had used the colloquialism and gotten by with it. "You of all people," her cousin had teased, "when you're so good in English, correcting me like you did when I was going to *carry* a cow! Guess I should have said *tote!*"

Embarrassed, Marvel had gone to the newspaper office, called attention to her poor diction, and suggested that they feel free to edit her work. She hoped they would. The editor had laughed and said absolutely not. Such words were acceptable in informal conversation—colorful, in fact—and helped readers identify with her work.

The desire to laugh made a quick exit. Why must everything be such a grim reminder of the grave realities closing in around them?...Mary Ann and her dreadful illness...the cows and their morbid fate. A drumfire raged within her as if she were standing along a battlefront in the line of discharging weapons. War! Was there no escape?

Suddenly she welcomed her mother's rush of words, meant to comfort, to cheer, to override any situation of gloom. "Oh Marvel, I have good news, honey," she whispered, even as Marvel heard Mr. Bumstead's response to the stranger (after all this delay, because of sickness, treating the water, and the like, the cows would be—*ahem*—taken care of tomorrow. *Tomorrow!)* Swallowing the lump in her throat, Marvel turned to face Snow Harrington.

"Good news, Mother? I'd like that."

"Oh *lots* of it," Mother said, obviously glad that she had captured her daughter's attention. "Your grandmother called— nothing unusual, except that we'd talked and I just *knew* it was good news. And guess what! Mary Ann has gone through the crisis—is better, honey—*better*! Jake talked Dr. Porter into letting him in. Maybe her life depended on it, she was so sick. Somehow he was able to get through to her, get her to nod. They wouldn't let him touch her, had to wear masks—you know the rules. But she heard, opened her eyes—Oh, it makes me want to cry. But out of the blue, she asked for fried chicken! Rae's had no sleep, but *she* called, too, she was so happy! There, doesn't that make you feel better?"

"Oh Mother! Oh yes, yes, *yes*!" In a sudden rush of affection, Marvel threw her arms around her mother, letting herself become that little girl she'd missed so long. For an enchanted moment neither moved.

Marvel was the first to stir. "And Daddy—does he know?" she asked, lifting her head from the hollow of her mother's thin shoulder.

"Yes—yes, he knows. He was happy, too—until all this. I know they mean well, these men, but I almost wish—wish they'd stop bothering him with every little problem."

"This isn't a little problem, Mother. It's a series of big ones—problems which affect us all. We can't hope to cope without each other. I understand how you feel and I share in those feelings, but we can't shield Daddy from the world."

"Not you, too, Marvel—not you. You're always so hopeful—"

"I still am—"

"There's my girl. 'The darkest hour is just before the dawn' and," Mother sighed, "I guess this is it. But wait! There's more news. Don't you want to hear about your grandparents—their patients?"

Marvel sighed, too. Of course she wanted to know.

They were fine, they really were. Said they were too busy for germs to catch up with them. Thank goodness Mrs. Sutheral and Brother Greer were snapping right out of it. Doctors said they both had light cases. And now they were waiting on each other. Wasn't that wonderful? That meant that Fanny could have a break, come home, bringing Prissy with her. Grandmother still needed help, so Sula Mae and Casper could replace them. Fanny would look after the needs of her own family and then she would be ready to help out here. What did Marvel think?

What did she think? Marvel's mind was traveling at the speed of light, reaching out for guidance for tomorrow. Only God could see her through it. This was an emergency, one Mother and Daddy must not face alone. A fig for exemptions, she would simply have to miss a day's school. Oh, but tomorrow was Saturday! In contradiction, she wished it weren't, that she could go on with her routine, close out the horror, as one deals with a bad dream. But this was reality—stark reality.

Plan ahead, that's what she would do—plan ahead and continue her columns about the Great Plains Agricultural Council, headquartered in Manhattan, Kansas. Its program was designed around hope—long-range planning to urge farmers to leave farms which failed to return a profit even in good years. Oh, but she mustn't mention leaving to Mother. She had never understood the necessity and, in her panic, would not hear the rest of the plans—never knowing that the abandoned farms would be returned to grass for grazing, planted with trees and cattle. In more arid regions they would convert the farms into wildlife refuges where fish could survive in fresh water, and rabbits, squirrels, quail, whippoorwills all could have food, be safe from animals of prey, free from disease-carrying fleas and ticks. Only then could the broad program, with man's cooperation, be restored to a near-perfect environment, *the Garden*....

Marvel must have mumbled something, for Mother was talking again...too much...and too fast. She was purposely trying to drown out the departing words of the men. Someone was thanking a Dr. West. The stranger?

"They need to plan without us," Mother said hurriedly, attempting to recapture Marvel's attention. "I wanted to tell you that our sweet Rae laughed—actually found the strength to laugh about Mary Ann. Rae told her she'd get her chicken leg in broth—and like it. Of course, Mary Ann's fuming, but her mother says that's a good sign. And it is. I love Rae—she and I are closer than we are to the other sisters-in-law. We think alike, like you and Mary Ann. But the others move in different circles."

Marvel nodded absently. "Aunt Eleanore and Aunt Dorthea *are* different, but I guess they're what Uncle Emory and Uncle Joseph want—need. They're different from Daddy and Uncle Worth."

"*Very* different—heads in the clouds. Would you believe they're still talking about your Uncle Alex and his senseless dabbling with hops, whatever that is, 'way up there in Oregon? How harebrained!"

"Maybe it isn't," Marvel said slowly, immediately regretting it when she looked at her mother's stricken face. "It's all right, Mother. Don't worry about what they do. Oh, here's Prissy!"

Prissy looked adorable in her pink pinafore, old but starched to stand out like an inverted mushroom at the hem, and pink ribbons on her corn-rowed hair. "I come—came to show y'all how good, well, no, *nice* ah talks 'cause of Billy Joe." Prissy brought an ebony hand from behind her and took a generous bite of raw biscuit dough. "Guess what we gonna have fo' suppah! Daddy done—did shoot us uh rabbit fo' stew!"

"No!" The loud protest came from Daddy. The men were gone and he stood alone like a one-man army. "I order you to bury it. No, I'll do it for you, Prissy. Go! The rabbits are sick—full of fleas—could kill—"

The wide-eyed child fled, her skirts rattling like the dry cornstalks.

"Oh Dale, why did you do that? You scared the child out of her wits," Mother cried out in protest. "We don't *know* that!"

"We know," he said in defeat. "The doctor—you have to accept this. No domestic meat—no game. All carry disease: pork, trichinosis—dysentery's rampant—food poisoning. We have to dump all our canned goods, on account of soil tests finding botulism. Meal? Unsafe—seems to be one cause of pellagra. Then there's jaundice—Erlene's folks, Marvel. Water's got everything from salmonella. It's gone—every morsel of good. *Oh, dear God in heaven! What's left for us now?*" Daddy rushed to find Prissy.

"The darkest hour—" Mother began. Then she, too, stopped. . . .

# 18

# *Tomorrow*

Tomorrow came. Marvel had lain dry-eyed with wretchedness throughout the night. Wrapped as she was in a cocoon of anguish, it was impossible to think. Nothing made sense anymore. She felt trapped, defeated, and afraid as the tightly wound threads of desperation sealed off every exit. Oh, that she could emerge a beautifully painted butterfly, allow herself to be lifted high above all the ugliness and horrors ahead, floating weightlessly on the wings of the wind to join Titus in their private world.

On the contrary, when the telephone cut shrilly through the predawn, Marvel shrank away and, pulling the covers over her head, felt a wild need to crawl back into the cocoon's protective dark. But, once emerged, a butterfly can never go back. There was a mission to perform ... promises to keep ... others to serve. There was no escape.

Jumping from bed, she reached the wall telephone first and ran her fingers up the cord to find the bell-shaped receiver. "Hello?" Marvel's voice was guarded as she spoke into the transmitter. Let Mother and Daddy rest if they could. She must be strong for them.

"Marvel?"

She recognized the editor's voice immediately. What could the man possibly want at this time of day on Saturday?

"Good morning, Mr. Corey. What can I do for you?"

"Forgive the early call, but it seemed important."

"I wasn't asleep. I'm an early riser. So?"

"So I have an assignment for you, an important one. I didn't get in touch before because I didn't know this was the day. The truth is, Marvel, I'd like to have you cover the story out there."

"About the cattle?" Marvel asked when Mr. Corey hesitated.

"Yes," he answered quickly, sounding relieved. Did he think she didn't know? "But now that I think of it—well, if you'd rather somebody else covered the story . . . I mean, you're so close to it—"

Close to it? Yes, both ways—nearby and leading their own to slaughter. Could she? She *must*. No outsider could know how these people felt, the losers.

Marvel's hand on the receiver shook as she responded, but her voice was steady. "I'll cover the story, sir. You see, there's so much behind the scenes which might lead readers to criticize the drastic move. None of us like it. But contrary to what others read in newspapers and hear on radio, we—we—we and our cattle never had a chance! Our former president's preventative measures didn't come soon enough. Mr. Hoover foresaw a depression, but who could foresee the drought and all its effects? Sorry—I'm writing the story already."

"And I'm liking what I hear! Can you give me a quick preview of just what you meant then? I know the local story is yet to come—"

Marvel found herself doing what she would have thought impossible just minutes before. What better proof that God always had a plan—a way out? How could she have thought there was no exit? True, she was a helpless victim, like the cattle to be slaughtered today, but just to be *thinking* was like salve for an open wound.

Yes, she could tell him—and quickly. Livestock elsewhere was brought on foot and shipped to be prepared for table use. Or if the herd was of a good breed, shipped to less-stricken areas, greener pastures. Already prices were rising—sadly, because of war talk. "Wartime prices," wasn't it called? And more favorable weather *would* come eventually.

There was silence at the other end of the line, and then a whistle. "What a story!" the editor said.

"Oh, there'll be other focuses—lots of them: the human interest, the—the carnage—without getting too gory, too maudlin," Marvel planned aloud, excited now. "I can do it, yes! I *want* readers to understand!"

"You understand that this is—how shall I put it—an honor? That you can stand on a pinnacle of pride?"

"Oh no—no, sir! I don't want that, Mr. Corey. I—I just don't!"

"No—no, I guess you don't... one in a million," he mumbled. "All right," and there was a soft chuckle, "*be* humble. Just keep writing!"

"Oh I will," Marvel promised, her mind already reaching to embrace the barrage of problems Dale Harrington had rasped out in a few painful sentences. "The Four Horsemen," she would call the emotional story. For they were all there, all crossing the finish line in one wild stampede. But not now... not even a whisper of a hint. Today was sufficient unto itself....

"Marvel, I thank you. I wish," Mr. Corey near-groaned, "that I could pay you what this is worth. And I promise you—you *and* myself—that I'll make it all up when you're ready for a career. We never really talked about this. Now's not the time, but what *do* you want to be?"

"Helpful," she said.

"That's no answer and you know it," the editor scolded. "You're a bright young lady—good with words. You know *helpful's* an adjective. I wanted a *noun*. I referred to a career! (*And my feet are cold!* Marvel thought.)

"All right then, I don't know. How's this: The Lord hasn't told me yet! And I'd better ring off. There's a finger of light prying underneath the door, and that means (Marvel gulped) the day'll be in action—soon."

"I've kept you. But Marvel, are you *sure*? I can send a reporter out, a man who can stomach this kind of thing—"

"No!" Marvel's response came quickly. "There can be no spectators. We have orders about that—dangerous in more than one way—"

"Wait! You mean no photographers either? We'll need pictures."

"I mean *nobody*—outsiders most of all!"

"But you know our rights—freedom of the press. We'll smuggle a man in if we have to!"

"I wouldn't advise it! You don't know what you're asking. I know these people. They're *my* people, on my own territory. The Harringtons have been around so long we're accepted. As for rights, laws— Whatever reason—forget it! The law, *their* law, is their code—Christian, yes, but Judaic Christians obeying laws in both the Old and the New Testaments. 'An eye for an eye.' I told you I'd do it, and now, I really *must* go. Thank you, sir. Thank you so much!"

And with that, Marvel Harrington rang off, breaking the connection by the local signal of a one-bell ring saying the party line was no longer in use. The young girl gave no thought to how independent she had sounded in her peculiar mixture of humility and self-assurance—or how convincing! But it was obvious that the newspaper editor noted each word and sent no aid. The next day's edition was to devote the entire front page to the stories wrung from her heart. And there *were* photographs of the hauntingly tragic pyre of burning carcasses—photographs taken by state officials who must, they declared, show proof of proper disposal if owners were to receive payment for the hides.

But that would be another tomorrow. "First," Marvel managed a lopsided smile at a breakfast nobody tasted, "we'll get 'shut' of today!" Yes, shut it out—*completely*.

# 19

# The Vision
# of Reality

All day the report of gunfire continued. By mid-morning a hazy blue smoke ring circled the sun. And by afternoon smoke had thickened the air like gravy—thickened it to such a consistency that breathing was almost impossible. And then came the stench of burning flesh. Buzzards, the vultures which had given up hope of finding carnage in a land where there was no life and disappeared, were back as a final touch to terror. The winds increased in velocity, pushing the great beasts of the air in backward flight, in futile effort to sweep away the impure air. But more smoke boiled in to refill each empty pocket, followed by more, until the atmosphere became a near solid. Then the wind—helpless against the immovable object—groaned in defeat as if mourning the dead. All else stopped breathing.

A sprained ankle or a dislocated shoulder one could handle, almost welcoming the physical pain to seal off the agony from within. But *this*? This was almost like fire from the nostrils of heaven, raining down the brimstones of displeasure at man's inhumane treatment of those over whom he had dominion. There was nothing one could do now.

But Marvel Harrington would have disagreed! There was *always* a way. God provided it. One person's strength was insufficient, but there was strength in numbers. "For where two or three are gathered together in my name, there am I in the midst of them," was the promise of God's Son. Already God had used one A. Thomas Corey as an unknowing instrument. There would be others—some as helpers, others in need. She must write not as a prophet of gloom but factually—black-and-white with bright beams of hope, reassuringly and confidently, that this would never happen again! She must retouch the rainbow of promise God had painted in the sky. Meantime, those around her needed attention.

So thinking, early that morning Marvel had pinned on an imagined Solomon's seal. That mystic symbol, she smilingly remembered from her studies of ancient philosophy, supposedly would guard against fever and other diseases. Why not stress, anxiety, and depression?

"Mother," she'd said without looking into her mother's pale face when she said a good-bye to Daddy, "there's so much we need to do—you and I. You know I'll be busy writing, but we can talk. I'm never too busy for that! I know people are told not to visit and we've been good girls, right, up to now? But the men will need something—maybe not food at first, but coffee and a chance to talk. And they'll come here. You know they will. Then there are other people—and here's one of them now. Oh Fanny, *Fanny!*"

Mother came to life. And suddenly the three of them were embracing. There were no words. They *knew*. Breathlessly, Fanny burst out, "Oh, Miz Snow hon, ah'm in need of you-all. Ah's—I's—I got me no right to ask, but I'm in desperate need. You-all knows—know—how scared the little ones are of fire! They's—they're plum crazy with screamin'. And, sho' nuf, Miz Snow and Missy—Marvel, honey-chile, I'm not up to talkin' 'em (in her agitation Fanny had slipped back into the softly slurred vowels of her native speech) into being-have (*behaving*—Marvel and Snow Harrington exchanged amused glances)—like coverin' up dem chock'late ears or coverin' up eyes agin' whut's mean'n ugly. Oh, dey say 'dis world's a-fire—the deb—devil's back—or *him*—the evil one—" Fanny's voice broke and she burst into uncontrollable tears—the first tears either of them had ever seen the black woman shed.

The miracle of the day commenced. Snow Harrington said warmly, "Marvel has an assignment to do—a very important one, Fanny. But I'll come with you. You know I will! And there are some matters you can help *us* with, too. Oh, I'm glad you're back! You're needed here. First, (she was shrugging into a coat and draping a scarf expertly around her wealth of golden hair) we'll need to think about something for the men to have when—when their work's finished."

"Oh, I got somethin' fo' you-all. Yo' sweet mammy sent *mo'* stuff. Oh, thank you-all—an' may de good Lawd bless us'ns all!"

"He will, Fanny, He will!" Marvel hugged her tightly and whispered a quick "I love you!" in her mother's ear before closing the door behind them. And in her heart was a strange peace.

The pencil took wings in Marvel's hands, and later she was to wonder where the words came from. Surely, they were too inspired to be her own. She wrote compellingly and flawlessly, her reasoning destined to create solidity, each word and each phrase shining with hope.

Twice the telephone interrupted her, but the calls were welcome. One call came from Grandmother.

"Oh sweetheart, I'm so sad about this fix we're all in. I wanted to come—you know I did. You need support and love—" Grandmother Riley said, her voice lacking its usual lilt.

"But we *have* it, Grandmother. Don't you know that? You're still under quarantine. The 40 days of isolation aren't up, are they? Another week to go, unless you've had another case?" Marvel hoped she had counted right.

She had. "No more cases—all doing well. But we want to see you, hug you—and we *will*. I feel it in my bones—my wishbone, I suppose," she said wistfully. "Of course, I—we, your grandfather and I—are awfully taken up with—things we'd hoped to share. Fanny can tell you part. Oh, and I sent a few items—canned oysters for soup. It sticks in my mind how your daddy loves that. So I sent evaporated milk. I knew you—uh, had no—uh—none fresh. Oh Marvel, is it so awful—as bad as I imagine? And this wind—this everlasting wind. Oh, stinkin' on it anyway! 'Pneumonia wind' Dr. Porter calls it—so many are down."

"It isn't like you to worry, Grandmother dear. Bear up, keep a lid on things!" Marvel said, purposely making use of one of the older woman's expressions. "Believe it or not, I almost welcome the wind today. It—it muffles sound." It was true: the guns... Captain Bumstead's former milk truck laboring past with the ghastly loads of animals stripped bare of all skin, to be burned like animal sacrifices at a location other than the site of their slaughter. "Oh," she continued quickly, not trusting the churning in her stomach, "we'll be in touch with Fanny. In fact, Mother's there, helping calm Old Uncle Ned, Heliotrope, Prissy, Blossom, all of them. Brother Hezzie's gone with Daddy, giving a hand. And the others are frightened—fire, you know."

There was a gasp at the other end of the line. "Elmer! He's put away to the best of my knowledge. Still, with a twisted mind like that poor boy's, he just could make a break—turn up out there with a 'howdy' like nothing ever happened. I don't want to upset you more, but darling, you'll be careful?" she begged.

Marvel—startled—promised to be careful. Then, to change the subject, she reminded her grandmother that it was Elmer's father who gave her the pearls—"pearls of wisdom" that taught her caution.

Had Grandmother laughed softly? Her voice had faded and Marvel realized that others on the party line had taken down their receivers to eavesdrop, taking the sound of other human beings as a comfort.

Unfortunately, Grandmother chose that time to say knowingly, "Oh yes, I understand, and I'm so happy for you. Frederick told us about the young man. Duke and Thomas know him and hold him in high esteem—"

*Oh Grandmother, we have an audience!* Clutching at a straw, Marvel interrupted quickly, "Oh, before we're finished, I have a big story to do for the newspaper I'll tell you about later. Tell me about the rest of the family, the other cousins—*all* of them. And how's Grandfather?"

Her scheme worked. The Squire was in the pink . . . her Uncle Worth hoped to go back to driving the bus Monday (Aunt Rae promised to call, she said) . . . Emory and Joseph kept pretty much to themselves, but others said they planned a major change, something the Squire used to think he wanted—but times were changing. His oldest, Alex Jr., was still "out West" dabbling around with Clarinda's husband. Strange? Emory's two boys still expected to make it into the Royal Air Force . . . "As if we didn't have problems enough right here without poking around in Europe for more!"

Leah Johanna Mier Riley's call gave her granddaughter much to think about—but not now. She *must* remember her geometry: "The shortest distance between two points is a *straight line*," and it must be applied—no detours of the mind. Marvel did remember with pleasure, however, what Grandmother said about Mother when she had shared her whereabouts and commented that the older woman could be proud of her daughter and how she'd measure up in face of the present crisis. "She'll always measure up. Mark my word! Even in bigger ones—and they'll come!"

Shaking her head to clear her mind of other matters, Marvel picked up her pencil again. But the words would not come. Something was unfinished—not just facts, the end being sanitary disposal of the charred remains (a common grave for the ashes and then the running of wheels over and over the scarred ground—no reminders were needed!). And not the quick summary of how the community and those surrounding it rallied in time of need to accomplish a task far greater than themselves.

What then? Chewing her eraser didn't help, and it spread germs! Guiltily, Marvel scrubbed her cramped hands with soap and, as she wiped them dry, tried the radio. There was static, of course, but she was surprised to find that it worked at all.

Louella Parsons, high priestess of Hollywood where gossip was involved, was on the air and divulging one of the "exclusives" of her weekly radio show. Marvel sighed at the empty-headed scoop on a movie called "Flying Down to Rio." How could anybody of sound mind get caught up in sometimes-indecent unrealities while the real world crumbled about their expensively shod feet? Right now the brassy-voiced woman was smacking her gossip-loving lips over the scenes in the "flying film"—a line of leggy chorus girls in gauze skirts dancing away on the wings of airplanes in flight ... *while other planes were flying over Europe*!

How sad ... Hollywood's brand of heaven on earth! It was a deliberate and, if one could believe the woman's words, an enormously successful effort of escape from thinking which would pay off: 85 million viewers a week! It couldn't be—it simply couldn't—when the slaughtered cows brought in 35 cents apiece. So it cost only a dime for a theater ticket? So did a large-size packet of notebook paper, and Marvel was running out.

Listening broke her heart, so she changed stations. The agricultural department was reporting progress on developing hardier crops—some new to the United States, others improved and more drought-resistant. Rice, always a staple in the Orient, could—in its new strain—adapt to the damper states and maybe replace wheat as a breadstuff. And Africa made use of a root called cassava. Could it feed our own people, with a surplus one day to help in other lands of hunger? Our country had always helped others—that was our calling. So instead of aiding in war, why not in famine? Perhaps we could help our president make good his promise, "Our boys will never be sent to war overseas again!"

An idea was taking shape in Marvel's mind when Auntie Rae's call came. Her voice sounded weak from fatigue, but there was an undercurrent of excitement even as she, too, expressed regret at being unable to be with them this day. And she had heard the terrible news about all the other diseases. If only she and Worth could help!

"But you *are* helping, Auntie Rae—you are! Pulling our Mary Ann through—and mostly alone—"

"Never alone, darling, never alone!" she said reverently. "The Lord was with us, and He sent us *you*. We all did it! Jake took your words to heart, and we all prayed over our precious daughter's bed. And then Jake made her speak—commanded her, Marvel, in the name of the Lord! Oh, she wants to see you—to tell you she's *engaged*! Watch out now for our little matchmaker. She'll have *you* married, too!"

Marvel was exhausted. Suddenly she was caught up, carried away from the lurid scenes of this day, and transported to a land where trees danced, stars spun and then fell on a field of white— white *veiling* in which she and Titus were one in a land they had helped create. . . .

She only half-heard her aunt telling about an "arrangement" between Grandfather Harrington and Grandmother Riley—taking in boarders. Yes, including one Oriental and one Negro, Chung Foy Su and Abraham Lincoln John-Paul Jones—both veterans. Government paying until a facility could be built. Hence, all that food. Oh Marvel, how wonderful when people cared. The former landlady was bedfast—sad, but—

Sad, yes. All afflictions were sad. But had she heard her aunt correctly? Her paternal grandfather and maternal grandmother took over?

She needed an assessment—a sorting out of facts and feelings, then a rearranging of the fragments into a mural of understanding. So much had happened, and the day, like the newspaper

story, was unfinished. She would know more when Mother
returned and the men came home. Marvel decided to postpone
her writing until then. Meanwhile, back to the news on the radio.

A faraway voice told of grand-prize winners in senseless mara-
thons, the torment they endured, some for sensationalism
(always hoping to be "discovered" by some movie scout and
starred in a high-intensity drama), but mostly driven by stark
hunger. So they stood on their heads atop flagpoles, they danced
the fox-trot until their shoes were without soles and their exposed feet blistered and bleeding . . . no rest . . . no food . . . eyes
blank and unseeing . . . until finally they collapsed. And the winners? Crazed with pain, many shot themselves or jumped—

Marvel could bear no more, so a turn of the knob brought this:

Hitler is a man of moods! Nobody feels comfortable
about the view of Austria from his beautiful Swiss
chalet. . . . How do we translate the Czech question:
"Do we go willingly to the butcher's block, ignoring
the cries in the bloodbath so near?" The Mother
Country is preparing, you say? Is a smiling negotia-
tion over a cup of afternoon tea proof-positive? . . .
Death row is tucked comfortably away inside the
Reich! Thousands rot in concentration camps, awaiting the executioner. Nazis *kill*!

Her throat constricted. The gunfire could be *here*. The slain
cattle could be our own boys, and the moaning wind, the wails of
the women who waited—unless the world learned to come
together in love, hold hands across the seas, share foods instead
of scrap iron. All this she must say.

Daddy came home. With him were the other men. She'd
known they would be. And somehow, in the strange scramble,
Mother came—bringing Fanny! And then the other women were
there, bodies crowded into small quarters like animals in the
holding pen—or *human beings* . . . all to be exterminated. Except
that they *were* together, and it was over! They had accomplished
the grim task and survived. Wordlessly, all heads bowed in silent
prayer and found solace as the smell of fresh coffee and nourish-
ing oyster stew rose up to meet them. It was a paradox: misery

combined with a sparkling glimmer of hope turning men not to martyrs, but to saints! It was a vision of unreality, followed by one of reality.

Marvel knew then what she must write. The miracle was complete.

# 20

# Forgetting
# Those Things
# Which Are Behind

The week following was eventful. Morning Glory Chapel lived up to its name, blossoming in spirit. The opening up to one another, the talk, the prayer, and the shared food and drink with the long-dreaded ordeal ended served as a catharsis of emotions. The slate was wiped clean. Remembering Brother Greer's last sermon in closing the church until the crises was past, they were to repeat his text often among themselves: "I count not myself to have apprehended; but this one thing I do, forgetting those things which are behind, and reaching forth unto those which are before, I press toward the mark." Right! What Brother Paul said to "them Philippines" was jest as true today. They'd press with 'im!

How *was* the preacher doing anyway? And when could they visit?

Grandmother answered that. She called one evening just as Marvel laid her burden of books on the kitchen table. "Oh, thank God, it's over—that awful ordeal for all out there, sweetheart! And just about over for us, too—the quarantine, I mean. Brother Grady's chompin' at the bit to be up and about." She smothered a small laugh. "Still spoon-feeding Mrs. Sutheral custard like a baby—sort of 'spoonin',' the Squire calls it! And Mary Ann's begging to see you. Let's see, can you come in next Monday? Worth'll be driving the bus—that is, if you can sacrifice one night's writing to that lad in Austin. I heard—"

149

"Grandmother, what big ears you have!" Marvel laughed. "Yes—yes, I'll be there. And here's Mother."

* * *

Erlene came back to school just as her mother contracted the intestinal disorder herself. The dysentery left Erlene pale, wan, and too exhausted to pick up her studies where she had left off. She just had to graduate, simply *had* to. Did Marvel understand?

Marvel did. "You'll feel stronger—believe that, Erlene. And you'll find Mr. Phillips more understanding than you think. I know it's the geometry you're fretting over. You're doing fine in all else."

Why wouldn't she be? Erlene fumed. Practice makes perfect, and she'd repeated twice already. They'd have to burn the building down to get shut—er, destroy—*her* records. "All the time I laid—*lay*, right—there dying, I kept muttering that stupid theory as far as I could."

"Good for you," Marvel laughed. "And then the cows, the wind, all of it—but you've stored some of the problem on a shelf there in your brain. Mary Ann'll be back and we'll work together. You'll graduate."

"Boy hi'dy! I appreciate *you*," the girl said gruffly. "I'm going to do something to pay you back. I must look awful. More rouge?"

Marvel shook her heard. "I wouldn't. You know how proper Mr. Phillips is, and you'll be going to domestic science, too. Remember the lecture on discretion? Some of us looked like signboards—all that?"

Together they managed a laugh. Then Erlene asked if Marvel knew where her mother could find help—just someone to fill in for awhile?

"Fanny's available, I think. She's been with Mrs. Bumstead. I— I'm still amazed about his allowing that. He—he's mellowed, I'm happy to say."

Later Erlene reported that Fanny *was* coming. They'd make it right with her, do something for the younger children. But would Marvel *believe* that the Captain said, "Now, looky, she's t'come in the *front* door!"?

It *was* hard to believe—as was Mr. Angelo's excitement when he summoned Marvel into his office to say: "You've made it big,

Miss Marvel Harrington. Yes, you've made the big time! *The News* office is covered up with letters—some coming from other states. Even the syndicates want to pick up the columns you wrote from your area as it reflects 'Mainstreet, U.S.A.' Then, of course, the 'Heartland' series you and young Smith do. This speaks so well for the school, such an honor—and a feather in the local paper's cap, if the editor's head hasn't gotten too big for a cap! I'll need an address for Titus. His sister's not answering her telephone. Is she ill?"

"I don't know, Mr. Angelo. Editor Corey has the address, but yes, I'll give it to you. Thank you for telling me all this, sir."

The man hesitated, his dark eyes studying her face. "I thought I'd see your face light up, see you excited. Do you realize what this means to your future? You may want to change your plans—"

Marvel smiled. "I have no plans yet. I'm happy that everyone is pleased. But as to whether the columns did more than attract the attention of editors—well, we'll have to wait and see. Newspapers deal with the sensational, then tend to forget. I—we—Titus and I want to set the pyramid upright, put the peak at the top then encourage the masses to reach for it. Forgive me," she said, feeling her face color under his long scrutiny. "I—I tend to dream aloud. It's so important."

"Go ahead," the teacher said quietly. "How do people reach that peak?"

"By helping each other. And we have to let them know someone cares!"

"And that someone is?"

"Our Creator—God and His faithfulness. We all need reminding."

Mr. Angelo shook his head in perplexity and then defeat. "I'm disappointed. Is this a final decision, without thinking about it?"

"It's final. It has to be. And I *have* thought. Thank you, sir."

*   *   *

When Marvel went in to see Mary Ann on Monday night, she was amazed at the change. Her cousin was so ethereal-looking, so angelic. Her crown of black hair fanned out like a dark angel's wing and her eyes were glowing instead of fever-glazed as one might expect. Gone was the elfish smile. Replacing it was a look of complete joy. Where had she seen that look before...the peace that outshone the misery? Marvel asked herself fleetingly. Oh yes, on the faces of the men on that awful day.

"Mary Ann—oh, you look *wonderful*. It's hard to feel sorry for you."

"Marvel—Marvel darling—I'd like to hug you, but 'no touch,' they say. I have shadows under my eyes, but no shadows in my heart. I'm in love—I'm in love—*I'm in love!* And I'm alive. Oh Marvel, it was a hard trip—" her color deepened with ill-concealed excitement.

"But you made it. God saw to that. And," Marvel found herself laughing, "as for being in love, that's hardly headlines. You and Jake have been in love all your lives—probably as kids in three-cornered pants."

"And how! Still this is different. We're engaged. He popped the question real formal-like. It's *different*—just you wait and see. Oh, I want you to be this happy! Has he asked you to marry him?"

Marvel felt a little uncomfortable. "I—Titus, you mean?"

"Of *course* I mean Titus!"

"Mary Ann, please— I told you we understand each other. He came Thanksgiving, and there's a small chance of Christmas. But look, I'm only 16, and there are things I have to do—and he has to do. And, for that matter, *you* have to do—" her words were disjointed, incoherent.

"You're glowing!"

Marvel felt her own face color. "We'd better talk school—"

Mary Ann sighed. "Leave it to *you*! I'm not going back. I've missed so much I'll never catch up, and Jake and I'll be married—"

She stopped when her mother appeared suddenly at the door. Auntie Rae's eyes focused on Marvel pleadingly. Marvel understood.

"Don't be silly," Marvel scolded gently. "Jake's job is just a promise of someday. And you're daydreaming. He'll need an educated wife, so let's take inventory. Erlene's back, so we'll conquer that geometry theorem. And as for that research paper, I have made notes on hops, something new, and you have Clarinda's letters—"

"And her Uncle Alex's," Auntie Rae broke in encouragingly. "That's up in Oregon. And Marvel, have you heard about your other two uncles?"

Marvel had not. "I seldom see Duke and Thomas—never see Cindy—"

"*Lucinda*—that's her name now—leads Erin around by the nose—"

Marvel laughed. "My turn to interrupt, Mary Ann, and correct! 'Dominate' is a better word. Do you mean they're avoiding us?"

"They sure enough are, now that they're under their Big Sister's thumb. One must associate only with the upper-crust now, and we're not rich enough for the Cohanes. Tell her, Mother—tell Marvel I'm right."

Auntie Rae bit her lip. "Don't be too hard on the girl. Amanda, isn't it? She probably was a help. You see, Marvel, their father and the boys' father have gone to Dallas. Mr. Cohane packs a lot of weight with big business there—"

Shocked, Marvel listened as her aunt explained about Uncle Joseph and Uncle Emory's hopes for "executive" positions with Sears Roebuck and the streetcar line—didn't know which one where. Aunt Dorthea and Aunt Eleanore agree to *that*? Oh yes, they'd move there gladly. Both belonged to a *bridge* club (Auntie Rae's laugh was a bit brittle when she said that until recently she herself thought the word meant a bone in the nose or a manmade means of crossing over water—if there *were* any!).

Marvel felt her own mind wander, remembering the two times she had been to the city—once to attend the Dallas State Fair when an excursion train gave Titus County residents a discount on fares, back when Pleasant Knoll was prosperous and banks were thriving along with cotton. And the other time was to visit Mother and Daddy's friends, she believed. She had been overwhelmed by the elegant stores and the commanding view from atop a balcony overlooking the ant-crawl of traffic from 32 stories high, called the Magnolia Oil Building. Was it the tallest building in the world, or did it just seem like it? The heights made her head swim and her toes clench to keep from falling, even while holding on to the guardrail with both hands. She'd been frightened—frightened, too, of the clang and clatter of the streetcars, the earsplitting sirens, and the blast of taxi horns. City life was not for her—not for Auntie Rae either, judging by her pursed lips. Of course life went on, and each must "press toward the mark" according to the calling. But she hoped the Lord didn't call *her* to city life. For the first time Marvel wondered how big Austin was, feeling embarrassed by such thoughts.

They talked on until Marvel was able to steer the conversation back to school and, eventually, the hops. "I did the research simply because I was curious. But," she said, removing the notes from her loose-leaf notebook, "*you'll* do the writing, and enjoy it. Just stop killing me with your eyes and listen: 'Green cone-like blossom clusters on the vines take on a yellow tinge and rustle like paper flowers...most aromatic...produces *luplin*...medicinal substance...grows in Pacific Northwest...perennial climber has male and female plants *(See? I told you it would interest you!)*...Used in malt beverages...belongs to nettle family."

"*Nettle* like in *the thistle*—like in Elmer!" Mary Ann gasped. Her face turned frighteningly white. "I—I'm scared. I *must* warn you—"

Marvel didn't want to be warned. And Auntie Rae's eyes signaled that Mary Ann was too tired. Gratefully, Marvel deposited the materials on a nearby library table and, blowing a kiss, hurried out.

\* \* \*

A week later Marvel read in the newspaper that Sears, along with other far-flung businesses, was on strike, with employees "toting" signs: Thou Shalt Not Pass. The burly union leader, John L. Lewis, wrote: "Labor, like Israel, has many sorrows. Its women keep their fallen...and lament for their children."

# 21

# Gone—the Pearls and the Hope!

The feel of Christmas came early. Nobody talked about it. It was too soon. But amid the pressures of upcoming midterm exams and the push-and-shove to be on time for this class or that, there was a subtle change in atmosphere as if a part of the sky had come down. There were no decorations. But the grocery stores had received their annual shipment of apples, and Piggly-Wiggly's were the reddest and most pungent Marvel could recall from past displays. Everybody should have an apple on Christmas: a fat one, so radiantly red that it gave off light, forced so deep into each hanging stocking that the recipient had to tug a bit to remove it, and then an English walnut. But this year, although apples were more plentiful because of refrigerated cars, money was not. It was sad. But those who understood could lean on memories, plucking one at random from the packsack of time, as small children plucked the coveted apples, and forgive the world, other people, and themselves for all they had done wrong. Forgiven, they could move on in a spirit of hope.

But small children did not have the resources, did not understand. Auntie Rae told Mother about Billy Joe. And Marvel knew Mother was crying softly when her sister-in-law said, "Billy Joe asked, 'Is it Christmas today, Mommy?' and I had to tell our baby, who thinks he's so grown-up now and then, 'Not today, sweetie—but Christmas comes.' That's all I can promise."

Marvel felt a bit of the shine of anticipation tarnish. Poor dears. Theirs had been a trying generation, too. She resolved anew to find a way to make things better for the two she loved so much. They must feel utterly helpless and hopeless—wanting so much for their children, to *give* when there was nothing to give. Auntie Rae, a child of an orphanage, and Mother, a child of rambling parents—both needing security they'd missed . . . both denied girlhood . . . and now, each still more child than woman, in a sense. Then suddenly (perhaps because of the season), Marvel felt as if she were holding her breath. Something good would happen.

It did. But first came two incidents that tore her heart into fragments. And, in putting it back together, life applied a mortar of reality that chafed with disappointment, fear, and hopelessness.

* * *

Mary Ann was back in school, fragile but starry-eyed. Occasionally, Marvel caught those starry eyes focused on herself as she assisted with the troublesome geometry. Once when she caught her cousin's gaze, Mary Ann seemed about to say something, but quickly changed her mind. "Oh, you'll be glad to know the research paper's almost finished, thanks to you and Jake. Sort of interesting about the vines' romances and their heart-shaped flowers," she said instead. "Jake's Uncle Russ is still in Oregon 'hopping' around. Life's strange—like Clarinda's husband and Russell Brotherton getting together. Oh, and our bachelor uncle's managing their finances. Uncle Alex did get back into banking. I guess our grandfather's pleased with *one* son."

Erlene was conveniently five minutes late, which afforded time for Marvel to reply. "Grandfather's pleased with all of them, Mary Ann—read his eyes. But what about Uncle Joseph and Uncle Emory?"

"Home—both of 'em. Strikers used to march, and now they're sitting down in Dallas like they did in whatever big city makes auto—"

"Flint, Michigan. They left Dallas—went near *there*?"

"Yeah. And guess what! Uncle Joseph got caught betwixt and between. Police stampeded the place, spraying the men with buckshot and eye-watering gas, beating them with clubs. And that C.I.O. union was hungry and cold but fought back with pipes, door hinges, coffee mugs—anything they could find. Awful, *awful*—everybody bleeding. Duke and Thomas are *really* riled now—just itching to join up with the R.A.F. Anything for a fight! Oh, police even grabbed food the Red Cross brought!"

Marvel's heart was pounding. Imagine such a thing in America. And it was almost Christmas!

"Uncle Joseph—was he hurt, Mary Ann?"

Mary Ann nodded miserably. "One cheek cut, and caught a terrible cold when somebody turned the company's fire hose on in that icy wind. The National Guard came and—well, that's all I know."

That was enough. "But what about Uncle Emory?" Marvel whispered just as Erlene came hurrying down the hall.

Mary Ann turned palms up. "Nothing doing," she whispered back. "Streetcars are changing over to buses. Oh hi, Erlene! Ready for a bonehead class?"

The other girl was panting. "What will they do? What *can* they do?" Mary Ann whispered through clenched teeth.

And it was Marvel who turned hands up at the complex question.

Even as Dr. Porter bandaged Joseph Harrington's wounds, the eloquent John L. Lewis was busy other places, taking on big business and small: coal, steel, and all its by-products from ammonia to cement. He was inside the mills and mines and out, stretching from America to Canada, to Brazil, to the railroads, and to all the ships at sea. "Organize *here!*" he boomed. "And the rest will follow. If the crouching lion can be routed, it is a safe bet that the hyenas in the adjacent bush may be scattered along the plain!" Some were charmed. Others were furious. And all were scared. There were bloodbaths as the "hyenas in the adjacent bush" were not so easily scattered. Men who betrayed their own government (some called them "reds" or "rebels") were massacred, their hungry wives and children trampled in the streets. But the mellifluous war of words flowing from the labor leader's lips was not to be silenced. Franklin D. Roosevelt heard loud and clear—so did the rest of the nation. It would take a long time. But through the work of one man (hero or villain?) and the cooperation of workers around him, the poor—once scattered and beaten by the "industrial goons" and ignored or opposed by politicians—held hope for assuming their rightful place as first-class citizens. The world of the underdog was changing.

"Dale, is this good? What will come of it? Oh darling, will it help *us*?" Mother, white-faced and wringing her lovely hands, cried out.

Daddy didn't know. "Lewis may be deported. Anything can happen—even another civil war. It's a stalemate. And the bad part is that Germany, Hitler, and his utensils are hearing! Will it help *us*? I can't see how, but then the vets' march on the White House did. It helped my father and your mother, if I understand right. I mean some of their roomers—wish I knew more about all this—are disabled war veterans and turned out to be lifesavers for the Squire and his duchess!"

Daddy tried to smile. His effort was no more successful than Mother's attempt. "What's your opinion, Miss Marvel?"

"I—I have none, Daddy. I don't understand it all—the rights and wrongs. I dislike violence," Marvel shuddered, "and lack of justice in equal amounts no matter where prejudice and unfairness are. About Grandmother and Grandfather—yes, I think you're right. There's to be some sort of government housing, including a hospital—somewhere, sometime. I guess what interests me most is how those people pulled together. Right or wrong? Only God can say. But one *can* make a difference."

*And two can make even more*, her heart wanted to sing out. *Oh, Christmas, hurry!* Billy Joe was right. "Is it Christmas today?" In the heart, yes.

\* \* \*

As the days hurried past, Marvel felt more and more certain that Titus was coming home for the holidays. He had sounded doubtful, but he loved to surprise her. Almost *all* their meetings had been surprises. And it added to the excitement, that element of surprise. Well, she would surprise *him*, be ready for that anytime-now meeting. Good grooming was a part of her daily routine—no change there. What to wear would have to depend on what hung in the closet. Cold weather dictated wool. Titus liked what blue did for her eyes, she dreamed on, and found herself humming carols as she sorted sweaters: one blue, one pink, and a white turtleneck. All were suitable if she used the blue silk kerchief-scarf. The scarf was old, but so were the sweaters. Then there was the ancient blue wool princess-line dress. The simple style did not tattle age. And with it—

Marvel stopped short, a sudden inspiration filling her heart. She avoided jewelry for school. It was discouraged and considered "poor taste," but the domestic science teacher likely referred to the bangles from the dime store worn by the girls who heaped on makeup and bathed themselves with Blue Waltz perfume until Miss Ingersoll put her foot down with a thud as if laying a fly to rest. "There'll be no more of that cheap stuff in this cottage! Go scrub yourselves until I say *when*. I'll sniff periodically, and when I can resume breathing, you're excused. Why, the very idea. Women of the night would be more subtle!"

Smiling in remembrance, Marvel followed through with the dream. The pearls! She must be wearing the pearls. Titus had remembered. She had stored the precious necklace away carefully once it was located after the terrible dust storm. Several times following Frederick Salsburg's last-breath wish that the pearls be hers, Marvel had thought about their loveliness— wanting to have another look, longing to touch them, admire them, and pinch an arm to convince herself they were hers! But there had never been time to indulge in youthful frivolities.

Now she lifted the lid of the carved chest, inhaled the scent of cedar, remembering Christmas wreaths before the few evergreens died, and lifted the piece of chiffon under which she had buried her treasure. The velvet box was not there. Mother had probably shifted the necklace in removing something else. Why then should she feel a sudden panic? Hurriedly, she lifted another item, then another. They had to be there—they *had* to! But when her cold hands scraped on the impersonal coolness of the chest's bottom, she knew.

*The pearls were gone!*

Mother and Daddy were listening to the radio more now that the coast-to-coast network had turned a dream of the Roaring Twenties to a reality of the thirties. Times were getting better, Columbia Broadcasting System claimed through the lips of a new male voice with a Bronx accent.... Surely everybody had noted the steep increase in Cuban cigar sales.... Soon the nation could close the door on the Depression. It was over, done with, "if people lived by that day-by-day credo"...better and better.

...Depression would meet the same demise of vaudeville.... Audiences were packing the theaters.... Talkies were new to some, "old hat" here....

Marvel wished there were no need to interrupt. Let them dream, her wonderful wishing-will-make-it-so parents. But the muscles in her throat were tightening. She was looking into a dark cavern of despair. Never mind what the all-knowing announcer from New York said. That was where Wall Street was, and there the crash that couldn't happen did. For the common man the Depression was *not* over, and here it was compounded by the drought. But here—right here—in this house a drama was unfolding. What if—just *what if*—Mary Ann's fears were justified. And Elmer had come for the pearls? The stepcousin considered them his mother's.

"Mother—Daddy!" Marvel cried above the blare of the radio. "My necklace is missing—my pearls. Could you have moved them—forgotten?"

Mother was amazed. And Daddy, busy at turning the radio off, looked equally concerned. "We'll find them, baby," he promised. But his face was blank. "If the newsmen are right, I'll buy some more if—"

Mother interrupted to say the necklace would show up. Nobody could have taken it. Nobody had been here—well, nobody who would *steal*!

"You stored the pearls when I—I put my violin away until I could afford— Oh Dale, you don't suppose—? If *it's* gone, I—I'll *die*." Mother's voice was desperate.

"It isn't!" Daddy said quickly, too quickly. But Marvel was too upset with the loss and what it might mean to notice....

Marvel, feeling torn between withholding news of the missing pearls and the need to confide in someone who understood—*truly* understood—what it could mean, told Mary Ann. "It's not only the awful loss—it goes deeper, much deeper. The pearls are valuable in themselves. More valuable because of Uncle Frederick's leaving them to me—a symbol, and that's exactly what the precious gems have become to Titus and me. Then (more slowly) I—I feel a little scared—all goosefleshy—wondering who intruded."

Mary Ann's face had bleached of all color. "I tried to tell you— oh Marvel, I tried. And he'll be back, I know it. Actually," her cousin's voice was shaking and her round chin quivering, "I saw him. I just know I did, when I was so sick. I didn't tell you—because—I protected you!"

"It was the fever, Mary Ann. You've nothing to blame yourself for."

Opalene Love, Angie Stone, and Clara Lynn Martin, friends to both girls from Pleasant Knoll, rushed over for a rare exchange of greetings. And there was no more time to talk....

\* \* \*

And then came the second blow. Titus was not coming.

Marvel felt the bad news before she opened the envelope when his letter came. The air, so recently filled with the star of hope which appeared at this brush-of-the-wings time of year, became weighty with dread. Her Christmas carols became a dirge. She knew exactly how Mother felt about the violin. Loss of anything so precious brought a death of sorts.

Titus' letter was chatty and sweet, carefully explanatory. Marvel scanned the contents quickly: how a ceiling-sweeping evergreen dominated the busy hall of the state house, all roped in red and green replacing the paper chains held together with paper clips of their childhood... and electric light bulbs—ruby-red like the dahlias Lucille once grew—instead of candles. But it wasn't the same. The heart goes home at Christmas.

> But this time, darling, it can't be. I watch the colored bulbs tunnel through the wintertime dark and try to hope that what I'm doing here will reflect through the coned light. Certainly there's a need... all the unemployment... the labor disputes... on the one hand wanton poverty; on the other, the blatant finery of a nation "down in the dumps"... and then the misguided, idealistic boys volunteering to be slaughtered overseas—*for the wrong side*! Dictators over there don't want peace, they want money, land, oil, *power*. I can pray that the pen *is* mightier than the sword, Marvel—I can pray! Hoping—always hoping—that the time will not come when we must employ the tacts of CIO leader Lewis: "They smote me hip and thigh, and right merrily did I return their blows." It can't happen here the

soothsayers tell us in language as archaic as its onetime definition of *true*!

The Titanic sank...Wall Street tumbled...and there's talk of a cross-Atlantic lighter-than-air transport balloon that *cannot fail*. Impossible, they say (out of Germany yet!). Impossible? "Nothing is impossible with God," and there impossibility stops! I feel so lonely...sitting here watching a thousand lights blink on in a toy city below. So unreal, all of it. Do those lights spell hope, Marvel—*tell me*, or are we heading into another dark age worse than that of the Middle Ages because it's brought on by *sin*? There, which do I sound like: evangelist or reporter? My part in all this is what keeps me away from home—and *you*. Once elected, Representative Norton is wondering if it's wiser to try again as senator, or consider running for governor.... Cliff's a quiet guy, not given to small talk, kissing babies, and complimenting ladies' hats. So the weight of writing speeches he'll make in the rounds of Decoration Day programs, box socials, and such falls on my back. It'll be tough enough on him just putting on "the polite shoes of politicking." So my job depends on ghostwriting. In a word: *Stay!* Anyway, no car—Bill Johnson gave up and dropped out when Amanda turned a cold shoulder. Oh Marvel, don't ever—but you wouldn't. I need to see Sis, but I need more to see *you*, to talk. *I have to.* I dream....You will be wearing blue...and the pearls.

Marvel could read no more. Her eyes blurred and a rebel tear, too long withheld, splashed on the letter. So pearls *were* for tears, after all.

# 22

# Games, Gimmicks
# Gadgets—and Gifts

Hope. Titus needed hope restored, and Marvel felt helpless. Theaters all over America, battling the immovable force of the Great Depression coupled with the irresistible force of radio, had resorted to giveaways. But they were finding few to accept their gimmicks and gadgets in the dwindling audiences. Her problem was the exact opposite, Marvel thought desperately. An audience of one-in-need waited for the gift she herself had lost.

Mother found escape and renewed hope in radio's first serial drama to be heard in and around Pleasant Knoll. "Can this girl from a little mining town in the West find happiness as the wife of a wealthy and titled Englishman?" the announcer's emotion-packed question pleadingly asked as an opener for "Our Gal Sunday." Overworked housewives hoped so, but none knew for sure. Their burdens were lightened by the big box in the living room—everybody's ticket to adventure, near-forgotten laughter, sweet music, and romance. Tears fell, but they were the tears of release. Mother found the strength to go on in that wonderful, manufactured world where one was able to supply mental pictures while radios supplied the sound. But that was the demise of movie houses.

Daddy, along with millions of other meek "volunteers," joined police forces to clean up the dangerous streets of gangbusters. But it was Fanny who surprised Marvel most. And she was to provide a setting for the real-life drama which was to take place without anybody else knowing. Fanny's smiling face appeared at the door just as Kate Smith, the hefty "Songbird of the South," called her cheery "Hello, everybody!" and belted out her theme song, "When the Moon Comes Over the Mountain."

Fanny nodded in satisfaction. "That's it!" she said excitedly, her diction back to its practiced clarity. "Dis—This *is* Thursday! News is over, I take it. And y'all can sit back an' listen. When I done—did work for your friend, Erlene's mama, dat—that deah woman stopped everything—even de clock, I'm thinkin'—when Amos 'n' Andy come on—"

"She and 30 million others," Marvel nodded. "Come right in, Fanny. That wind has a terrible sting. Let's understand, Fanny," she went on slowly after the front door closed behind their heart-of-gold neighbor. "Are you wanting to hear that program. Is that it?"

"Yessum. Now I sure 'nough shouldn't be asking. But if me— the children and I—*could* be hearing it, I'd thank you for a most *wonderful* Christmas present evah I got. I've told the little ones— and it's their too-big Christmas gif'. Do y'all reckon?" Fanny's voice was that of a pleading child.

"Of *course* you may listen, Fanny dear. You're welcome to bring as many as this house will hold. Just be awfully sure it's what you want."

Marvel explained quickly then that the comedy was not what a listener might think. Yes, it sounded "black-voiced," but it was created by a pair of white men, Freeman Gosden and Charles Correll, who used to be in vaudeville. Fanny *did* understand and was not offended?

"Oh no, Missy—uh, Marvel honey-chile. No, *no* it tickles my funny bone! Those folks got a dignity. Brings to mind th' fo' men with song book singin'—remembah? One was blacker than a crow and made us laugh right out of our chairs. Some laughing's a heap of a gift. *So* funny, Amos 'n' Andy and dat—that bossy Kingfish man orderin' meek-as-a-lam' Lightnin' round while th' po' soul's totin' stuff out of that big meetin' place fo' Mystic Knights of the Sea! I bettah run—be back!"

CBS programming was interrupted briefly for a special report. A man by the name of Kaltenborn was to make comments on Britain's attempt to postpone further movement by Germany into Czechoslovakian territory. A "great deal" depended on a meeting now underway. Peace or war? "And now," said the announcer, "we resume our regular programming."

The house filled up with faces like caramel candies (and they were just as sweet, Marvel thought), framed by hair standing out like whisk broom straw in excitement. Fanny, as excited as her charges, admonished, "Y'll be good now—yah heah?" just as Lightnin' lamented: "I ain't got me no money-friends. All I got's sympathy friends. Dey listens an' feels right sorry fo' me but den dey's gone!" There were peals of laughter which Daddy covered for the delighted audience by turning the volume higher.

And so it was that amid the whoops and hollers of needed laughter the all-too-familiar pale, ghost-like face with leaden eyes appeared at the single-pane kitchen window where Marvel was trying once more to begin a reply to Titus' letter. For a moment she was unable to move. As if drawn by an irresistible magnet, her eyes met his, expecting to see danger written there. But there was nothing—nothing at all. And as she watched, the face faded, leaving only the eyes which turned to burning coals, as if left over by the fires set by this twisted creature.

*Hurry. She must hurry.* Quickly, she cranked the box-phone once to signal the central office. "Emergency!" she said in a guarded tone, "I need help. Call this number," and read the number Frederick Salsburg had given for the sanitarium for the insane. The call went through and a faraway voice, registering surprise, assured "Miss Harrington" that help was already there. Officials would explain, if she would detain the patient. Without a wrap, Marvel slipped through the one door of the house to where the intruder stood, hardly feeling the sharpened-steel stab of the east wind. If only she could get through to him—

"Elmer, what brought you here? How can I help?"

Elmer Salsburg heard and understood. "Th' pearls," his tongue was thick, his voice, without emotion—dead. "My mother's— they're here. He took them—had no right. Who was that man laying claim? Putting them on the throat of some other woman, when a knife needs to be put on his—his throat. Knife? You have—knife—do I know you—how do I know? You can be—be trusted—how'd you get 'em—the pearls?"

"The pearls aren't here, Elmer. And you can trust me. I'm Marvel, your cousin. It's all right, Elmer. We'll look for the pearls—"

Through the square of light escaping from inside, Marvel saw a wavering, an uncertainty. "If I had the pearls I'd give them to

you," she said truthfully *(to save my life and the lives of others!)*.
"Come with me," she coaxed gently. "It's cold out here—" Marvel
took the white-coated arm.

Somehow she was able to maneuver this now mumbling and
frightened-by-the-world creature to the front of the house. And
there, without lights and the sounds muffled by the wind, a car
pulled in almost simultaneously. There were explanations....
The patient had slipped through the fingers of a new guard....
Probably rode out in a laundry truck... gone a week, no food
or water.... Officials traced him through descriptions of his
garb.... Baffling, but who knew the evils lurking in a twisted
mind? It would never happen again.... The patient must be
sedated at all times. Marvel scarcely heard. She was aware only
that Elmer had crept willingly, almost gratefully, into the waiting
car. The lights blinked on. And they were gone.

Only then did her legs begin to shake.

* * *

For reasons Marvel would have found difficult to explain,
writing to Titus seemed easier after her dread of Elmer's return
ended in the nightmare of reality—a reality of darkness and cold
which she had undergone alone, where nobody could tell her
everything was all right—until she saw Mary Ann. "Nothing to
fear but fear," the president had declared. Well, Marvel Harrington had faced that enemy and *conquered*. And now she could
write Titus.

Yes, the world managed to look beautiful, in spite of itself on
Christmas, she wrote. It was colored by memories and by hope. It
had been a troubled world into which Christ, the Savior, was
born—a world of fears. The shepherds had been afraid of the
star which lighted a troubled world, but they trooped over the
hills to find the crib where God's only-begotten Son lay. The
common people quaked, but among them were the trusted few
ordinary ones who sought forgiveness and pledged to spread the
Word, Marvel wrote from her heart.

> And we mustn't be afraid either, darling. Have you done
> the right thing in following your calling? you ask. We have
> to *believe* you have.... No, *know* you have. Your sister and I

want the best for you, and both must be unselfish in wishing you home for the holidays. Look at that lighted city below you, so beautiful from a distance—as is the world, if we see it through closed eyelids. But what of car thieves who have an easy time on empty streets because ears are deafened by radios for escape from a world of want and need or drown out the awful possibility that maybe times are *not* getting better... that they could get worse? We have to keep informed. John writes: "Ye shall know the truth, and the truth shall make you free." How can we know without opening our eyes, seeing as well as hearing? When radio announcers tell us x-number of men lie choking on their own blood from bullet-ridden bodies, their women and children trampled on by conquering boots, do we *see* them? Germany Moves into Austria... Spain Shoots Its Own in Civil War... Italy Submits to Enslavement.... Our own President tries to reassure us that we will send money to the suffering—but not our boys. Did it ever occur to you that even he distrusts Hitler and the other raging terrorists, sees their hunger reflected in the worn faces of migrants or in our breadlines? It would be so easy to fix blame, but is it important? It is better that we light candles in the dark. You and I are fortunate (or is it unfortunate? I ask in my weak moments—like when I long to see you!). We see. We hear. We *care*. And caring to us means more than "the pursuit of happiness." If the "better world of tomorrow" promises *only* health, wealth, fame, it would be an empty life without *love*. God has planted something more noble than existence, more enduring, and we cannot bury that entrusted talent. It is up to people like us to fulfill His purpose... building back... restoring the land... but reshaping hearts, also, with the purpose of His love. There! Now who sounds like the evangelist, or essayist, or maybe a dreamer?

*Dreamer.* Laying aside her pen, Marvel let her head fall into folded arms, admitting that she was weary of the tumult which raged within her like a mighty river. Should she tell Titus how much she missed him, dreamed of him, and longed for their next meeting? Yes, she must! He needed that reassurance, too. And so she continued:

And now on the personal side, yes, I look forward to your next visit! Do you have to ask? Forget Amanda's mistreatment of Bill. He should have her arrested for breaking and entering his heart, I guess. I will always be here for you, and we can have our Christmas then. Meantime, I'm nibbling on the greatest gift of all, God's love, which recognizes no calendar. Surprise me . . . make my dream come true! In it, our oak tree is moved to shade a towering mountain peak, far across a misty border of magic without the realities of grief and heartbreak. All is tranquil there, for disappointment is unheard of. Far below lie rainbow valleys, meadow-carpeted and sweet with flowers we have helped to grow. White unicorns with peppermint-striped horns drink from crystal-clear waterfalls brought on by gentle rains lighted by sunbeams to twist hues of reappearing rainbows in promises—His and ours. Our unicorns are waiting and so am I! And yes, I will be wearing blue and—

*The pearls*. How could she promise that? Mother had asked Fanny about the necklace. A horrified Fanny told Mrs. Bumstead, for whom she continued to do the Monday wash until her strength returned. Time was when the Captain would have muttered "thievin' niggers!" But that was past. "We'll turn th' place upside down. They're bound t'show up!" he promised. His mood was contagious. Believe . . . she would *believe*!

—I will be wearing the pearls you remember, for pearls will *not* be for tears! *Your Marvel*.

Grandmother called on Christmas Eve. "Christmas gift!" she cried out happily. "Now, don't go thinkin' 'She got me' and worryin'! Turn it around this once and know we—I—well, *both* of us have a gift for *you*! Jake's coming," she chuckled over some secret, "so he'll be one who *gets* you! We'll have a feast right out of Mrs. Sutheral's *Stretching to Survive* book with prayers by Brother Greer—both being family. The sky's squeezin' out a few snowflakes. It'll be a beautiful Christmas, I'm here to tell you!"

# 23

# *"Merry Christmas!"*

Dawn had not brushed the sugary glaze of powdered snow when Marvel awoke on Christmas morning. The light dusting was Mother Nature's gift, her way of covering the ugliness beneath. If only it were that easy to ease one's heart. She pushed herself a little deeper into the piled-on quilts, still feeling the bite of the cold, and tried to pretend she was still a little girl back when the world was "normal." For a blessed moment, it worked. The thrill of anticipation prickled her backbone. And then it was gone, as before.

It might have worked, Marvel thought miserably, if only she had not turned on the radio last night in hopes of hearing some beloved carols. Instead, in the "Christmas Around the World" report came news of the brutal beatings of those confined behind the walls of German prisons. How dare they—how *dare* they sing their stupid praises, their hopes of deliverance, in defiance of the guards whose god was Adolph Hitler? And still they sang, knowing they were marked for death either way. And now they were dead by the thousands, their starving mouths silent, their blood staining the cold, dark streets. But their hearts were one with God! *And it was Christmas all over the world.*

Forcing herself from the maze of covers, Marvel pretended that she caught the smell of frying sage-sausage. She prayed then, thanking God for the freedom that was America's hard-bought heritage, asking mercy for those still imprisoned. But she could not bring herself to pray for the cruel dictator, that prince of darkness, the madman who, in a tirade of words, declared that he would rule the world one day—rule for a thousand years! She wished instead that she owned a shovel big enough and sharp enough to bury all the world's evils, as the light snow had buried the ugliness around her. A little rhyme came back then, a memory of the childhood lines taught her by dear Mrs. Key, her Sunday school teacher:

> God made man and man made money;
> God made bees and bees made honey.
> God made Satan and Satan made sin;
> God dug a little hole and put Satan in!

God would take care of it. And Christmas made its own melody in her heart. Pushing aside the frilly curtains Grandmother had made to cover the small bedroom window, Marvel saw that the snow clouds had moved on and the sky was filled with dimming stars. One star—the morning star?—bigger and brighter than all others shimmered like a newly lit fire. "Merry Christmas, Lord!" she whispered, and the music in her heart grew louder.

Grandmother, her gypsy-brown eyes as bright as the early stars, embraced them fiercely one-by-one at the door of the old boardinghouse. She smelled sweet and clean, her soft bisque skin scented with body powder and dried apple strudel.

"Merry Christmas!" everyone sang out at once, clustering excitedly around the newcomers. The others were assembled. The "chosen ones" for the rosy-dawn breakfast included—in addition to the beaming hostess' daughter, Snow, and her family—the Worth Harringtons and all the boarders. Others, namely Grandfather's other two sons, Joseph and Emory, and their families, would join them later. "Merry Christmas!"

Billy Joe had put away his childish ways of whining and complaining and, looking for the world like a miniature angel ready for trimming the scrub pine in the long hallway, was all virtuous and giving.

> Up on the housetop, click, click, click—
> Down the chim-ney comes Old Nick!

"*Saint* Nick," Leah Johanna Mier Riley corrected gently as if she, too, had forgotten all the two's petty differences. Never mind the gloomy forecasts, the dark valleys through which they'd passed. Today they were filled with streamers of sunshine, and the world was more good than bad. And children were God's greatest gift, beginning with His own!

"Saint," the child repeated meekly. "And we know some *secrets*, don't we, Gran'mere?"

"Secrets we aren't going to tell until the proper time," she said, clearing her throat warningly just in case. "Gran'mere'll be needing a big boy like you directly." The two of them disappeared mysteriously.

"I wish," Auntie Rae, lovely in her old but becoming holly-green rayon coatdress, said softly, "that children—baffling little burdens that they can be—never had to grow up. I'd rather worry over earaches and tantrums than—than their marching away. We devote 20 years to them—gladly—then lose in just a single—single—"

"Flash of the lightning or break of the wave—I know. Marvel had to learn that poem—it's some elegy. But you almost lost Mary Ann to fever," Mother protested. "So, honey, forget all that. It won't happen!"

Auntie Rae sighed. "I was going to say single burst of enemy fire, but you're right! There aren't any enemies on Christmas!"

"Oh Marvel, what do *you* think will happen?" Mary Ann whispered desperately. "The other cousins will be here soon and—"

"So, let's put on our brightest smiles! You look beautiful. Jake has proposed, and one day you'll wear that wedding dress and tuck orange blossoms in those storybook curls—"

"Don't *say* those words—not now—about orange blossoms, I mean—"

Her voice was lost in the confusion of conversations. Grandfather, excited over something (the news?), was pounding his cane on the hardwood floor where the carpet stopped. Mrs. Sutheral, still pale but glowing, moved over to chat with Mother and Auntie Rae. And then Grandmother and her "big boy" helper were back. Breakfast would be simple fare, she announced, because of the need to take care of those "secrets" before the others came. And then the *men* could do dishes.

A dandy arrangement. Nobody would remember food anyway—not with all the excitement that lay in store.

"Squire Harrington," she said formally, and rang a small silver bell to signal silence. Grandfather rose immediately. Coffee could wait.

"Merry Christmas, family! We bid you welcome—the Duchess and I!" (*Duchess?* Grandfather had given Grandmother a new name.) "The two of us had promised a surprise at Thanksgiving—most of it has leaked out since. But repeating (and *repeating* is one of the indulgences allowed to us older and wiser ones!): the two of us are in charge here now, operating a joint business, a hotel, Pleasant Knoll's only home-away-from-home, and old soldier's home—the only one of its kind in the great state of Texas! You'll meet the guests, and please be advised that they all have their surprises tucked away for sharing. Do I hear applause?"

He did. And there were plenty to follow. The sun came up in all its glory. And the clouds of scrimping and saving, Dust Bowls, Depression, and the haunting echo of a world at war just faded away.

It was a day to remember—a day from which to draw strength— a reminder that love is stronger than any of these. It was a day whose joy in togetherness could never be repeated—certainly not duplicated.

\* \* \*

Grandmother had baked sweet cakes and sugar cookies for all. And there were bright and shining toys for Billy Joe, whose face took on a peculiar green tinge warning that he was about to be sick with excitement as he screamed wildly, "It *is* Christmas today! No more promises—*it's Christmas today!*" There were big, fat red apples, one apiece. And then Grandmother told a story so funny that all at the long, linen-covered table held their sides in laughter, people being mesmerized like they were by the magic of radio that had emptied the movie houses. Picture shows would be a thing of the past unless drastic steps were taken. Some were simply turning off projectors and piping in pure radio! They'd go broke . . . close their doors forever. No self-respecting citizen would resort to bankruptcy, become a second-class citizen, and all that. So they'd try gimmicks and giveaways, furnished by Culverville merchants who were feeling the pinch of credit to customers out of work. But first there had to be an audience. What was the reason for showing old heroes like that square-jawed, horse-riding Tom Mix (the star could be *heard* now, yep! selling cereal on radio!) or the few newcomers like the Great Garbo who couldn't speak a word of English? Not even much help for that National League of Decency with their long list of taboos: naked babies, kisses, and double beds, to make shows fit for children. Oh, no more guns either...or criminals triumphing over decent people! Out with all the old, in with the new!

"And so it's door prizes—ummm—sometimes good enough to eat. Food—lots of it, by the bag! Just everything from free finger waves for the ladies' hair to brand-new cars as bright and shining as Billy Joe's new toys. Oh!" Grandmother had become as excited as the owner of those "bright and shining toys," too. "Another enhancement's the double, sometimes *triple* features— all at reduced admission. Exciting?"

"Hardly," Daddy surprised them all by saying drily. "Just who can afford this 'reduced admission'?"

Grandfather Harrington accused his son with narrowed eyes. "*You* can—thanks to *me*. Right, Duchess?"

"Right, Dale son," his mother-in-law said, "The Squire's right. But let's get on with the merriment! We didn't ask you here to go cryin' over the plight of the theaters but to give you gifts! So let me tell you that your father worked hard for the tickets you're about to receive!" Her brown eyes twinkled with mirth and mystery, and she loved it!

There was a chorus of *Ooooooooo's*.

And then she told her story. If word could be spread about all these giveaways, why not assemble all the merchandise, mark tickets with coupons at the end of each, and those holding the lucky-numbered stubs which matched their tickets would receive one of the gifts, and then try to toll in an audience who *would* spread word of their good fortune? Two nice men came to the hotel right then (all other places pretty run-down and looking for the world like "The Deserted Village"). Oh what a night! They led in all kinds of parlor games and tricks, prizes being free admission tickets. (Yep! with those promising stubs!) Well, the Squire here (Grandmother rolled roguish eyes to a now uncomfortable Squire) was a right good sport. When it came to charades, he was to be a snake, had to propel himself, crawl on his belly—without his cane, arms, or legs, mind you! And they should have seen him—

"They should not!" Alexander Jay Harrington exclaimed, bringing down his cane to punctuate his objection.

His duchess ignored him. Shaking with laughter, she said, "He never so much as made it out of the kitchen and—(she wiped her eyes) and—come to find out, he *won*. Snakes *crawl*, don't they? Well this one did, and this snake won us tickets for Dale and Worth's families. A slew of us'll go. While Billy Joe hands these winning tickets out, Snow's to come with me. Billy Joe, get the chopsticks and the hymnal of old-time spirituals. You know where those go, too."

More confusion, some laughs—and some tears. Mary Ann reached a hand underneath the starched cloth to curl icy fingers over Marvel's. "Don't let on," she whispered without meeting Marvel's gaze, "and for goodness' sake, don't open this box. Keep a straight face. And I'm so sorry—I had no right—"

What could her cousin be talking about? And then she knew! The square velvet box was unwrapped. Open it? There was no need. The pearls—the precious pearls she had rashly promised to be wearing for Titus—were inside. Mary Ann had taken the necklace to protect her. The lump in Marvel's throat was too big to swallow, and her tongue felt frozen. But her heart could speak—speak silently. *Dear God, You had a hand in this. You provided an escape from Elmer—made it possible for me to speak the truth when I told him the pearls were not in my possession.*

Mother and Grandmother had been gone too long. Auntie Rae said she would make fresh coffee. Did anybody want more waffles? Nobody did—they were too excited. But talk was beginning to lag. It had to be pushed along while eyes kept looking at the doorway through which the hostess and her daughter had made their exit. Daddy did not seem anxious, just eager. He would check on them, he said, his blue-blue eyes telling Marvel that he knew the secret. But she would never have guessed. Her mind was everywhere at once: the tickets...the pearls...*Titus*.

When the three of them returned, the faces of both the women were swollen and red. Nobody noticed and nobody questioned, for Mother was clutching her most cherished material possession: *her violin!*

"Dale—Dale—" Grandmother hiccuped, "knew—helped p-pull it off—and Chung Foy Su here and Abraham Lincoln John-Paul Jones—go on—"

The two elderly veterans rose on cue. The short-of-stature Chinese Chung bowed low, his round-as-a-full-moon face beaming. "Pleesed to tell you, Missy Harrington, Chung Foy Su's honorable ancestors teechie trade well. We feex all musick-makers—likee new. Likee pleeze?"

Abraham Lincoln did not wait for "Missy Harrington" to answer. "Ah dun got me heah uh book fo' harps o'heben! Ah hepped mah frien' hol' de fiddle 'n de bow. An' iffen I kin beg y'all's fangers t'play, ah'll sang. *All* uv us'ns will jine in an' praise de Lawd fo one big Merry Christmas!"

Grandfather added another log to the fire and tongues of flame leaped up hungrily. The parlor glowed brightly, rivaling the sunlight filtering through lace-draped windows and the happiness-glow of those who watched. Gently, as if she were alone with her memories, Mother caressed the bowed-in back of the shining instrument, turned a peg or two, then lifted the violin to its remembered place on her shoulder and brought the bow across the strings tenderly. If there was a flaw in the sometimes moody instrument, Snow Riley—true musical performer that she was—failed to notice. She played each note of "Rhapsody in Blue," Gershwin's greatest claim to fame, with emotion and pure joy.

The audience was spellbound during Mother's solo. Then came a thundering applause. She smiled charmingly and responded with a medley of belovedly timeless carols. Then, as if on cue, Grandmother joined her at the piano, her fingers lightly touching the keys, and the two played the opening bars of "O Come All Ye Faithful" in delicate balance between violin and piano. How like mother and daughter to never overshadow one another . . . another great gift of Christmas.

*"Everybody!"* Grandfather's invitation was an unneeded command. The audience joined in. On and on they sang, first softly, and then triumphantly, until there was a near frenzy to their song.

The finale was "Jingle Bells," light to rambunctious, for Billy Joe. Christmas was drawing to a tired but reluctant close. Mary Ann's eyes were filled with tears as she leaned toward Marvel to whisper, "Do you get the feeling they think it'll never happen again?"

"They *know* it won't," Marvel whispered back, knowing it was true.

They must hurry now, Grandmother said, bright-eyed and breathless. The men, obeying previous orders, began to clear the table. Grandmother's reward was a ravishing smile. And then she began a colorful exhibit of charming outfits—some made by her own fingers and instructions from Mrs. Sutheral, others by Erlene's mother for Fanny's brothers and sisters. The ladies would wrap the outfits for surprises while the men had some time to themselves when the others of the family came.

"But before that, let's slip out—you know, where the others won't follow." Mary Ann's hand was already tugging Marvel's elbow.

Outside, she spoke quickly, first to apologize, to explain. Marvel waved the words away, then told her that Elmer had come already. It was all over, settled, finished. But something else troubled Mary Ann. "What is it, Mary Ann? No time to deny something's wrong. Tell me."

"Oh Marvel, I'm so scared," Mary Ann blurted out, looking over her shoulder to make sure the two were alone. That's why I—I couldn't talk about orange blossoms. They're *there*—upset with me—he'll go—"

"Let me understand. Who's gone? Who's upset? And who'll go?"

Mary Ann's composure crumbled. "Don't be cross. I need you—oh, I need you! The Brothertons—they listened to Jake's uncle Russ, and he—my Jake—wouldn't leave school—the job with a future at the bank—and me—he—he loves me. But they're mad—angry—at us both."

"I do understand and I'm not upset with you, or cross—just concerned about you and a lot of things. But this is Christmas!"

"And *I* am Jake's family. All of us are! Gran'mere knows and asked him to dinner. I hear voices. But listen. Remember that our Uncle Alex is there, too—up in Oregon, wherever that is—"

The voices were getting closer. "Sh-hhh—quick, where's Jake staying, Mary Ann? His parents lost their home, so they had to go somewhere."

"Yes. Jake's with Newlands, working with Arch when school allows."

Without ever reaching the bathroom, they managed to dodge through a side door as Aunt Eleanore and Aunt Dorthea tossed coats on the bed.

Grandmother was still talking. She planned another gift for Fanny. That girl needed food for "those adorable darkies," and the government allowance would cover a widow's mite. Anything would help.

Mother and Auntie Snow looked up quickly. Even a widow's mite— But Daddy and Uncle Worth exchanged glances, communicated with those Harrington-blue eyes, and Marvel had never seen their faces so dark. *We will support our families! A woman needs a man!* She felt oddly comforted.

All guests had assembled. The Harrington men clustered together, talking in low tones, except for Grandfather. He looked agitated and used his cane a lot. Duke and Thomas waved and then joined them, but Jake came to sit by Mary Ann. The women hurried to wrap packages for friends of the bottomland with Aunt Eleanore and Aunt Dorthea showing little interest. The two kept looking at the men, straining to hear.

"And just where are Erin and Cindy, Dot?" Grandmother asked when the last ribbon was tied. "Too busy to spare time for their grandfather?"

Aunt Dorthea, her hair tattling a recent peroxide bleach, looked a bit flustered. "The girls are much in demand, but they'll manage dinner with the family. Then on to a small invitational dance—in Culverville."

"At Amanda's?" Mary Ann muttered. Aunt Dorthea may have heard. She became very busy brushing her red wool dress (didn't it fit a bit snugly?) free of imagined lint. Marvel remembered then how Grandfather had had to set things aright between the Cohanes and Mary Ann's father.

Auntie Rae remembered, too. Conveniently, Billy Joe showed signs of fatigue. "Nap, honey? Your toys may need one, too, so bring them."

"I'll catch a wink, too—rest and be fresh for the meal," Mrs. Sutheral said. "I'm still trying to regain my strength. That typhoid's draining."

Brother Grady leaped to his feet, his face concerned. "I'll see you up those stairs. You'll excuse us, ladies? I need to think on my prayer."

Grandmother winked. "Much to tell you, but it can wait for the mortgage burning and church dedication in May. All paid—and *more* land, thanks to Frederick, rest his soul. The secret belongs to those two."

Brother Grady and Mrs. Sutheral. *What* secret? It glowed in their faces as in Mary Ann's and Jake's—like the glow in her own heart with thoughts of Titus. God was wise. Maybe He planned their lives this way, holding them apart long enough to make them see that they could not live without each other...giving them time and space in which to examine the foundations of their faith in Him, themselves, and in the "selves" to form a common thread: strong, service-filled, and everlasting. Look at the persimmons. Everything worthwhile took patience. Every love, like every plant, was different. She and Titus needn't be like Mary Ann and Jake. The creator wanted His every child to develop a certain gift. Only then could they "forsake all others."

Marvel's private reverie was interrupted by a soft, rhythmic snore. Ah, there was the source. Abraham Lincoln and Chung had had their moment of glory and retired to rocking chairs by the fireplace, filled with waffles and molasses (a little rivulet of which still trickled down Abe's shiny-black chin), war tales, and recognition. Abe's long legs reached to the hearth as he had sort of slumped down, dozed off, and now gave out little snorts of satisfaction. Chung sat straight, head nodding in perfect sync.

The icy winds had picked up speed again. But the skyline took on a deep purple, with red streamers streaking against the Christmas sky. In the cozy warmth of the great hotel parlor, wonderful smells wafted from the kitchen to mingle with the little pine's aromatic boughs.

Grandmother said softly: "Soon we'll gather about the table for Brother Grady's blessing, and I'll praise God for more than a lifetime of love—and for family: blood kin, in-laws, step-kin, and adopted, walking abreast...stumbling but picking each other up...and singing against the wind.

# 24

# Sing a Song
# of Money

In those frantic, fumbling mid-thirties, only one thing was certain: the inevitability of change. Big industry was learning from the common man. After all, ultimately it was the "little people" upon whom they must depend to consume their goods. That meant money. Money meant work. Work meant jobs. And jobs were few and getting fewer.

Motion picture industries were among those hardest hit— especially in Small Town, U.S.A. "Talkies" had been in for years now. But only "the Wall Street folks back East" could support increased admission, so middle-American towns had been denied the magic of talking actors. But they kept up on such matters through the shared radios and newspapers, paying particular attention to the Harrington-Smith coauthors who talked their language in "Heartbeats of America, U.S.A." Their Marvel was going places, and "Don' y'all forgit it neither." Anybody with one iota could tell by her "Eyes of East Texas" writing, and that Smith boy knew what he was about, they agreed—referring to Titus' "Ears of Austin" column. Why, they would recognize old Will Rogers on sight!

Midterm exams were uncomfortably close. Both Mary Ann and Erlene redoubled their efforts, spending hours in frantic recitation of the troublesome geometry theorem they knew would be included. Marvel *had* to help—she just *had* to. And that isn't all Marvel *has* to do either, she thought tiredly. Her own overloaded schedule included preparing to assist Brother Grady when he came back with the first bluebird of spring. By then Mrs. Sutheral would be Mrs. Grady Greer, a preacher's wife! The Morning Glory Chapel congregation would want to pitch in and do something nice for them. That would take planning, as would the wedding, no matter how simple. And then there were all those columns. Grandmother's suggestion that the family postpone using the theater tickets until she and Fanny could get her own house in order and the Squire could "spruce up the yard" a bit suited Marvel just fine.

Meantime, Dallas radio announcers, eager to grab at anything new, spent a lot of time with movie talk. Dallas had boasted of the talking pictures for so long it was "old hat" now, they said. But every indication was that outlying towns would be compelled to update, too, or close their doors forever. They'd done a good cleanup job but:

Cleanin' out won't make new! Dialogue's cleaner so we can rightly dub the billin's "family movies." Titles on the billboards are more decent, too . . . like takin' the "Too" off and advertisin' only "Good Girls Go to Paris" and changin' "*In*fidelity" to "Fidelity." Makes a miraculous transformation. "Banned in Boston" is spreadin' out like Bermuda grass. . . . How do you feel about that, folks? Why not spend a minute and a penny postcard and tell us? Do ya'll feel right about all this trash and corruption glorified in the eyes of our children? Or do you think, like some politicians claim, that we Americans are on the verge of losin' the rights and freedoms guaranteed us—hmmm? Minds need refreshin'? All right, remember "Little Caesar" back in, let's see, 1930 or so? Well, I'm here to tell you that film opened up a keg of gunpowder! Yep! Edward G. Robinson, riddled by machine-gun bullets, set off a spate of gangster films. Crime doesn't pay? Uh-huh, sounds good, *is* good us Texans think. . . . But it paid big money to a place called Hollywood. Multiple murders meant multiple box-office dollars. We have to wonder though if accusations are true that these swaggerin' punks set off a real-life generation of imitators. "Glorifying the underworld," like some mighty powerful folks claimed. Hollywood had to duck fire or go under. . . . You movie-goers know the outcome, how they've knocked off the crime lord in the last reel. Okay by censors? Not on your life! Those censors were unmoved. . . . So just where is all this leadin'? Could it be the *battlefields*? . . . That brings up two questions *we* have to decide while celluloid paradise sings a song of money. Write us your feelin's on the rights issue, sure. But examine your own conscience and ask these questions. Should the church step in—as well as enter into politics? We never did resolve that. And how far should *education* go? Where does it all begin? *And where will it all end?*

Marvel had sat for a long time, chin cupped into her upturned palms, gazing into nothingness—which, unless somebody cared, *really* cared, might be where the world was heading: into nothingness, oblivion. There was so much here for the editorialized columns. But oh how it needed talking about—if only she could see Titus!

*Titus.* Thought of his name lined all the planets up, making them one great shining light to send all dark shadows slinking from the face of the great planet earth. A billion lightyears ago he had written to say they could not spend Christmas together, that he had no idea when they could hope to see each other again. Well, Marvel thought suddenly, *she* could hope. And hope she would—hope for a miracle and *believe* in that miracle. With God all things were possible. So she would represent Culverville High as no school had been represented before—enter that county meet in all fields of competition in spite of her resolve to pick and choose if she competed at all—and concentrate on declamation, of course. Marvel Harrington would win county, district, and *state*! That would take her to Austin for the greatest "meet" of all.

A pale February sun pushed aside January's sleet curtains to let the new month enter. A few brave bulbs speared the still-frozen ground. Midterm exams had come and gone and, although the east winds still shrilled hoarsely of winter, hearts turned hopefully toward spring.

Mary Ann and Erlene were ecstatic with triumph. Both had "squeaked past" the first semester of geometry. Their daily work left a lot to be desired, Mr. Phillips told them darkly, but he was both pleased and surprised that the "less than excellent" pupils had done a commendable job with what most considered the ultimate test: *the theorem!* And (shaking his head in perplexity) a few of his more able failed.

Marvel felt relieved and happy until one of those "more able" stopped her in the hall and chokingly confided—and the routine renewed.

"Marvel, I—I'm desperate. I messed up—fooled around with Amanda's crowd—and now I may not graduate. Please help me!"

The girl had blurted out her heartbreak with such a rush of desperation that Marvel was caught off-guard. Recognition came with a shock.

"Kate Lynn!" she exclaimed at sight of Dr. Porter's daughter.

The girl was unduly hard on herself, filled with self-loathing, desperation, fear, regrets, and embarrassment. But if only Marvel would help her, it would never happen again—never, *never*. Could she forgive her?

"I am not the one to forgive you, Kate Lynn," Marvel told her gently. "You need tell me nothing more. You owe me no confidences. I'll help."

Dr. Porter came to see Mr. Phillips on behalf of his daughter. After the conference, the doctor made a point of walking to the bus with Marvel. "Kate Lynn has permission to retake the test, due to several matters we had to settle. She is not a bad girl, Marvel—"

"I never thought that, Dr. Porter. I've promised to help, but Kate Lynn will have to work. It won't be easy."

"My daughter has learned a valuable lesson—and, without knowing it, you were her inspiration. You might like to know that she has stopped smoking. Mr. Phillips was impressed by that—says it shows determination and a strong will. I personally can't thank you enough. If there's anything, anything at all, that I can ever do, you'll tell me?"

Marvel smiled. She liked the doctor and she liked his daughter. Kate Lynn was too good for Amanda's crowd. "Thank you, sir. You've done quite enough already—coming to help others in need. You care!"

She boarded the bus and prepared to take roll for Mr. Bumstead. But her mind was still on the strange turn of events. Life was filled with surprises. Each day held its own miracle. God saw to that with every sunrise. Marvel shook her head in wonder, realizing suddenly that the bus driver was looking at her strangely—and that she had failed to check off names of some ten or twelve riders. She set to work, little realizing that one day the strange encounter would mean more—much more.

* * *

Grandmother thought it would be "sweet" for them to make use of those theater tickets on Valentine's Day. Uncle Worth's family had agreed, she said. "That falls on ticket-drawing night. And judging by the news, any movie could be the last picture show on silent screen."

She was right, Marvel felt, and looked through her bulging file of clippings saved for future columns to find an article she had saved:

Movie houses, in spite of their drawings for prizes which make the deprived into "instant millionaires," continue to play to empty houses. In order to stay in business, producers are compelled to reach out and explore the new. "Think big," they call it. Sherwood Anderson in *Home Town* says differently: "The big world outside now is so filled with confusion. It seemed to me that hope, in the present muddle, was to try *thinking small*." All media needs to remember that Americans at all levels stand in need of something affordable to shoo away those Depression-time blues. Be that as it may, the days of the silent movie are in the past. Giveaway days are indeed giving way! Voice along with action is no longer a novelty. There has to be something more glitzy, while Hollywood keeps a keen eye on the purse. Musicals, bits of froth that they are, cost less to produce as producers can draw from the chorus lines. Most previous productions have centered around the perennial lovebirds, Dick Powell and Ruby Keeler. And now comes another sticky-sweet variety starring Jeanette MacDonald and Nelson Eddy in schmaltzy operettas.... But word comes now of the biggest money-maker of them all: Fred Astaire. Never give up hope. Astaire didn't, even when his reviewers wrote: "Can't act. Slightly bald. Can dance a little." But after playing some bit parts, the *can't* man has teamed up with a nimble-footed young beauty called Ginger Rogers. The team's first hit is such a smash that RKO insured Fred's legs for a million dollars. Bravo for hope! But hope's not what it's all about, unfortunately. The light-on-plot films center around the making of money, and dollar signs replace eyes for Hollywood producers.

With a sigh, Marvel returned the clipping to her file. The rest of the lengthy item could wait. For now, *she* could hope. "My hope is in thee, Lord, not in *money*—truly the root of all evil!" she whispered. The words were a promise of her heart.

And so it was that Marvel Harrington awoke with a tingle of excitement on Valentine's Day. She and Mary Ann had talked about the big night all week. "This should be a red-letter day on the calendar," her cousin insisted. When Marvel reminded her that it wasn't a legal holiday, Mary Ann had tossed her dark curls little-girl fashion and declared that it wasn't *illegal*. "Anyway, it's a holiday in my heart."

*A holiday of the heart.* Marvel tasted the phrase and liked it. Valentine's Day, the day of hearts and flowers—a day for love! She would wear the red turtleneck sweater and the matching skirt. The pearls? Not for school—but wouldn't they look lovely? As she fastened the clasp, Marvel looked at her reflection in the mirror and gasped. Why, she was blushing: two round telltale spots staining the whiteness of her skin in the way that prompted others to ask if she used rouge.

And then she knew the truth. She was dressing for Titus....

Throughout the day the sense of excitement lingered, making her pulse race and alerting her hearing. When Titus came, she would hear his footsteps—even sort them from the constant shuffle of other feet around her. She'd *know*, and she'd run to meet him...never mind curious stares.

But the day wore on and Titus had made no appearance— unless he was waiting outside. He was not. She must overcome her disappointment and be ready for the gala affair the family wanted and needed. She *must*.

Bravely, Marvel put a smile in place before calling out a cheery "Hello, I'm home!" to her parents. The rest was easy, for Mother responded with a smile as she held out an odd-shaped envelope and hurried into the kitchen. They'd have an early supper, she said, making ready.

Again the rapid pulse, the *knowing*, and out fell the most beautiful valentine Marvel had ever seen, made to open outward in a tissue-fluted crimson heart designed to stand alone. To the left was the usual question: Will You Be My Valentine? And to the right was a verse that she knew with all her heart had been chosen with care:

> I want a friend whose heart is true,
> Someone, my dear, as sweet as you!
> I want a friend who'll one day be
> *A great deal more than a friend to me.*
>
> —Your Titus

The purchase meant sacrifice of other needs, but sacrifice for the sake of love was a willing sacrifice. And in return she gave him the gift of her heart. *Oh Titus, my darling, my darling... forever...*

"*Mother!*" Marvel cried out, overcome with joy. Mother's eyes were rimmed with tears when she rushed from the kitchen. Wordlessly, they embraced. It was the first time ever they had shared in the way only a woman understands. They were closer than ever before—in a new way.

\* \* \*

The evening was star-studded for Marvel. And it was a night of magic for the other Harringtons—magic which turned to a miracle, which was strange, for it had brought disappointment to Marvel. And that was followed by a kind of melancholy that springs from watching a final curtain come down. It was the end of movies as Culverville had known them, and the end of something else she was unable to call by name. There would never be another time like this—together. How then could joy overcome?

Attendance was sparse—strangers who patted yawns in practiced boredom with the triple feature. First came a lovable little tenement-based "Dead End Kids" comedy followed by an ancient Bob Steele cowboy movie. The Harringtons, in a little world of their own, applauded for the "white hats" and jeered at the "black hats," while Billy Joe clapped in glee. And then came the timeless "Les Miserables" taken from Victor Hugo's classic novel. Its gripping plot held the audience spellbound in its mixture of the bizarre and beautiful. Oh, to be able to write like that! With that thought, Marvel turned full attention to the celebrated social novel of the titanic genius whose pen was so mighty.

Set in nineteenth century France, the story began with a dying man's confession to two lovers, separated by his bed: "Once upon a time, my children, a man stole a loaf of bread...." It would have been easy to weep throughout, but Marvel's mind centered on plans to use the message for a critique required in English class, including the book's want of needed humor in contrast to the heavy drama. How different—and yet how like— were conditions in today's world. Hunger existed then and now. Titus could use that point, weaving it into the complexity of the varicolored tapestry of the four horsemen and political efforts for extermination.

In the theater the unforgettable silent film ended where it began with little change in spite of the suffering between. Objection! People in America *cared*, Marvel thought fiercely. It was up to this generation to perpetuate that kind of love. They *must*.

An endless flashing of still ads followed: ...Cars, New and Used, $57.50 to $500.00, *buy now!*...New A & P Grocery Store, sirloin steak 29¢, Cornflakes 8¢, Buttercrust bread, *sliced*, 5¢. *Shop where it pays to buy!* Billy Joe squirmed, others groaned, and then houselights!

The manager importantly took his place in the spotlight. "This will be the last silent movie, folks. We're merging with the other Culverville theater for your convenience. When we reopen after enlarging, we promise the newest and best in supercolossal productions—in all delicious flavors!" The man waited for expected applause, bowed, and continued: "And now! Lad—ees and gentle-men—comes the magical moment when, blindfolded, I will draw a winning ticket stub. Make ready!"

"This small group increases our chances, so watch those numbers!" Grandmother confided and leaned forward, sable-brown eyes glowing.

The very first number called matched Leah Johanna Mier Riley's. Grandfather's cane pounded the floor as Grandmother accepted the two armloads of fancy groceries brought by the usher. Let others stare. Alexander Jay Harrington could yell

"Bravo!" if he chose. And he chose. Some ungrateful lady received a floor lamp, calling it "cheap" and saying that perhaps she could use it as a booby prize in a bridge game. And then it was back to Grandfather's wild cheering, for the unbelievable had happened. Uncle Worth received two bulging bags of groceries, and then Auntie Rae. She looked ready to cry, and when Mary Ann's number won an identical prize, she did! "But it's unfair," she whispered to Mother.

There were brooms and mops, chocolates and silk hosiery, Havana cigars, family coupons for Cy's Corner Cafe—and tickets for the grand opening of the combined theaters. Trivia to some, so the audience thinned. The Harringtons stayed on. Then when Daddy's number was called, followed by Mother's, Marvel entered a world of unreality. This was a miracle, a miracle absolute: food not by the sack but by the bushel basket, when once upon a time a man stole a loaf of bread. Heretofore, they lived from the rapidly dwindling foods stored in the cellar and dried peas saved for seed. Oh what a celebration—a red-letter day indeed! Titus' beautiful valentine floated right off the mantel to dance before her dazzled eyes . . . and Mother's violin refused to be silenced. Understandably, when Marvel's number was called, it had to be repeated. No groceries, the manager said, just a coupon worth a month's supply of foods of her own choosing. *Just* a coupon? Oh, praise the Lord. . . .

The Harringtons' silver cup of happiness overflowed when Billy Joe received an all-leather catcher's mitt Grandfather said would cost over a dollar! Why, the new prosperity had come! In wild abandon, the family—all packed for going home like a tin of sardines into the great, black car left to Grandfather by his stepson—sang out "Beulah Land": "I'm feastin' on a mountain underneath a cloudless sky. . . . I'm drinkin' from a fountain that never shall run dry."

# 25

# Not by
# Bread Alone...

With the lovely valentine before her, Marvel read the sentimentally beautiful words over and over. *She* was the friend Titus sought—friend and *more*. Never mind the "one day" phrase. That was a sealing of a relationship both knew existed already. A—a—why, it was almost a *proposal*, coming from Titus. He had meant it when he said so long ago, "I do not jest about matters of the heart!"

When the card came, Marvel had longed to call a message to Western Union, making use of a single word: YES! The telegraph office would have no choice but to add a "STOP" since there was no punctuation in the Morse code. But, Marvel thought dreamily, I'd have preferred DON'T. All right: DONT! DONT STOP! But a telegram was out of the question, of course, for the minimum charge was 24 cents, and if she had a quarter, it would be spent on notebook paper. She had three sheets left in her notebook, and her supply of ink was so low it was necessary to tilt the bottle. Oh, wouldn't a pen be nice? Marvel sighed. Wistful thinking would not change things. Anyway, deep in her heart she knew that Marvel Harrington would *not* have sent such a daring message.

But she would write! The newspaper was as generous as A & P Grocery who had furnished the manna, for it had to be a gift supplied by the Lord from heaven. Gratefully, Marvel took a sheet of the pale lilac paper the editor had given her, along with stamps and envelopes.

My dearest Titus: The beautiful valentine was like a breath of fresh air—and I needed both. I will keep it in my box of memories and display it each February fourteenth. Not that there's a need for reviewing, as the words I've memorized already, but to savor as one savors a photograph or a pressed rose for the *feel* of the moment. Will I be your valentine? Did you need to ask? And our "one day" is *now*, my darling, for what we have is precious and priceless.

Marvel laid her pen aside. The words had come straight from her heart, but had they been too personal? Suddenly it seemed unimportant. She was in the grip of a strange sense of timing, a sense of urgency resembling an uneasiness mixed with excitement. The feeling, although unexplainable, was not new, she realized. It had swept over her at Grandmother Riley and Grandfather Harrington's Christmas party, and again in the theater. How strange. No—not like that. It couldn't be. *Dear God, not a last time!*

Quickly, her writing turned to other matters, questions Titus had posed so long ago and she had felt unable to answer until now.

You must be very busy now with the responsibilities the senator has delegated to you. Such an honor, however, and I am proud of you and know that your sister feels the same. Once you were questioning what part churches and the educational system should play in politics. I felt that you were questioning yourself during the preparation of Senator Norton's upcoming speeches and perhaps his platform. I know the two of you will decide on that, but I'm thinking of our columns and have tried (in vain!) to get some opinions. I am amazed, Titus, that people of far more knowledge, education, and wisdom than mine have taken so much for granted for so long—and without question! "Separation of church and state," they declared—convincingly because they all believed that phrase. I've heard that all my life, but I'm not old enough to vote (until someone lowers the legal age to 16!). But I was made to feel silly—as if they felt threatened in education, or as if I were questioning a higher authority in theology. *I* have no need to be right for the sake of my ego, but, as columnists, we have a vital need to research our statements. Our readers have a right to know. My efforts were not in vain. Do you realize that "separation of church and state" does not appear in any of the legal documents upon which our laws are based? Not in our Constitution. Not in the Declaration of Independence. The only place I could find the phrase was buried deep in a *letter* from Thomas Jefferson in his presidential campaign back in 1803. My goodness! Do you realize that was in colonial days, back when the Bible was used as a textbook to guard against "ye olde deluder Satan." Well, these are a few of my observations, and they lead me to say a loud "Yes! We do need to involve the church in the educational system." Read Romans 13 and see if you agree. I'll rephrase it for my column—together with, oh, so many other matters....

Marvel told him then about the merging of the two theaters, the promise of updated "family films," adding the news of the Harringtons' winning stubs. Perhaps it was pride which kept her from telling just how badly the food was needed. Instead, she moved into other, more exciting matters. She had entered the upcoming contests for county meet, senior division this year, and would win at county level and at district! Didn't she sound smug? she teased. Smug? No, more like motivated—because that meant state. Austin!

And so, my darling, our "one day" will come in May—even though you may be unable to come if you're with Senator Norton when he makes his platform speeches. I'll go, if possible, to one of the many cemeteries here. One is tucked around each bend of the road in groves of persimmon trees and brambles. We'll renew our dreams when we're together—there or here. I long to see you, but I'm glad you turned down the job in Greenville.... Onward and upward, that's you! You must help Lucille just as I must help my parents, no matter what the sacrifices are. And then there's the Smith Hotel for you and reconstruction of the Culverville Baptist Church where you graduated and I will graduate ... where you made your commitment to God and your promise to a suffering world. . . . Enlarge, make needed changes, but keep those stained-glass windows where sunshine comes streaming through the blues and yellows to reflect the face of the Good Shepherd and His sheep, while I try here to recapture enthusiasm the winds have blown away . . . trying in my small way to bring light from those stained-glass windows to some irascible, cantankerous (but believing!) old coots, shaky though my knees feel. Would you believe that most out here are softening toward our African neighbors? We have to grind prejudice with our heels, but it takes patience. So *one day* . . .

Until then, I am now and forevermore: Your Marvel!

Marvel read her finished letter through and found that it was not finished after all. Certainly, it needed two additions. She must lightly (Titus understood her, would see her smiling) mention that those numerous cemeteries were not there, hidden haphazardly and forgotten. Each was situated behind a chapel, what had once served as a church and a school before this "separation of church." Certainly she didn't wish, she wrote, to give the impression that Morning Glory Chapel was more *dead* than alive (except, her second P.S. read, for the sad condition of the land!). That was her dream, Marvel reminded Titus, that one day the garden it once was could be restored: peaceful, happy, and in harmony with the Creator. It had always been there, waiting, and it was still waiting to be rediscovered. "Mercy me!" she said aloud with a laugh that sent Titus' valentine twirling until her heart was pinned on every wall, making all things beautiful. "Mercy me!" she repeated, "will one stamp be enough for *this*?"

And yet she added another postscript: "I will be wearing the pearls when I come to Austin to win the trophy—and (daringly) *your* heart!"

\* \* \*

Time was at a premium. Personal communications must grow more brief and be spaced farther apart between her and Titus, Marvel knew. But their constant flow of column materials kept them in touch, and always there was time for a word or so to keep her heart glowing. She failed to recognize that those messages grew more and more personal. She had always understood without the "analysis" so in vogue these days.

"Oh, the beautiful lady in blue!" Titus wrote once. After quoting the lyric that he'd crooned beneath their oak, finishing with the line, "She kissed me then fled..." he posed a silly riddle, asking how a kiss sent by mail resembled a straw hat. Titus got the laugh he had reached for in supplying the answer: "Neither is *felt!*" He would always remember her running to catch that always-in-a-hurry bus...blowing little fingertip kisses—tantalizingly, he added.

Then came demanding days in which Marvel could personalize only by closing with "Your Marvel." Miss Robertson was compelled to return to Wichita Falls—without saying goodbye!—to care for her aging father who had broken both legs in a fall. Mr. Caldwell came to replace the teacher who had contributed so much to Marvel's success in Culverville High School. Of course the spirited redhead had related well to all her students, Marvel remembered of Miss Robertson. Then Marvel granted herself the same ability! She had never come into conflict with a teacher.

But Mr. Caldwell was different. Something in his manner warned that he must never be challenged or made to feel uncomfortable. The man was tall with lean cheeks, and his eyebrows lifted as if questioningly yet all-knowing. And missing from his pale eyes was any hint of humor or message of reassurance. His greeting was curt, his expectations unrealistic. And there would be more to add if students hoped to graduate. Did she imagine it or did his eyes focus on her?

She did not imagine it. The English teacher, seeming to feel that she was a threat (and Marvel never knew why), goaded her at every opportunity. "So you are Marvel Harrington—*the* Marvel Harrington. I must caution you that it will be dangerous to rely on past achievements"..."I see by your record that you are trying to conduct newspaper columns in your spare time—of which there will be none in *my* class!"..."Entering every competition for county meet, are you, Marvel Harrington? It surprises me that you forgot baseball and high jump! I suggest you drop all except declamation. I will be judging and screening entrants and am not easily impressed"..."Did this entry in your diary *happen*?"

Marvel knew that any response would be misinterpreted. It was wise to remain silent, even try to act dull-witted—even though in the process she must bite her lower lip until it bled ... like her heart.

Kate Lynn Porter was in the same class this semester. "Oh Marvel," she whispered one day. "That man's impossible. Why is he centering you out? Not that he's exactly lovable to the rest of us. Is there anything I can do? You can't take this. See Mr. Phillips—"

"Thank you for caring. I—I need a friend," Marvel managed to say. "How will I manage? I have no intention of backing down. I— I'll avoid Mr. Caldwell as much as I can, but I will *not* change my plans."

"Oh Marvel, I admire you! You're responsible for my getting through geometry. Oh, you're in touch with Titus. Tell him I'm seeing his cocaptain and buddy—he's back. We're enjoying a friendship! Amanda's seeing a guy—fellow—from another town. Older man, I hear."

Kate Lynn *hears*? So her association with Amanda *was* over. But even more surprising was the news that Duke had been tossed aside. She wondered about Erin and Cindy—and how their mothers felt about this. Oh well.

True to her word, Marvel continued with her columns. And she did not withdraw her name as a contestant for county meet. It was close at hand, she was prepared, and that was that. She would do what she could to meet the teacher's other demands, however, and shrug off the hurts. She had been hurt before and she would be hurt again. With that thought came another. Why not make the most of a trying situation and use it in her column on education? Jesus had said: "It is written, That man shall not live by bread alone, but by every word of God." And the Word of God was love. Feeding the hungry was not enough. There must be compassion and caring. Couldn't the same be said of education— that students at any level did not learn by books alone, but by the compassion and love, the gentle guidance of caring teachers? "Let the little ones come unto me ..." God's Son had said. Some- where, somehow, it all tied together: legislation, education, religious faith, and more: a *working* faith, a caring faith, held together by the invisible thread of love. Those in the high places, teachers most of all perhaps as they helped the minds of tomor- row, must realize that vital to the success of every significant pursuit is the handful of inspired leaders who encourage the turning of dreams into reality. Those notes she sent to Titus without making mention of the new English teacher.

# 26

# For of Such
# Is the Kingdom

The early signs of spring appeared in spite of the stubborn east wind and its cold invasion of houses and human bodies. Marvel continued to wear her winter coat in spite of its aging condition. The wind seeped through, and she was stiff with cold at the end of the 40-mile bus ride to school. But the cold could not touch her heart. It was springtime there. Spring *was* coming. Graduation was coming—and so was Titus. Somehow he would find a way to see her. She just *knew*.

And so, undaunted by all else, she watched the valiant efforts nature made to renew itself. Silver buds fattened on the willows' wind-whipped branches. Buckeye bushes took on the color-promise of crimson blossoms. Hickory, black walnut, and chinquapin trees donned wigs of green catkins. "One day, *one day*," Marvel renewed her promise to the land, "you too will be renewed." And she thought of time as round, like the earth. It would lead back to the beginning. There might be wandering ...exploring...*learning*. But the barriers would come down, the "flaming swords of the cherubim" of pestilence, war, famine, and *death* would be extinguished. Mankind would learn from those wanderings how to care for that over which God gave him dominion, though not by going the shortest distance. But then, there was only one point: home... "on earth as it is in heaven."

What, then, did it matter that she must borrow notebook paper from Mary Ann? It was only a temporary condition. ("I sound like Mother," she thought in surprise.) Grandmother was taking Mother shopping tomorrow. Possibly the new Atlantic and Pacific store carried school supplies. The baskets of staple-grocery prizes had been adequate until now, but Marvel's own prize was a month's supply of whatever groceries they chose.

She was to learn that while, yes, the store did stock a limited few items, clerks could not honor such a request. They must adhere to the chain store policy of groceries only... of course, they could be fancy. And fancy they were, Marvel was to find out as well. For, in addition to the usual coffee, flour, sugar, and cornmeal, there would be Daddy's favorites of canned oysters (and evaporated milk to make the soup he so enjoyed), canned meats, crackers, and so much more. Most of these, sad to say, people had taken for granted as gardens were lush, poultry and dairy products plentiful, and what one neighbor's larder lacked the other provided. Well, there was nothing to divide now.

But this day kept mum about tomorrow's secret. And so Marvel accepted ink from a girl across the aisle from her who had noticed that her bottle was now dry. It was blue and Marvel had used black, but she accepted what the other girl offered to share—mostly to keep from hurting her feelings. She would borrow from Mary Ann again, or Jake. He'd be more than glad to share. But, finding neither of them, she was compelled to use the blue. At least it was dark—a near-match, in fact.

Grandfather Harrington and Grandmother Riley came for Mother and Daddy after Marvel had left to meet the bus the next day. Mother made no effort to conceal her almost childish excitement. Did her hair look all right? Wasn't it nice of that young man who cut the men's hair to learn to "feather" ladies' hair as well—just to be neighborly, and, of course, express appreciation for reading Marvel's complimentary copy of the newspaper? And did her dress need pressing? After numerous reassurances, Mother relaxed. Daddy was going to Culverville, too, but he was unusually quiet, Marvel was to recall later.

Grandfather and Grandmother were still there when Marvel came home, and everybody was talking at once. There seemed to be no end to their talking. The small house overflowed with groceries and laughter.

The older couple hugged their granddaughter soundly, Grandfather saying what fine reports he was receiving and commenting on her columns. "Like a true Harrington!" he announced, while Grandmother repeated over and over how lovely, how stately Marvel was—"like true royalty, which she is, on the *Riley* side!" Marvel laughed and, embarrassed by what she considered flattery, hurriedly asked to be caught up on family news.

"There's not a whole lot of time for talking," Grandmother said in her usual breezy way, "but we'll take a minute as Fanny—the jewel—will have the evening meal underway. But—well, there are no secrets now. You know that our Mrs. Sutheral is to change her name on Memorial Day. So guess what, Marvel dear! She wants to be married at the hotel, with your grandfather giving her hand in marriage. And you and Mary Ann are to stand up with her. It will be wonderful, wonderful, with her descending the stairs and a big crowd, that being the day set for the decoration at the cemetery, the mortgage burning—and *our* surprise!"

"Quite a spiel in one minute, Duchess," Grandfather teased, fingering his gold retirement watch. "We could have had coffee— and my mouth feeling like a dry-cell battery. Dale, let's you and I put away groceries—you know, on the high shelves the weaker- but-wiser sex can't reach!"

Nobody objected. Grandmother continued to tell of the family, with Mother and Marvel listening eagerly. She never saw Aunt Eleanore or Aunt Dorthea. They seemed to avoid her purposely, but wouldn't you think the grandchildren would come to see the Squire? Of course, they had been tossed aside like long undies in summertime by the snobs in town.

"I don't know what to make of it all," she said slowly. "Joseph and Emory have talked with their father on occasion, and the Squire goes to his quarters afterward. Worries me because that man skips meals and eats like a canary for days. He shouldn't either, what with this new outbreak of influenza. Better make a note about that for your local column, Marvel dear. Back to the sons... they're up to *something*—"

Grandmother stopped in mid-sentence when a low-pitched exchange of words sifted through the kitchen door. "It's about the boys," she said.

"They've taken leave of their senses, both of them," Grandfather said with an expected thud of his cane, "won't even listen to reason. Well, nobody jumps a sinking ship but rats, and you know it!"

"Until the passengers are safe, Father." Daddy sounded tired.

Alexander Jay Harrington cleared his throat with a rumble. "Have it your way. But I'd say even then their chances of survival would be nil if the crew was packed into lifeboats in cattle-car fashion, like those roads are packed with rovers. Might as well be hoboes, gypsies, *tramps*. No son of mine's going to become a tramp if I can help it!"

"There are some things you can't help, Father!" Daddy's voice had heated up. "Not when our president has been unable to keep his promises. The New Deal's not working, and men do desperate things when their families are hungry. A man, a *real* man—and that's the kind of sons you tried to bring up—won't sit idle and wait for his cow to come home, back up, and wait to be milked—if there *were* cows—"

"I know, I know," the older Harrington conceded, "he'd go after the cow. But cattle don't go straying way up to Oregon. So Alex Jr. and the Brothertons go looking for cows anyway. Well son, you listen to your father. Call FDR wishy-washy, whatever, I'll never forget what he warned when he took over that monumental job: 'We'll concentrate on one thing—*save the people!* And if we have to change our minds twice every day to accomplish that end, we should do it!'"

"They *are* trying something," Daddy said a little desperately. "And yes, sir, I do recall the president's words: 'Take a method and try it. If it fails, try another. But, above all, *try* something.'"

"And the man in the white house is *still* trying. It'll happen—wait and see. There's that new social reform coming up, promising a retirement plan for all workers, even the self-employed."

"And when there is no work?"

"There'll be something else. At least *you* haven't abandoned ship!"

"Not yet," Daddy said. And there was defeat in his voice.

* * *

After a flamboyant sunset, the sky empurpled with twilight—a reminder that days were lengthening now. Marvel watched from her window, forcing her mind to concentrate on all that lay before her. She had managed through prayer to lay aside the troubling thoughts (perhaps even then she knew that a crisis lay ahead), as she had laid aside Mr. Caldwell's unwarranted taunts.

Laid aside, yes, and yet they hung there unresolved. One day they must be reckoned with, but not now.

It was impossible, however, to ignore *time*. Some voiceless whisper warned Marvel that it would be wise to send all notes for further columns to Titus now. The English teacher's seemingly unnecessary requirement for keeping a diary proved helpful as a reminder of matters she had never mentioned. She mailed everything to Titus. The bulky envelopes held her factual notes and her secret hopes and dreams concerning the land's future. On the positive side were reports of attempts already in progress to rid the soil of poisons, making gardening again possible as soon as the rains came. On the negative side was the frightening news of the flu outbreak. For yes, it was true, she had discovered from the county health department, subsequently writing a column to alert local residents to the danger and advise them on precautions to take (avoiding fatigue, replenishing body fluids, and eating a balanced diet) because there was no known treatment.

Titus' forthcoming columns were masterpieces. Marvel's heart swelled with pride as her words echoed throughout. Demands on their time robbed the young couple of coveted opportunity for personal letters, except for occasional scribbles like Titus' saying, "Don't wander too far—I couldn't do this without you" ... "I fight the *blues* by remembering the blue of those eyes!" ... "Someday (always *someday*, isn't it) you and I must coauthor a 'bestseller'—sounds good, the *you and I*!" ... "'You're wonderful, you're marvelous' (*my* Marvelous!)"

Just a fragment of a song, but Titus had added the words that made it meaningful: *his Marvelous!* And so, longing to say more, she refrained. He had never said the words her heart cried out to hear. Until then, she must not be the one to say "I love you," just "Your Marvelous" as a signature, and the affectionate use of *my darling* that he used.

Marvel read Titus Smith's follow-up to her column on the church's role in politics. She had challenged the figure of speech "separation of church and state" that churches had accepted without question. His column said in part:

> Difficult as it may be to believe, the historical "shot heard around the world" exploded from the fiery tongues at the reverend gentleman, one Jonas Clark's church. The

date was correct, of course April 19, 1775! The resistants? Members of that church. In the battle with the British Army, eight were killed.... Once upon a time the church was very much a part of the great mission of Christianity. Why have we proven to be deserters? There should be, there *must* be a rediscovery of our Christian heritage, a demand that we reestablish a righteous government. Then and then only can we denounce tyrannical, godless rulers elsewhere.

And where does education fit into the political arena? (Titus began another column, in response to Marvel's notes). We Americans are immigrants, strangers on a foreign soil, bound together by a Constitution, a republic with a democratic form of government. While a democracy lays no claim to perfection, it works better than any other. Abraham Lincoln declared us indivisible, founded by the people, of the people, and for the people, declaring that a house divided cannot stand. But those words go back in history to the beginning. In the Old Testament's beginning book, we find that our Creator divided the light from darkness—and still we walk in the dark. *E pluribus unum*, our nation's motto, means "one of many" so we are of all backgrounds and we continue to pour in—believing, trusting, and finding basis for that trust on our medium of exchange, "In God We Trust." And so we are indeed a Christian nation as well for, updating the late great president's words, let us turn again to the Bible, on which our Constitution was based. In Luke 11:17 we find: "...and a house divided against a house falleth." So much for history. Where do we stand now? In need of money...in need of legislation which provides that money for the basic needs here and to others even more unfortunate across the seas...and to provide money for schools where educated teachers who *care* are trained. For books alone are not enough.

The words began to swim. Either she was too weary or too overcome by emotion. Marvel laid the newspaper column bearing a Smith-Harrington byline aside until her eyes could focus. But her mind busied itself with the growing question as to how their controversial probings would be received. The subject of money was a sore spot. Did they sound too altruistic, creating another hated "dole"? On the other hand, Texas was a liberal state—or had been. Did voters feel more conservative now? Titus would need to decide whether to pepper the senator's campaign speeches with such views—not an easy decision. Platforms must hold practical promises, not expensive dreams. Election depended on that.

Years would pass before she knew that Cliff Norton's decision spelled his demise. But, mercifully, the curtain of time screened away the future....

As the days wore on, teachers became increasingly edgy. At home there was the same feel in the atmosphere. It was not limited to her parents, Marvel felt, but affecting her grand-parents as well—as if they needed something and didn't know what they needed. Reassurance? Past, present, or future? She had a strange premonition that they had made or were to make a journey—a journey they regretted or would come to regret. *Stop it*, Marvel willed herself, *or you will become confused and afraid*. Her mind *must* remain clear, otherwise, her schedule would become a nightmare, a succession of horror stories instead of lovely expectations and dreams.

Local tryouts came and went. Marvel was among the winning contestants to represent Culverville High at county levels, but declamation came last. Several other students had entered and, while wishing them well, she felt driven to win. This was her ticket to Austin, and she had promised Titus. She was well-prepared, accustomed to competition. Why then the queasiness, the feeling that her body was put together with Tinkertoys by the fumbling hands of children and was falling apart as she spoke? Gratefully, she sat down afterward, only to be asked to leave the room while judges made a decision.

It came as no surprise when Marvel Harrington was asked to return.

"You've been chosen," Mr. Caldwell said coldly, "although the choice was no easy matter. And there remains doubt in my mind you're more qualified. It's more of retaining the status quo with other teachers—"

Mr. Angelo cut in sharply. "That could have been left unsaid! Marvel was head-and-shoulders above the others!"

There was enmity between the two teachers, an undeclared war, Marvel noted with little interest. Without checking on the identity of the third judge, she stumbled from the room. She was about to be sick.

Maybe the small victory would please Mother and Daddy. But they scarcely noticed, both murmuring the kind of "that's nice" phrase one uses when told a person you don't remember asked about your health. And later that night she heard Daddy say, "I told my father that crews are not deserting when they pull a sinking vessel into port for repairs!" Still talking about ships... or Daddy was. Mother was saying little these days. Somebody would have to tell Daddy that dream boats were myths, that they didn't "come in." Or did he know? He probably did.

Pushing herself all the way, Marvel kept up on her assignments, not daring drop behind. May had slipped in almost unnoticed because of no spring planting. But buds had opened in more protected places, and green leaves spoke of Austin, Decoration Day, June, graduation...and Titus! Titus—dear, faithful Titus who kept up the flow of columns even when she'd been compelled to curtail submissions to help.

He wrote of the country's needs, struggles, and growing disenchantment...his personal struggle to understand and help conquer the demons of "bureaucratic red tape" in restoring hope, peace, and security...and preparing today's youth for a better tomorrow.

They troop into our overcrowded classrooms with visions of a better life dancing in their heads like sugarplums. *Save our children!* We *must*, for (and he finished the quote Marvel had begun)... "for of such is the kingdom." These are the immigrants—almost the unknowns in America's heartland, for our population remains virtually unchanged. This is home, settled with generations of determined people filled with an unyielding sense of purpose to overcome, to build back with the pickax of determination. That will be our crowning achievement if we widen the horizons of education, religion, and social reforms for our young. The winds of change are blowing, just as the whirlwinds which steal our soil and our hope. So let

us renew our hopes, become the most that we can be,
serving as models for younger ones who must care
again.... We must teach them to care, *make* them
care... care *about* themselves, *for* themselves—and
more. The gritty streets of Chicago... the slums of
New York... the barren deserts right here and over
there...

Marvel clipped each column and filed them all away with
Titus' precious letters, his valentine, and her memories.

\* \* \*

And then Daddy took ill. The day had begun like any other,
with Marvel planning ahead what she must accomplish. The
signs of his approaching illness had gone unnoticed: his pallor
and the hacking cough that had become a part of him. Mother
insisted that he stay home instead of going to baseball practice
in "this evil wind." But he had forced himself to carry on, just as
Marvel forced herself in spite of weariness.

Mother wrung her hands at his gasping for breath. *What could
they do?* Marvel took one look at the high color which had
replaced his former pallor, his feverishly bright eyes, saw that he
held his chest in pain, and she knew what they *had* to do. "Dr.
Porter, this is Marvel. Daddy's very sick, and we can't pay—"
He'd be right out, he said in response to her telephone call. "Of
such is the kingdom..." she whispered to the Lord.

# 27

# *The Ugly Face of Reality*

The white maze of unreality closed in on Marvel. She moved in it gratefully. She braced her shoulders, stiffening the muscles to accept the inevitable pain of reality. The pain would come, she knew by horrible insight, but for now she was numbed by shock.

"Dr. Porter," she had managed through stiff lips that first night, "what *is* it? Is my father dangerously ill?" Foolish question, when she knew the answer.

"Yes—yes he is," the man Marvel had come to regard so highly said. "As to the diagnosis, it's pneumonia." Putting away his stethoscope, Dr. Porter motioned Marvel to a corner, away from the bed where Dale Harrington lay, and away from the ears of his wife, who knelt beside it, her lips moving in silent prayer. "Your father will need his family standing by, which is better medicine than I can offer. Although there are a few precautions (he named them and then continued). And I will stay with you until after the critical third day. Nobody else must come in. And Marvel, I want you to trot along to school like a good girl. Now, now, no objections! This is what your father would want, and I know the pressures you're under in school. I'll call if there's any change."

Pressure? Nobody knew how much. But the doctor was right. This is what Daddy would want. She would do it for him—and for Mother. Her education meant so much to Mother. Somehow they would get through this....

Marvel tried to pray and found herself unable. But God knew her needs and met them. She must have made sense when others spoke, given the proper answers. And evidently her speech had been well delivered at the Titus County meet, for it was Marvel Harrington who won first place in declamation. It was she who would represent the county and the school at district competition in Texarkana...later, state...if...

Ice—Daddy must have ice to break his dangerously high fever, the doctor said. Marvel called Mr. Bumstead. "Bring it on th' bus? Not on yore life. I'm gonna git it right now!" he said, sounding happy to serve.

Marvel prepared hot water bottles, Vicks-saturated chest cloths, and shaved ice, while managing meals for Mother and Dr. Porter. And there were the never-ending telephone calls. The doctor dozed in a chair between medicines and forced Mother to bed after a sedative. But Marvel kept vigil with him the first two nights, sleeping almost none.

Daddy slipped into unconsciousness the third night, a state which was not that unusual, Dr. Porter tried to reassure them. And Mother was surprisingly calm. White-faced, she gripped Daddy's hand and unashamedly declared her undying love over and over, always saying how much, how very much Daddy meant to her and Marvel. "And my darling, when you are well and strong again, we'll see that your dreams come true. *That I swear!*"

There was a nightmarish moment when Daddy's labored breathing stopped. Dr. Porter, his face ashen, barked orders— orders which Marvel, capable only of automatic, trancelike motion, obeyed but never recalled...except his order of *"Pray!"* She tried and failed. But Mother was more successful, and then continued her words of gentle reassurance to the man she loved.

And Daddy must have heard! "Coffee—I want a cup of coffee—"

"You'll get fruit juice—and drink it!" Dr. Porter said curtly. And then Mother broke into tears. The doctor joined her. But Marvel collapsed at his bedside. She was tired...so tired...and her body was now on fire. The crisis was past, but she had glimpsed the ugly face of reality.

In the days that followed, Marvel was vaguely aware of her mother hovering over her like a guardian angel. She dreamed of a great, dark forest which one moment promised peace and security, such as she had felt before the crash, and a longing to wander back to find what she had lost. And the next moment it was black with despair, filled with people who were hopelessly lost, wailing out pleas for her help. But in either case, it was Mother who guided her back, cautioning that she must never wander too far into the forests of the past or those of the future— and never alone. It was hard to tell what was real.

How did one reconcile reality and unreality into a shape when life is neither—or both? But throughout the white stupor there emerged an awareness of certain moments that would last a lifetime.

She knew when Dr. Porter came back without being asked. "Your daughter has had a terrific battle with influenza—but she's a fighter, that one! Now she must recuperate, as your husband's doing so well. Throw away those blasted books, tie her to the bedposts, resort to anything that will keep the young lady home! No company. This thing takes root like Bermuda grass and goes around looking for bodies to invade. And oh, here are her assignments Kate Lynn sent—and a bottle of ink. Some gift! Has our other patient depleted all the makings of soup?"

"Just the oysters, milk, and crackers. He's back to solids now."

Mother whispered something about late payments, and the doctor came close to being offended. "Not on your life! After all she's done for Kate Lynn— By the way, tell her my daughter told Bill—that's Bill Johnson she's seeing, nice boy—and he wrote Titus Smith about Marvel."

Bill had been Titus' cocaptain. Yes, Titus would write. The expected letters came, but reading them would have to wait. She was sick, so sick. Mother held Marvel's head while she retched. Then, with a kind of tenderness, her mother stacked the letters in full view.

Weakened, Marvel drifted away again. But she knew when Daddy called in to say, "The doctor won't let me in, baby— doesn't want you and me involved in a gift exchange of germs! I feel like sneaking in, except I know the medicine man's right. But there's one thing that's hard for me to resist, you know and that's temptation!"

Mother's laugh was like music. Daddy was trying to joke. Marvel would get well. She must—for them.

That night when Mother brought broth, Marvel tried to force down a swallow. It was the only way she could regain her strength.

After one gulp, she signaled for Mother to remove her arm from beneath the pillow. Then she closed her eyes and tried to hold it down.

Mother soothed her with words as if she were a child again. But her words were not childlike. "Easy, sweetheart. Lie still for Mother and Daddy. You're going to be all right. You're back from that forest you talked about when your fever was so high. It's down now, *praise the Lord!* You talked about Mark Twain's Huck Finn, and I found the copy you had checked out of the school library. I guess it's an assignment. Yes, I see it is by Kate Lynn Porter's notes. Anyway, honey, it had been years since I'd read the book, so I thumbed through it while I sat with you. But," she sighed, "we can't escape into that never-never land of his where there are no restraints. We need responsibility, as you and your friend have pointed out so wisely. Are you listening?"

Marvel felt a faint stir of emotions. She nodded.

"Oh honey, I've learned so much—I mean, what's important. We need home, but there's Mother's sampler: Home Is Where the Heart Is."

Marvel spoke her first words then. They were weak, almost inaudible and spoken haltingly, but they were words! "A man—named Blackstone, I—I think—said—Oh, I—remember—Sir William—said—uh—'Home is the—the place from which—when a man departs—is a—a wanderer—until he—he returns.' I—I guess he—meant both places: heaven and earth. Is—is the broth—still hot?"

"Oh, my darling, you spoke—you spoke! I'll warm the broth. And yes, *yes*, that's what I'm trying to say. That hymn says it: 'If Jesus goes with me, I'll go.' And if my family's with me, I'll go, hoping—always hoping that—that we *can* come back. Oh Dale! Don't you dare try to come in. But she spoke—our Marvel *spoke!*"

Mother cried then. Even with her eyes closed, Marvel knew. But she lay very still, filled with the miracle of Mother's promise—whatever it might mean. She would face that later. It was the realization that Snow Riley Harrington was not fickle—that she *was* capable of deep emotion, that she *did* have depth of feeling. She had light-touched life because, for her, otherwise it would have been too much to bear.

Mary Ann called repeatedly. Marvel was unable to walk to the wall telephone, but Mother took the messages. "Thank goodness," she reported, "Marvel's safe as far as exemptions go. Used to be we were ineligible to skip the silly things, but Mr. Phillips has mellowed—so much sickness. She can be out a week. It means a lot to her."... "And no need to worry over the district meet—it's over, and who cares? All they won is a trophy."... "We'll all help like she helped us—and, Auntie Snow, there—there are some things—we need to talk over."

Mother relayed the messages reluctantly. "It doesn't matter, darling. Remember how you felt about Mary Ann's illness? What's important is your getting well, and then we'll *all* talk—the family and us."

With a heavy heart, Marvel gulped back her disappointment. So the contests were over. Now there was no hope of Austin, but there was Decoration Day...and graduation. Now she must get well, qualify for exemption—

But that didn't happen. Marvel tried, but her legs crumpled. It would take more time. The ugly face of reality reappeared.

# 28

# For No One Knows the Future

Snow Harrington had made a mistake. It was foolish and impetuous of her to spend precious money on luxuries. Her daughter's prize on the closing night of the movie house should have gone for staple groceries instead of squandering it on frills. Now, overcome with remorse, Mother spoke in guarded words to Grandmother, confirming what Marvel should have expected. They were out of food. Well, almost.

"It's my fault—I knew better. No, Mother, you did not overpersuade me.... Yes, you're right about that. Dale *did* need the oyster soup.... And yes, there were meals to prepare for the doctor, but (and her voice dropped even lower) I—I simply don't know how we'll manage."

How *would* they manage? Marvel wondered, putting down the pen she had worked overtime in an effort to catch up on the assignments before returning to school. The ink Kate Lynn had sent was green—not a deep color she could hope to get past Mr. Caldwell like the dark blue, but green-green. It was a horrid color even to her eyes. The entries taken from Mother's reports to Dr. Porter would have to serve for entries in her diary. Illness was no excuse in his unforgiving eyes. There was no choice. Families without funds for food could not afford ink.

Grandmother Riley called back almost immediately. Apparently she and the Squire had wasted no words. They were coming right out!

Mother looked bothered when she reported the news, but Daddy was pleased. Marvel thought in some far corner of her mind that the two of them had reversed roles. Daddy was glossing over while Mother faced facts. Then her mind went back to the task before her, the task she felt too weak to do but must be done. The grandparents' visit would be short, but every minute of her time counted. She had lost out on the news completely, giving her time instead to reading Titus' letters over and over. Nobody could blame her surely, but she must make up for the time now. She needed to stay informed, and her diary could use some kind of seasoning. Quickly, she switched on her favorite radio station.

While the set warmed up, Marvel caught the sweet sound of her father's voice. "I love you...love you...love you," he said softly to Mother, punctuating the words with a little cough that turned brassy.

"Me too," Mother said absently. "That cough's getting worse."

"I'll be fine, so don't go havin' yourself a conniption fit!" Daddy tried to laugh, but the attempt ended in a spasm of coughing.

The news boomed on:

"History repeats itself," they say. It's true in Washington, D.C. Remember 'way back in '32 how veterans and their families stormed the gates in hopes of getting themselves a bonus? Sad day in history. They were welcomed by one single man, Police Chief Glassford, who knew the nerves of the then-President Hoover who had tried and failed to appease the hungry human beings, were jangled. The chief would do what he could, he promised "his boys," bein' a vet himself. But what power did he have—other than gettin' 'em to believe him and move out? The evacuation proceeded all that day, but the "highest authority" wasn't satisfied, so ordered a parade of infantry and cavalry with formidable, deadly weaponry to pursue feeling women, children, and legless veterans—victims of the Depression many felt Hoover caused. "A challenge to the authority of the United States government has been met!" Hoover said proudly. But the bloody episode cost dearly. Marchers never forgave him—neither did hordes of sympathizers who voted the infamous man from office. When the second veterans' army assembled in Washington—'though it, too, failed—the men received far gentler recognition. So "Hoover sent the army," the desperate people applauded, "but Mr. Roosevelt sent his wife!" And Eleanor Roosevelt walked among them, listening to their songs and tasting their humble chow. Excellent politics...but, tired of waiting now for a New Deal which won't work when there's a combination of depression and drought, there's a new crop at the bottom of the economic ladder, on the march again ...destitute...while their rejected "doles" go out to foreign countries where there's a distant but sobering rumble of gunfire amid promises that our boys will never be sent overseas. *Believe?* Promises we've had all along, but can we believe? Ask the starvin' Appalachians and you'll like as not hear, "Now, don' thet fry yore 'tater!" Well, give the man on the hill credit for tryin'. It's the unparalleled twist of the times that's hog-tied the president. And there *is* hope—the hallmark of the present administration—if you can wait it out, or even if you have to search for it elsewhere until our state bounces back on its feet. There *will* be changes. They're inevitable.

Had she heard all this before? Marvel wondered. If so, she had forgotten. Or was she seeing it all in a new light? She needed to review Titus' revealing columns. And oh, how much her heart longed to reread his notes, beginning with concern about her illness and gradually becoming more personal—almost but never quite saying what she needed so much to hear. But there was no time. Dipping her pen into the green-apple ink, she scribbled hastily, wishing all the while there were a way to put such broadcasts on recordings such as singers and musicians used—or, wistfully, that she owned a fountain pen.

The announcer told of the opportunities now opening up—most of them out-of-state, unfortunately. And, sadly, the openings were due in part to the threat of war. Take the defense plants. They were turning out ships and planes—all for use overseas. "So don't get scared off, ladies and gentlemen!" But they were paying good money to a few. Prices were picking up on farm products—some exported but a good amount kept here at home, making good FDR's promise to "feed and seed" the new generation. More yield meant more employment—better wages, too, as the labor organizations tried to finger the pulse of the blue-collar laborers. And speaking of big—gee-willikers! Were listeners familiar with the name DuPont? That company was working on a manmade fiber that was bound to be the greatest thing since sliced bread! Rayon had replaced silk now, and this material was apt to replace rayon—a wonder product called nylon. Funny name? Yeah, funny—some claiming it was an acronym made from the words "Now You Lousy Old Nipponese." Just some wag, mind you. But it's a slap at the increasingly unpopular nation of Japan which breeds silkworms for ladies' stockings. We could be paying too much attention to Europe's problems and not enough to China's and our own. We continue to send scrap iron to Japan, knowing it's used as weapons against our friends, the Chinese—and all for the price of silk? No wonder Japanese were critical and a little on the huffy side. Silk would be obsolete if the DuPont experiments proved successful, and the company had faith in it. Otherwise, would they have invested over 27 million dollars in hopes of perfecting the fabric? It's another promise of the bright new prosperity of tomorrow. Tough row to hoe, but "We've come a long way, baby!" Of course, Americans may be forced to wait a long time to make use of these and other synthetics if we have to go tooling up for our own defense. We need time to reassess values, shed old habits that got us into the black days of the 1930's—shed them like snakes shed their old skins making way for the new, but not blindly like snakes act in the dog days before that shedding. We must do more than earn a day's wages. We must manage to keep our political balance, so vote, citizens! Regain economic health . . . and *stay out of war*!

Involved as she was in taking notes and trying to make sense of a senseless world, Marvel failed to hear her grandparents arrive. The wonderful pair was almost devouring her with kisses before her eyes and mind could focus. "Oh Marvel, little sweetheart," Grandmother cried, "let me look at you—fragile as a butterfly and twice as lovely, wouldn't you say, Squire?"

"Cute as a bug's ear!" Alexander Jay Harrington declared.

"My goodness!" Marvel said breathlessly, managing to get on her feet but feeling light-headed and giddy. "You'd think the two of you were saying good-bye instead of hello."

"Never! *We'll* never leave you," Grandmother whispered almost fiercely. Then, burying her face in Marvel's hair, she added, "Little silk-head." There was a hint of tears in her voice.

*"Nylon,"* Marvel smiled, knowing that Grandmother did not understand.

Grandfather was pumping Daddy's hand. "Sorry they wouldn't let me see you, son. We all wanted to come and Mary Ann was fit to be tied, wanting to see Marvel. Oh Duchess, I hope you remembered the medication and other items. I'll get it all if you did—"

Of course she remembered. A tonic for Marvel, lots of iron in it—she needed building up, Dr. Porter had said. And a syrup for Daddy's cough. The "other items" turned out to be a chocolate cake Fanny made fresh today, some sacks Marvel was sure held groceries, and an oblong package for Marvel herself.

"It's from Mrs. Sutheral—a gift she received and had no real use for. Dr. Porter's concerned about her, as he is for you two. She's not snapping back the way she should, not even able to partake of Sunday dinner and it was her favorite, a Gospel bird."

Gospel bird? Marvel caught Daddy's eye, and he laughed soundlessly. "An expression you never heard. Means chicken—the usual Sunday fare saved for the preacher who managed to show up at mealtime."

Marvel opened Mrs. Sutheral's gift and gasped. A fountain pen!

"It pays to be sick—" was all she could manage.

*"Pays?* That's hardly the word. Would that it did," Mother said wistfully. Then, trying to brighten, "We could do with some cash!"

Grandfather cleared his throat unnecessarily. "It may—it very well may," he said meaningfully. "Who can know the future?"

Grandmother looked at the stately gentleman in admiration. "Nobody, Squire, nobody. It's a guarded secret. So take your medicine, Dale son—and think of each day as an invitation to a fresh start."

"Thanks, Mother Riley. I'm sure there's a promise of untouched opportunity out there somewhere. I'll bank on that—even though right now I'd have to feel better to die!" Daddy's grin was on crooked.

"Don't talk like that," Mother protested. "I've done what I wanted to do for you and our daughter, but I do worry about the future—and you. I—I couldn't get along without him," she said to her mother.

"Stop that!" Grandmother said snappily. "You won't have to! I told you a long time ago you would measure up when the time came, and this was a test you passed. So think of any challenge ahead as an exciting adventure—like *(ahem)* the Squire and I do! Good that you have each other 'in sickness and in health.' You know," her voice softened and her velvety-brown eyes moved from Mother's face to the stack of letters from Titus, focusing then to include Marvel in her next words, "times, places, years make no difference when—when a couple's old enough to know what they both want in life yet young enough to believe—to *know* they belong together. That's called *young at heart.* I think a few have it!"

For a blessed moment Titus' profile flashed into full view, as if to show Marvel what she already knew: that, unassumingly, he was always there when she needed him—and those times were coming more and more often. She saw the determined jaw, straight classic nose, firm and serious mouth which reserved a smile for special moments, dark combed-back hair over the forehead so high she had to tiptoe to see the top, and those unforgettable gray-eyes-turned-black filled with emotion at moments when he looked into her blue ones. The symbol of tomorrow, that profile—emblem of their dreams.

Grandmother was looking at her knowingly. Blushing, Marvel made a flimsy excuse about stirring Mother's spaghetti sauce and stumbled out weakly. When she returned, winded from the exertion, the conversation centered on news of the family. Worth and Rae were fine . . . well, not really, considering changes for next year about the school buses. They didn't know? Well, dandy for the students—better vehicles furnished by state and federal matching funds ("FDR *does* live up to his promises. Senator Norton, too, due in part maybe to those columns, Marvel. 'Chickens come home to roost', you know!"). But not so good for Worth. Drivers would be appointed—sent in. So local men would be out of work again. Mary Ann seemed more woebegone than her mother. That set Billy Joe back, trying for attention with many a wile, the most recent being a threat to beat himself to death. Fanny put a quietus on that—said she'd do it for him if he didn't shape up right smart. And he did!

"What's Worth going to do, Mother? There are no jobs."

It was Grandfather who answered. "Hard saying, Snow White! Something's bound to break. And he's blessed with horse sense enough to have taken a good wife, like Dale here. Good family, too—show good raising and some good old Harrington blood! Well, I can't claim the same for Joseph and Emory. Dorthea and Eleanore are birdbrained snobs, and those girls are a disgrace! Erin and Cindy finally paid 'the old man' here a visit—dressed fit to kill," he sniffed, "with so much paint slathered on I asked my granddaughters what they'd charge me to haunt a house."

"Now, now, Squire, that's mighty colorful language," Grandmother gently reprimanded. Then both of them laughed at her twist of words.

Daddy smiled with them, but Mother looked preoccupied. Could she be thinking, as her daughter was, how much would be lost if the younger generation did nothing to preserve such colorful language, distinctly a part of the heartland? If teachers had their way, the descriptive words would be lost. And she was equally responsible. She regretted then having corrected Mary Ann as she herself had been corrected. Why, the grandchildren must preserve tradition. It must be included in the "one day" book.

"Yoo-hoo! Marvel! Contact!" Grandmother called as if she were turning the propeller of a pilot's plane. "You're a million miles away—"

No, strangely, she wasn't. In spite of the momentary drift-away, Marvel had heard. No need beating a dead horse. The other Harrington daughters-in-law had met the same fate as their "painted daughters." Yep—their one-time cronies' mamas up and dumped them like hot potatoes. Seemed the Cohanes started the ball rollin', "that Amanda" in lead. No more bridge parties, beauty parlor fingerwave sets, and silk stockings.

"Well!" Grandfather's voice sounded angry. "Emory and Joseph can't say I didn't caution against *that*, hanging onto their wives' coattails for jobs. Ugh!" Surely his cane went through the floor. "I'm ashamed of them—no way for he-men to get into banking. That's for men with character, courage, strength. Just where that leaves Duke and Thomas I don't know. Those two show some promise, only—Eleanore's fattened their egos with big ideas, made them feel like heroes with this Royal Air Force stuff. Not that it matters much. That future we talked about's here!"

What he said next reduced all other news delivered by Alexander Jay Harrington and Leah Johanna Mier Riley to the status of an overture. Both Grandfather and sons Emory and Joseph had received letters from Alex Jr. He *had* done well in that hop-yard experiment. Expanded it, in fact, to include twice the amount of land—up near the Oregon capital, yes. Salem, wasn't it? Working with mint now as well—planted between the wired-up hop vines and ("I'll tell you, it's paying off, too") got geese to saw off the grass (won't touch the mint, the sillies!). And what do you know? Now, everybody wanted those mindless wonders. "The goose that laid the golden egg!" Grandfather laughed with obvious pride. "Now for a gem of a wife—"

"Now, now, Squire, just because we—uh—" Grandmother, flustered, was behaving charmingly like a schoolgirl, "the other boys have found happiness gives us—uh, you—no license as a matcher. They'll find their way—aha! with all that rich Harrington blood!" she finished triumphantly.

Both her parents were leaning forward with interest, Marvel saw. But it was Mother who asked, "And Jake's uncle? Has anybody heard?"

"Uncle!" Grandmother exclaimed. "Don't you remember, honey, that Jake's daddy went to California, too? All the Brothertons are there, except Jake. He's staying with Archie's folks, the Newlands, for now. But I think that's what's bothering Mary Ann—what he'll do after graduation. Oh, they're all staying. Things *are* better there: more jobs, good gardens. Of course, it's not home—or is it? You see differently."

"I—I'm not so sure about that," Mother whispered brokenly.

Marvel gasped. She had heard wrong, imagined the words—or had the fever come back? Her heart beat wildly and she gasped again, this time because of knowing none of these were correct. She knew by the silence.

The grandparents left soon afterward. There was a sort of clinging in the farewells, a finality. It was as if the facades of make-believe had crumbled but in their crumbling had taken strength in their pile of ruin. But a spark of hope *must* remain, for Grandfather kept up his reassurances and he was not one for the game of pretention. "Something *will* turn up for you. That I promise!" he called above the weeping winds.

"It will take a miracle," Mother said in her new self-despair. "I'll pray for it—"

"*Play* for it," Daddy begged. "It's been a long time."

Snow Harrington looked at her husband, listened to his cough, and obviously saw him in a new way—this man who had had a brush with death. Dale Harrington, the man she loved and chose to obey. While the spaghetti stuck to the pot in the kitchen, she gave him her heart bound up in musical strings—happy, bright notes of joy to fill the house and soul and swirl out the window to challenge the ankle-deep dust of yesterday's folly.

Marvel would always believe when the miracle Mother prayed and played for came that God had heard and used Grandfather to bring it about. But how far-reaching that miracle he could not know. For who, save God, could know the future?

# 29

# Breaking Through the Barriers

A ceiling of low-hanging crimson-splashed clouds obscured the sky when Marvel returned to school on Monday, following her grandparents' visit. Lovely as it was, the blinding hues brought a strange sense of foreboding. "When it is evening, ye say, *It will be fair weather, for the sky is red.* And in the morning, *It will be foul weather today, for the sky is red and lowring.* O ye hypocrites, ye can discern the face of the sky; but can ye not discern the signs of the times?" Jesus had said to the Pharisees and Sadducees who mockingly asked for "a sign from heaven." Sign?

It was as if she had seen one. And the premonition proved correct.

Mr. Phillips welcomed Marvel back when she reported for a readmission slip. "You've had a harder case than most, and I am sorry about that. Are you all right? You could take more time, you know."

Marvel thanked him and said she had recovered, which wasn't quite true. She felt light-headed, and her legs were so weak she had to grip the banister when going up and down the stairs. But time was so short.

First she must see Mr. Caldwell and hand in her notebook, diary, and some book reports. She swallowed hard, dreading the encounter. She hoped he would ask her to be seated. He did not. Neither did he rise.

"Well, I see Marvel Harrington is back. You know, of course, that your malingering placed the school in an awkward position of having to send a second-place winner to district meet." When she made no answer, he continued as if piling up evidence for a trial. "There will be no exemptions either. You know the rules. However, I see that you were able to continue with those controversial newspaper columns, choosing to ignore our agreement that there would be no more. Don't say you forgot!"

"There was no agreement, Mr. Caldwell," Marvel said simply.

The man rose then, and she wondered if he would strike her in his anger. "I issued an order, and I expect my orders to be obeyed!"

Marvel felt beads of perspiration form on her forehead. But she managed to retain her balance and self-control in spite of physical weakness.

"I do not take orders well, I'm afraid."

The teacher's fist came down on his desk—hard. His eyes were burning coals—like Elmer's had been when he threatened her life.

"You are on the verge of failing my class—not graduating. It will teach you a lesson! All those lofty words and lacking subordination! Just wait until I have a look at the homework you turned in—*late*!"

"It is due today, Mr. Caldwell," Marvel reminded him. That was dangerous. But it no longer mattered. She had borne the lash of his words as the innocent Jews had endured the cruel whips inflicted on their innocent backs by jackbooted Nazi soldiers. That was how dictators were made...by those forgiving their tormentors, submitting, losing their rights to rule even their own minds and hearts. "And yes, I will wait," she said, as if the English teacher had meant "just wait" literally.

Had she *willed* him then to do what he did next? Marvel would never know. She only knew that the entire world was turned upside down with worry and fear. And somebody had to stand up against tyrants who by means of whips or red pens made heaven and hell one. "Stand up for Jesus."

No longer afraid, Marvel Harrington braced herself for the tirade of words that followed. Had he taught her nothing—absolutely nothing? Was she so smart that there was nothing left to learn...thinking herself above the norm, above *him* just because she could toss around a few empty phrases as placebos for intelligence... *because she was a Harrington*?

The problem then was his, not hers. For some inconceivable reason, the insecure man who totally lacked compassion felt inferior to the Harringtons. But reference to her family in an insulting manner was unfair and unwarranted—a sort of snobbery and discrimination in reverse. A kaleidoscope of colors exploded within her, colors which could have bleached to a white rage. But that would please him. She would turn the other cheek. There was within herself a part he could not reach.

"Have you nothing to say for yourself?"

"I was waiting until you finished."

"It is *you* who is finished! Look at this—this utter and complete disregard for instructions! Any freshman would know better than setting out intentionally to goad a teacher, ignoring directions, using ink of every known shade! Black, blue—and then this horrible, sickening green. What possessed you—the devil? Why on earth—"

Gone was any fragment of false pride. Marvel had found it necessary to humble herself to Dr. Porter, tell him the truth, admit that there could be no pay for his services to her father. And it hadn't pained her at all. All barriers were down. There was beauty in truth.

"Why? Because I was forced to borrow, Mr. Caldwell: borrow ink, borrow paper, anything and everything. We have no money. Try to understand that I—I did what a lot of us are forced to do: swallow our pride."

The man quailed as if she had struck him. It was easy to imagine things with the world swirling around her. Did he shrink in size as he dropped into the swivel chair, his sparse frame thudding as though he were overburdened with flesh? His face was chalky with shock.

"I—I didn't know," he said, more in fear than remorse.

"No, you didn't know." *But I was hoping you'd understand*, she thought. Marvel had intended to say no more, but the words came out in a rush, as if they had been held captive too long and demanded release. When he asked if she planned to report the incident, she looked at him in sorrow, the fierce hatred within her overcome. Here was this shell of humanity who could inflict pain and feel no regret, lack the grace to apologize or ask how he could help the student who was at his mercy. But he could think only of saving face—perhaps his job...as Grandmother would say, his *skin*! Marvel forced her eyes to focus and looked at him squarely.

"*Tell* other students, the administration, my parents? No, I shall not report you. I *pity* you, Mr. Caldwell. Never mind my own problems. I have learned the valuable lesson you did *not* set out to teach. I have learned that it is better to suffer than cause suffering. Good day, sir."

\* \* \*

Marvel went through the rest of the day with a new appreciation for her other teachers. Without exception they were kind and considerate, welcoming her in a way as refreshing as soft rain—Miss Ingersoll most of all! The domestic science teacher's behavior was amusing. It was as if someone had flipped on a switch behind her eyes, causing them to shine with a new incandescence of ill-concealed excitement.

"Oh Marvel!" she glowed. "Thank you for coming early. I want to tell you before anyone else. I'm going to be married right after the end of school and live in *California*! My fiancé has set up his law practice in Sacramento—land of sunshine, oranges, olives, and grapes," she went on breathlessly. Then, "Oh, forgive me. You've been sick—"

Marvel laughed. "You make me feel better," she said truthfully to her teacher-friend whose recipe book probably included black-olive crepes, orange blossom nectar, and stuffed grape leaves now.

But inwardly she was thinking that, should this migration continue, somebody would need to move the California line eastward. The thought bothered her a little. Not that it was new. She had always known. Known what? Never mind. She must cope with what is, not what is to be—for now, assignments and makeup work.

Marvel extended best wishes and again spoke openly about her inability to afford material for the making of a formal gown for graduation. Miss Ingersoll brushed aside explanations. It made no difference, she said. Time was too short to complete the project now. Why not make some more of those "darling rompers" for her friends out on the farm? Oh, she had "scads" of remnants that needed using. All right?

It was more than all right. Marvel had a feeling that Miss Ingersoll, in her euphoric state, would have agreed to anything. Dealing with her more personal questions was more difficult. Only months ago this teacher had pleaded with her not to be a stumbling block to Titus and break his sister's heart. She now did an about-face. Marvel felt confused, uncertain.

"Let me talk to you face-to-face, darling. You're far more mature in every way than any other student in this class, in this *school*. All your teachers acknowledge that. But that doesn't mean you're wise in the ways of love. Sometimes," her voice lowered as if walls really did have ears, "a woman has to—well, *push* a little—very gently, of course, just taking the initiative ever so subtly, delicately letting her true love know her heart. Wait, don't go! This is important, possibly the biggest thing I can leave you with—a fig for the rest! You and Titus are ambitious, but lucky—just plain lucky—that you met so young and face a future together. Life can be empty as today's rain barrel alone. Goals? What greater goal can there be than *marriage*?" She was too choked up to go on.

"But we're different. We can wait. If we ever—uh, do—"

Miss Ingersoll was in control again. "Do *what*? *Marry?* Marriage is made for couples like you and Titus. Love's not fulfilling all goals alone. Marriage is for having the 'object of your affection' to share the struggle, the defeats, and the victories. Break down all barriers while there's time."

# 30

# An Intervening Hand

"Marvel!"

Mary Ann's voice caught up with Marvel as their respective buses arrived. In the frenzied rush to get back on schedule after her long absence, there simply had been no time for the needed chat.

Now the cousins embraced and Mary Ann clung. "They wouldn't let me come in. You know that—and I needed to talk. You know about the letters from those uncles of ours—mine and Jake's. Boy, can they talk or can they talk! Tongues faster than greased lightning, and putting ideas into the heads of Uncle Emory and Uncle Joseph. And you *know* Cindy and Erin don't have the sense God promised a goose—"

Marvel stopped her. "There's the warning bell. Tell me quickly. Are you saying what I think you are, that—?"

"They'll be going West, too? Of course!" Mary Ann sounded surprised. "Didn't Grandfather and Gran'mere tell you?"

"Not exactly—" Marvel said hesitantly. *But I knew.* That was not what she said aloud. "That's up to them, isn't it?"

"What they do'll affect us all and you know it! Good riddance as far as I'm concerned, but I want them to—to leave Jake alone!"

Mary Ann was too agitated to be left alone in the hall. "Get hold of yourself, Mary Ann—you have to for—for your parents' sake. Remember our pledge that we'd take care of them? And we will. Uncle Worth is carrying a load—about a job with the changes in transportation. And it's only right that Jake would hear from his parents. But trust him, he has a good head on his shoulders. We're going to be late—"

"I don't care!" Mary Ann wailed. "They'll go. You know they'll go!"

They parted. There was no choice. Marvel forced a smile and Mary Ann nodded, which meant she would try. But Marvel did not feel that smile. Inside her, the words echoed: *They'll go. . . . They'll go. . . . They will!*

All that day Marvel pushed the threatening words down deep in the pockets of her mind. What his brothers did had nothing to do with Daddy. Dale Harrington was his own man. He had proven that over and over, sticking with his dreams of farming even when his brothers scoffed and his father was enraged—at one time. But now even Grandfather was impressed, and the two of them were father and son—as if—as if father, not son, were the prodigal! And no matter what happened, father would stick by his son. There was comfort in the thought—comfort, too, in the plan she made to write to Titus. There was much to say, plans to make, and—although Miss Ingersoll would never believe that her words had nothing to do with this—she wanted to open her heart to him. It was a *need. . . .*

And then when Marvel went home, the unbelievable had happened . . . *impossible*, except by the intervening hand of God!

Dale and Snow Harrington could not wait for their daughter to come inside. They came to meet her, not walking but running, in spite of his cough. Marvel could not believe her eyes. Their faces were *alive* with a newfound joy! This was no game, the kind Daddy had played to keep Mother's hopes alive of late, or the kind she had played so many years before in order to make an unbearable situation bearable. This was *real!*

Daddy, his blue-blue eyes sparkling so much that one tended to be blind to the equally blue circles surrounding them, held an official-looking document overhead, letting it ripple in the wind like the flag.

"Me—they chose *me!*" he shouted with the glee of a child.

"A sum-mons—to serve on federal g-grand jury—" Mother panted.

"In Texarkana!" Daddy beamed.

The rest tumbled out in a duet, making it difficult to understand at first. But Marvel was able to glean enough to be reasonably sure the two voices said he, Dale Harrington, was hereby ordered to appear on the following Monday, be prepared to withstand interrogation as to fitness as a juror, and be prepared, as well, to serve for an indefinite period, depending on the nature of said case under investigation. In return for Mr. Harrington's "fulfilling his duty as a citizen," he was to receive six dollars a day (Did Marvel hear? *Six dollars!*), plus he was to be reimbursed for all expenses incurred. They talked on, growing more and more excited about how much this would mean financially, how much a day's pay like this would buy these days, what all they must do to make ready, and the honor of being selected! How could it have happened, *how*?

"The names are drawn from a hat, so to speak," Daddy said, shaking his head as if he still found it impossible, "but they can reject a name."

"They'd have no reason to reject *yours*, sweetheart!" Mother defended.

"You're an angel—taking it like this," Daddy said softly. "It'll be our first night apart since—since we married. I'm sorry, honey."

"I've thought—thought of that," Mother gulped, "but—you must."

"We'll be all right, Daddy—and I'm proud of you," Marvel said when she was able to ease a word in edgewise. "It *is* an honor!"

*But honors call for sacrifice*, she thought. *And Mother made it!* A miracle? That, too. A miracle in which Alexander Jay Harrington, was an instrument in the intervening hand of God....

Snow Harrington busied herself immediately with white shirts to starch and iron, socks to mend, her husband's flattopped summer straw hat to clean with cornmeal, shoes to shine. And she must check with Dr. Porter, make sure he felt the patient sufficiently recovered.

Marvel's offer to help met with immediate objection. Marvel must do her homework. Marvel had other things to do in addition. It was easy to see that Mother wished to make necessary preparations herself, and it would be a disappointment for others to deny her the chance—which was fine. Marvel did covet the time to write the intended letter to Titus. And now, in newfound security, she could plan on a future—a time when the two of them could be together. So, hurriedly, she took her pale lilac stationery from its box wrote and wrote happily.

(Who could know the future? Grandmother Riley had asked. Her granddaughter, then, had no way of knowing what lay ahead, else the course of history would have been altered. She would have been unable to write as she did, expose her heart because all barriers were down—"the veil rent"—and furnish the primary and secondary research to Titus Smith, which proved to be the inspiration for his most profound columns.)

"For, lo, the winter is past, the rain is over and gone; the flowers appear on the earth; and the time of the singing of birds is come..." she was able to quote from *Solomon's Song*. Not literally true, she wrote—would that it were, but it was the way she felt. She was completely restored, having shaken away the darkness of illness now past and all the tentacles that tried to lay hold and sap her strength—physical, spiritual, and emotional. She was *free*. And in her heart it was eternal spring. Now, free of all shackles that tended to bind her hand and heart—manacles to her feet, fetters before her eyes—she could scale the mountain's face with him at her side where, together at the summit, they would reach out and gather the dangling stars. For the victory must be shared, else it was empty, pointless, and without joy. "And, oh Titus, I want to share with *you*, so it is with anticipation and longing that I pour out my feelings to you tonight. For now I know we will be together, you and I, and the time does not matter, my darling. Meet your goals... dare to be right. And remember, *always* remember, the blessed words of our Savior, 'Lo, I am with you always even unto the end of the world'. That is His promise to His disciples, and we are His modern-day disciples and must follow the same commands. Remember, too, my dear, that I am with you, too, wherever you go, whatever you do—the part of me that counts. The other part of me remains here—waiting, watching, praying for your promised return. And you *will* return, for I know now that you meant it when you said lightly at our first encounter: 'I do not jest concerning matters of the heart!' So, as the song says, 'Take good care of yourself—you belong to me!' (then lighter) I love life—I'd miss it!"

Marvel told Titus then how absence from school disqualified her for exemptions from final exams, saying it didn't matter (and about missing district meet, which *did* matter). There would be no trip to Austin for state competition now, but he was busy, she was busy, and a surprise visit would be more exciting anyway! News? Departure of the English teacher (brushing lightly over her replacement)...plans for the domestic science teacher's marriage (Lucille would want to know, as they were friends)... her own friendship with Kate Lynn Porter (Had Bill Johnson told him that he was seeing the doctor's daughter since Amanda chose to stop seeing the former cocaptain?). Marvel told of her father's selection as a juror in federal court, adding: "He will be joining you in an effort to keep the wheels of justice turning, making sure that justice is blindfolded!" Very carefully she avoided mention of the family unemployment and changes it could lead to. Then she signed the lengthy letter: *Your Marvelous.*

Now for the notes and thoughts for their shared columns. Education? Certainly some changes were in order in this not-so-stable-after-all economy—changes before the next generation came of age, not waiting until all lay in ruins like the land. With 20-20 hindsight, people saw their folly. Learn from that. Employ foresight! It would take daring—even what others might shrug off as foolhardiness. Let them scoff! There must be more than curriculum, although literacy was essential *for all.* It would take a willingness on the part of teachers, parents, voters, *everybody*, to try the new without discarding the old. They must expect lethargy, embarrassment, ridicule. And oh, the price was high! They must be extravagant in a time which required tightening the belt, scrimping, and saving—extravagant in *caring*, and caring meant to love with wild abandon. That meant paying the price in the currency of a broken heart.

Marvel stopped scribbling from her notes at that point, realizing that she had said at the beginning what she intended to say at the end. But the words had been squeezed from her pen just as the feelings behind them were squeezed from a bruised heart. Oh, how Mr. Caldwell's words and attitude had hurt! But she must be objective, quoting from reliable sources: newspaper clippings, longhand notes from radio programs.

She began with a radio announcer's scalding attack on attitudes:

"You Don't Go to Heaven on a Choo-Choo Train" is an oldie in song we're all familiar with...and I might add that the same is true of the much-talked-about *Zephyr*, America's first streamlined train—a beauty, that! Until passengers—that small fragment of the populace who can afford a ticket—look from the windows of inside glitz and glamour to see the wastelands in the Corn Belt, where the first public tour of that stainless-steel racer took place. Yep! Right there in good old Lincoln, Nebraska. But, as listeners know out there in radioland, this is the time set apart for our weekly analysis and recommendation for our nation's schools. Today, let's take a quick look at reading, the most fundamental single area on which all other learning hinges. Is our methodology the very best we can employ? Our books updated? A recent poll indicates that we've dropped back two centuries from *McGuffey's Eclectic Readers* with their articulation, elementary sound, vocals, subvocals, and aspirates methods. But Muckety-mucks couldn't wait to fix something that wasn't broken. I declare, "Baby Ray has four ducks," makes less sense than the deathless dialogue uttered in the bizarre adventures of hack writer Edgar Rice Burroughs. At least there was progress! The white-skinned orphan boy and the girl he kidnaps from a safari must rely on sign language and his fearful jungle yodel: a mixture of five sounds which included his own scream, a soprano singing high C, and a recording of a hyena's howl played backward, 'tis said. Until the girl he loves teaches him meaningful words, progressing at last to "Me Tarzan, you Jane." Must educators jump onto every bandwagon that comes rumblin' down the road? Or does it begin with some upstart who aims at some political office's way of appealin' to voters about their children's education and says this book will do the trick? Time's about up, so if y'all will write this station, I'll send pamphlets with lists of men on the Board of Education—and some mighty fine suggestions on discipline for good study habits, as well as bills before the Congress aimed at remedyin'_a situation before it becomes a problem! We've got ourselves the potential for the finest educational system in the world if we utilize it *now*! Unless we want to become a nation of followers, and the world's full-up with them already. We're still in the travail of the Great Depression. . . . But above all

talk of immediate concerns, hear more than the reverbera-
tions of the crash on Wall Street. Listen to the rumble of
distant gunfire and know that it, like Wall Street, can come
closer!

Marvel had sent for the pamphlets and mailed them along in
the bulging envelope. She wished there were time to reread
them, but her own at-home columns must be prepared, her
studying done.

What part should the church play in politics? Titus had asked
her once. Well, she had more on that now. Marvel glanced at the
articles and again wished for more time. One in particular caught
her eye:

> According to national polls, the church now has
> more members than at any other point in history,
> more facilities, and the *promise* of more money. Why
> then do these members forfeit their right to a voice?
> More of everything—but influence in our national
> life? *Why?* Because Americans have abandoned the
> greatest mission of all: their political mission!

Quickly now, Marvel stacked clippings and notes on community involvement: making them care, getting at the cause before
the effect came, increasing sensitivity to differences and diver-
sities, and *equality*. These would bring responsibility full circle,
putting the burden upon individuals, homes, churches, schools,
and political arenas—not in vague terms, but hitting home! This
responsibility included the poor, the sharecroppers, the blacks,
and what was looked down upon as the "po' white trash" who
must accept doles.

"I guess, my darling," she added on impulse, "I'm just happy
today—filled with new hope. Solomon mentioned the 'voice of
the turtle' in the Scripture I started this letter with. I guess a
turtle would have to come out of his shell to sing! So I'm ready to
stick my neck out, knowing God usually lets us find what we're
looking for. I'm looking for *you*!" M.

# 31

# Loom of the Morrow

Daddy had gone. And Mother was adjusting to the jolt of loneliness more easily than Marvel would have expected. Of course, the telephone helped. Scraps of the conversations with both Grandmother and Auntie Rae told her that the women must talk several times daily. Later she realized that there should have been more questions on her part or that she could have been able "to discern the signs of the times," as Matthew warned. But school was demanding more and more: deadlines to meet, plus senior class meetings that all were required to attend. One might hope for mercy from teachers, more realistic assignments. Well, one would be disappointed. Instead of fewer requirements there were more. It was as if instructors either felt quantity more important than quality, or that faculty members were competing among themselves and would be judged according to pounds of production! With one exception—

Mr. Caldwell, of all teachers, added nothing more, asking only that his students endeavor to complete assignments on his syllabus sheet. *Endeavor?* They'd jolly well better, if she knew Mr. Caldwell! Which she didn't. She didn't know this man at all anymore.

In one of the rare moments alone with Mary Ann, her cousin said in a jumble of words, "How do you keep it up, with all you have on your mind? How can you *stand* that man after what he's done to you? How does he act since you made him eat crow— Caldwell, I mean? And how's Uncle Dale's health? Dr. Porter gave

Auntie Snow such a scare, but she's behaving like a brick. I wonder how she *feels* though? And I wonder now how—how my own parents c-c-can survive—no money—job. Go to California—like the—the rest of the tribe? Are you listening?"

Numbly, Marvel nodded. It was all too much too fast. Through frozen lips she managed, *"How!* Are we talking Indian language today?"

"How—oh, there I go again. Well, I don't care! How can you joke?"

*Because I'm scared.* Instead, Marvel said, "All right, my turn. *How?* How do I manage with Mr. Caldwell? There's no way to avoid him. And frankly, he has surprised me, now that I think about it. Treats me like Nebuchadnezzar must have treated Shadrach, Meshach, and Abednego—you know, in a sort of astonishment at their walk through the fiery furnace. But Mary Ann, I never tried to embarrass the man—*make him eat crow*, as you phrase it. I didn't!"

Mary Ann shrugged, her mind obviously elsewhere. "I'm the one in a rush. I—I don't know what to do. Jake and I have to talk—in case."

But Marvel detained her. "Don't leave. You've left too many questions. No, don't object and say they don't need answers. *I* do! Just answer quickly. How did you know about Mr. Caldwell?"

"Kate Lynn. She was just outside—"

Marvel's nod told the other girl she understood. Yes, she understood—just as she understood Kate Lynn was another source of information.

"And Daddy? How did you know?"

The natural upward swing of Mary Ann's dark brows arched even higher. "Why our mothers talk every day. It's no secret. Let go, Marvel!"

In her desperate need to know more about Daddy's health, Marvel unconsciously clutched Mary Ann's skirt and wadded the pleats. It would need pressing. "Sorry," she mumbled, "I'll take it—the gasoline iron's empty—and the REA hasn't so much as put in a pole—"

Mary Ann's *"Ha!"* reflected no amusement. "The power's turned off—the power in our house! They do that, you know, when you can't pay."

Another shocker, Marvel thought dully, lacking the ability to smile at her pun. Anyway, why were they wasting words about a skirt Mary Ann obviously couldn't take off and send with her? How foolish.

"What did you mean?" Marvel insisted. "I *have* to know."

"About Uncle Dale? Nothing—nothing special. Just—uh—a general question," Mary Ann evaded. "See you around."

"Mary Ann!"

"You'll know soon enough, and to save time let me tell you why I have to see Jake."

"That's none of my business. Daddy *is*!"

Mary Ann reached out and hugged her—hugged her tight. "Oh, I'm—I'm too mixed up to make sense. It *is* some of your business. I mean it *may* be! Uncle Joseph and Uncle Emory are going for sure!"

And with that, Mary Ann fled.

There was no further time for thinking. Two unscheduled events took Marvel Harrington by surprise, compelling her to give them priority, and set her one day's loom to weaving a new design—so new that at first she did not recognize it, and yet so old it was oddly familiar.

\* \* \*

Mr. Caldwell detained her at the close of English class.

"You know that one afternoon class is canceled to accommodate some speakers?" he asked as if addressing a stranger, polite but distant.

"No sir, I'm afraid there has been no time to check the bulletin board. The meeting is for seniors?"

"Yes, seniors—regarding careers, especially those who plan to pursue a higher education. You *do* plan to attend college?" he hesitated.

Marvel covered the embarrassment the teacher probably felt, remembering their encounter and her disclosure of financial difficulty. Her reply was immediate. "I keep working and planning toward it. College has been a lifelong goal. But I may be unable to afford it."

The man looked her in the eye for the first time. "That's what I wanted to explain—the funding, I mean. You are under consideration for a full academic scholarship. The speakers have the list. You'll go?"

The room spun about her crazily, beautifully. The eastern sky lighted up again with the Ralston-wheat-cereal-box orange that Tom Mix (the nonsmoking teetotaler now retired from pictures) advertised on radio. She smelled the remembered fresh, clean air from an imagined rain, and heard the hum of promised honey by bees, their legs gold with pollen of tomorrow's daisies. Her senses had recorded the fantasy during the brisk walk to the bus. And now it was back, along with the lush spring-green of meadows, the gentle lowing of the cattle....

"Marvel! Are you all right? Do you need to sit down?" There was genuine concern in his voice.

Marvel pulled herself back to reality. "No sir, I am all right. It's just—just that I am so overcome—so happy! Oh, thank you for telling me, Mr. Caldwell—giving me time to prepare, to try to measure up!"

Oh, the miracle of it all! She tried to imagine the joy of sharing this with Mother...Daddy...Mary Ann...*Titus! Oh, thank You, Lord!*

In a state of euphoria, Marvel would have taken her leave then. But again Mr. Caldwell detained her. "Wait—please. I wanted to tell you *(Did he gulp? Was he groping for words?)* that—that I won't stand in your way. I want you to have the scholarship. You deserve it."

Astonished, Marvel said quietly, "I wouldn't have thought you would, Mr. Caldwell."

It was then that the Mr. Caldwell she had never known—and later she suspected he had never met before himself—emerged. "Must you leave? I would like to hear more about your plans, your dreams. Would you—?"

Marvel sat down uncertainly, perching on the edge of the straight chair he had indicated with a nod. "My schedule is more flexible—with the change. Yes, I have the time." She remained perched as if for flight.

"You plan to go on writing, I imagine?" he said immediately.

"I—I don't know. I've given it no thought. Or maybe I have—"

"Tell me," he encouraged in a near-whisper.

Was there a hoarseness in the whisper, or was her imagination working overtime? There was such a thin line between fact and fiction, as search and research bound them together—searching the mind and researching the black-and-whites of what others called facts. Were facts *truths*?

A moment ago Marvel had felt herself transported back in time to the early morning. Now again came the *déjà vu*—this time to a scene when, with feelings of ambivalence, she sat with another man who begged her to stay. And, then as now, she had opened the door of her heart to a dying man.... This man was dying in a different way, and she was responding to a stranger—revealing to a person she had cause to hate the thoughts she had never revealed to those she loved.

Shifting to a more comfortable position, Marvel felt herself drift into another world, no longer aware of the presence of another in the stuffy classroom: "Sweet are life's truths remembered," she began. "Yes, that's how it goes."

> Sweet are life's truths remembered—
> Dreaming and yet not quite—
> As fabrics on loom of the morrow
> Weave words hearts hope to write.

"Do I know the author?" His question came from far, far away.

"You are beginning to," she said as if to Frederick Salsburg—once again reminded that for all things there is a purpose. "Someday I guess I shall write a book—yes, a book with a purpose!"

"Good. And the title?"

"Title? I—I don't know—nothing lofty."

She felt rather than saw him wince. When the verbal attack he expected did not come, he relaxed. "The title can come later."

Marvel hardly heard. *"White Flags of Triumph,"* she said with her eyes closed. "That will be the title because—" she paused, wondering where the words had come from.

"Beautiful," Mr. Caldwell said in awe. "But don't white flags mean surrender? It's hard—impossible—to think of your surrendering."

"One must surrender the ugliness for the beautiful to triumph—of that I am persuaded. That's as far as I can go in that area, but there are others. Readers will understand someday—"

Under different circumstances Marvel would have been unable to go on, too overwhelmed that this conversation was in progress. But for now the incomprehensible had become comprehensible.

Did her listener ask whether it would be fact or fiction? she was to wonder later. He must have, because suddenly she was unfolding a dream of the future to the English teacher as she had unfolded a tender memory of the past to her stepuncle. The same dream she would share in brief with this afternoon's speaker, and repeat to Titus in a letter she must write *tonight*. Time was a factor, even in her near-trance.

Writing took imagination, and imagination—a *seeing* heart— was a gift of God, Marvel said. A writer must rely on black-and-white words to convey colored imagery. Like Plato's shadows? No—not that, for shadows were black-on-white. But writers, real writers—and yes, writing was a calling—were artists... artists who used words on the palette of time. Facts, while essential, were but outlines and must be given dimension through use of imagination—a kind of fiction perhaps, but necessary in order for the characters to change from faceless paper dolls in bold print to living people in readers' minds. This applied to journalistic writing as well as to fantasy. And when there was a marriage of the two, the sky was as real—as touchable—as the earth. Was life just factual, or wasn't there more?

"Like *Huck Finn*?" he ventured once.

"Somewhat—not exactly. More like *Tobacco Road*. Did imagined dialogue in that book make the facts behind it less real? Right now I am thinking of horses—make that unicorns! Fact finders tell us the animal exists only in fables and in the minds of human beings with imagination—a white horse with one golden horn. Even reference Bibles let me down when I wanted to verify my findings—'wild ox' was one translation. *Ox?* The Bible itself doesn't say that! Maybe translators took liberties—"

"Interesting, but why wouldn't unicorns be around today?"

"I don't know," Marvel said soberly, "unless they missed the boat."

His chuckle of appreciation for her unconscious wit went unnoticed.

Marvel wished aloud fleetingly that she were a sculptor, able to chisel from cold stone a live, warm pair of the animals—a timeless sculpture of mother and child of the animal kingdom in purest white. Unblemished by earth, they would stand in long, graceful leg stance as models for mankind... dainty hooves flashing... tender eyes glowing with the nurturing warmth of eternal devotion to their own kind and for the world...golden horns reaching heavenward to their Creator. She could see them in kelly green meadows, pink noses nibbling daintily at the windswept flowers...hear the voices with which they were endowed speaking in a language of love, gentle and lyrical as poetry. Would man destroy or protect?

What such a sculptor could produce in stone she could chisel in words. But would readers appreciate, preserve? Or would they scoff, even sneer at her literary efforts to weave together the power of "fact" and the drama of fiction into *truth*?

"*Feelings* are what it's all about—about ourselves, about others, about the world. We have to live the spectrum, experience the agony of pain and the sweetness of healing. That's how miracles are born!"

"I stand in the midst of one," Mr. Caldwell said, his voice sounding more natural to Marvel's ears. "I—I don't know why you chose *me* as a confidant—"

"I don't either!" Alarmed, Marvel scrambled to her feet.

The teacher rose, too. "But I want you to know that every word is held in confidence. I want to thank you, too. Somehow I find myself believing that you will understand. You made me see what you described so eloquently. If a man like me can understand, the public certainly will be able. And your work will be a breakthrough. You see, I am a part of that miracle you spoke about. I don't understand it!"

"You don't have to, Mr. Caldwell. You are inside it because you have a *hearing* heart. I don't understand any more than you do the—the *why* of things. So, reach skyward...."

"Marvel Harrington," he whispered reverently. "You—are— just—"

"*Marvelous!*" she laughed and ran through the open door, *feeling* marvelous.

\* \* \*

The meeting for seniors planning to seek an education beyond high school graduation was relatively brief, leaving time for speakers to explain that they would be cosponsoring scholarships and under what terms. Most of the students, and that included Jake, knew in advance what careers they would seek, for whom they hoped to work. Their goals were specific. Marvel felt as usual that she was the exception. Hadn't she always been *different*? However, after all the strange events of this day, it did not strike her as strange that she should feel less embarrassed by that difference. There would be so much, so very much to share with Mother tonight.

Marvel took a quick glance around the room. Amanda was not there, but her father was. Of course—Mr. Cohane was in banking. Her eyes met with Kate Lynn's, and the other girl curled her fingers in a small wave. And Dr. Porter was seated beside her. Oh, if she could only speak with him, find out the truth about Daddy. But for now, she must concentrate on the meeting. It was getting underway. Marvel gave it full attention. Afterward, a soft-spoken, portly gentleman Marvel remembered to be pastor of the First Baptist Church in Culverville informed the group there would be opportunities for students to meet in smaller groups, asking questions of the speakers.

However, it was Editor Corey who sought *her* out. "Congratulations, my dear," he said, mopping his face and shrugging off his suit coat. "You'll get the scholarship from the newspaper office— and be offered others. Whew! Hotter in here than a six-shooter! But we want to get our bid in first. I have some ideas I'd like to mention directly, but first, let's hear yours. Surely you'll include writing no matter what else?"

"Yes sir, I will," she found it easy to say, and shared briefly thoughts expressed to Mr. Caldwell. "Of course," she added, "that may have little to do with you—my Defoe kind of thinking."

"Oh, but it does! Daniel Defoe was an English newspaperman back in the eighteenth century, so it's not new, just controversial—and," he laughed, "would you believe the public thrives on that! That's one secret to the high degree of success you and Titus Smith have achieved. Readers need shakin' up. Why, some are green as a gourd—don't even know how to cast a ballot. Women! It appears to me they'd rather stay barefooted and pregnant, laying claim on Dark Age stagnancy—saying women's place is in the home."

"Mr. Corey!" Marvel reprimanded gently. "I'm a woman, and proud to be!"

"Sorry, but I can tell by your work that you understand the necessity of getting everybody involved. So *make* them listen.

Get those poll taxes removed. Frankly, I think they're downright unconstitutional if ever the matter's taken to the Supreme Court. And after reading some of young Smith's work I have lying on my desk, I think it can happen. He warns of tax increases in these tryin' times when men can't feed their hungry children. What'll it take, another Boston Tea Party? Sorry again—I didn't want to get offtrack, it's just that I'm unable to separate the two of you—"

"Don't try!" Marvel burst out and could have bitten her tongue off.

Mr. Corey laughed indulgently. "Good! Now go on. Your plans?"

Marvel did not hesitate. "You know our thoughts on education and religion."

He nodded. "Titus belongs to the preacher there's church. Man's in touch with him, in fact, and plans on seeing you about your future."

"My faith is behind it *all*, sir. But besides my work with the church and the newspaper, I still want to experiment with fact-fiction for both adults and children. Think how much more interesting reading could be with animals talking. Only so far it won't sell."

"Fascinating—but how do you know it won't sell?"

"I've tried, Mr. Corey. Nobody else knows, but I have dresser drawers filled with rejection slips. They want reality. It *is* reality!"

The editor's mouth gaped open. *"Reality?"*

"Yes sir, it's biblical—both Old and New Testament writings."

"Pardon me," the minister Mr. Corey introduced as Dr. Holt said. "I overheard in passing, and the young lady's right. A mule speaks with a male's voice in Numbers and again in 2 Peter." Then he moved on.

"I see. If we could let animals speak, let them create a marvelous new world, fill it with adventure bordering on the ridiculous, get away from adults talking down to them about Baby Ray—even," he was becoming excited, "sometimes-rambunctious, improper but proper— Oh yes!"

Time ran out before talking! The editor was considering an invitation for Marvel and Titus to write an experimental ongoing serial, column by column—high-interest fiction based on fact—like "Twenty Dollars a Week," which appeared in a Dallas newspaper. Research was done . . . had appeared in the newspapers here and in other cities. . . . Marvel did remember that other newspapers were utilizing their work?

"Which reminds me," Mr. Corey said, pushing his glasses up into his forelocks and blotting tired eyes with his handkerchief, "I have a small check here. Not much, goodness knows, but something a newspaper from back East—Chicago, I think—sent our office. We figure it belongs to you. It's only ten bucks."

*Only!* Ten dollars. She would send Titus five dollars and use the remaining five for school supplies that were essential. That way she could repay what she had borrowed and still have money for Mother's cream pitcher savings. Daddy's pay would be slow in coming. *Daddy.* Marvel's heart sank at thought of what Mary Ann had said—no, what she had *not* said. She must talk to Mother, let her know how important it was to know the truth. Maybe things were not so bad, after all. It was not knowing that was torment. Yes, they *must* talk.

"So I'm all for it." Mr. Corey was beaming when he spoke. "We'll want that series. That can make our newspaper! Women have told us that they clipped those columns of 'Twenty Dollars a Week' and pasted them in old catalogs or wallpaper books and made them into books! Talk this over with Titus, will you please? And, Marvel dear, go ahead with the books for children—*do*. Give them rhyme and reason, but make them absurd while holding to a sniff of reality. Shall we say *logically insane*? Yep, that's it! Writers live in a different world. You have talent—genius!"

Marvel wanted to tell Mr. Corey about *White Flags of Triumph*, but there was no time. Jake came to tell her that the bus was waiting. As they hurried to board their respective vehicles, he said breathlessly, "It's all coming true—I'll get it. But you have to help me convince Mary Ann. *Please* make her understand. If they go—" and the wind blew his words into the loom of tomorrow....

# 32

# Sources of
# Understanding

The next few days carried an aura of unreality—a dreamlike quality, in which one moves from happiness to despair. When the surges of happiness came, Marvel wanted to hold onto the dream, bury it as an anchor. But lovely dreams fade as one awakens. The same was not true of the darker moments. They tended to stay with her even after she awakened, hanging there mockingly, as if daring her to seek a solution.

But Marvel knew the problem. She *must* find out about Daddy.

Dr. Porter had gone when her interview was interrupted by Jake. There was no opportunity, she thought with a seldom frown. The frown came from remembering Jake's words, for they added another concern. Or were they a part of the whole picture? Mary Ann had hinted that there was a connection when Marvel all but shook the words from her cousin. That left Mother. But there was no chance to talk to her mother, although she had run all the way from the bus stop home to be alone with her, pour out all the surprises and victories of her strange day, then gently lead up to coaxing confidence. The house had been overflowing with well-intentioned neighbors, however. Mrs. Harrington must not be left alone. She was unaccustomed to being without her "better half." Miz Snow needed understandin'... a slice of this special cake... a bottle of this Watkins' spice, the two-fer-one sale was in progress... or this bloodbuildin' tonic, kind of a chilltonic bought at a medicine show three years ago but "good now fer what ails you'all as 'twas then." Marvel believed *that*!

But, most of all, the thoughtful neighbors enjoyed the radio programs the Harringtons had invited them to share—and they considered this to be a standing invitation. Marvel was reminded of the words of critic John Gould Fletcher: "The American film has served as propaganda for the emotional monotony, the naive morality, the sham of luxury, the haphazard etiquette, and the grotesque exaggeration of the comic, the sentimental, and the acrobatic that are so common in the United States." True, all true. But these salt-of-the-earth folk who gathered around the now-aging cabinet radio needed the escape it provided. They could "picture" the faces behind the voices. And, although they had no desire to see that evil place called Hollywood, it was exciting to hear about the thousands of pilgrims who journeyed there to make reverent tours of the homes of the rising stars. Helped them escape the trying times in these parts, it did—the dreariness they accepted but no longer talked about. They needed laughter to shut out the sad wails of the wind at their door and the sound of distant gunfire which they *knew* could never happen here. But somebody's sons were dying.

And so they dried their unshed tears and listened to the "funnymen": W. C. Fields, in his Western drawls of "My Little Chickadee," slapstick comedians John Barrymore and William Powell, and pie-throwing, paint-spilling ignoramuses called "The Three Marx Brothers." Make no never-mind about "The Ultimate Glamor Girl," "Poor Little Rich Girl," "Vixen," and "Sirens" ("Them names sound like St. Nick callin' his reindeer anyways!"). These funnymen could make them laugh—just plan ole folks like themselves, who knowed what 'twas like out heres.

"We've made ourse'ves a reg'lar schedule—ain't thet th' word?—th' Captain 'n me has, so's t'know what's on them red 'n blue networks, yuh know? George Burns, Fibber 'n Molly, Major Bowles—why, hit's like bein' there. You kin *hear* 'em doin' what they say—'phones janglin', chairs scrapin'—"

Marvel had nodded, thinking once more of how *real* characters became in the minds of listeners and readers.

Mrs. Bumstead burst out laughing. "You stay so busy with them books, honey—but you need some gigglin' time. Have you'all heered th' new one—uh, Mr. Bergen 'n his dummy. There's uh a big word for hit—"

"Ventriloquist?" Marvel supplied, careful to make the word a question.

Mrs. Bumstead rolled her eyes. "Whew-e*eeee*! Talk 'bout folksy—'n speakin' uv bein' real-like, I heered one uv them newsmen a-sayin' that vent-trill—cain't say it—thet thinga-majig uv uh dummy up 'n fooled some king—was interduced 'n th' king up and shook his hand!" When she laughed again, others joined in.

One lady said the game shows were worth listening to... could be that one of them would make it big around these parts like the Harringtons that lucky night the movie went bust! Now that was something to hope for—and anything helped. And there were always Amos and Andy!

"Does Fanny's family still come?" Marvel asked.

"Oh, sakes alive, yes!" the Captain said. "Reg'lars, come Sun-day nights. Wish we could be gittin' Brother Grady back. We was so cocksure, but that was before all this other bizness—and before Dale got that s'prise call. We shore miss them ball games—" he said sadly.

"Buck up, Cap! Th' man wuzn't able doin' thet anyways—looked too peaked t'go if you-all ask me. But we'll manage—always have, always will. Th' Good Lord's on our side. Meantime, we ain't fixin' t'leave you-all's mama. We need our Snow, 'n she needs *us*!"

Yes, the need was mutual. Somehow Marvel knew then that her own mother was avoiding her, that she welcomed the pres-ence of others as a protective wall. Well, it wasn't going to work much longer—the insulation...the isolation...the *charade*!

Meantime, Marvel found solace in writing another lengthy letter to Titus. The fire of excitement rekindled within her as she wrote details of her interview with Editor Corey. Actually, it all centered around Titus' decisions, anyway—except perhaps for the children's "talking books." No, that too, since it involved education, reading, and more! Children were born with imagina-tive minds. It was adults who, in the name of "learning," stole it away—whizzing the little ones away too fast, preparing them for "life." Well, she would be different. She would dare to whisper beneath the door which closed behind them, let them know that growing up did not require losing their ability to laugh, to imag-ine, and to create. Others might confine them into a world filled with chairs that were too big for them and rules they were too young to understand. "I may not be loved by all—who is?—but I may reach out to a few and lead them to hold onto that other world, the wonderful world of childhood's mystery and majesty, fact and fantasy, and bring it back into play as they move into the *real* world of history and science. Oh Titus, if children can learn that books are among mankind's most marvelous creations and read, read, *read*, enriching young lives to color the black-and-white words of biographies, newspapers, and the Bible, they can recapture love, faith, and peace—the harmony of God's relationship to man, to prevent wars with one another and eventually the world...."

That seemed the perfect time to make mention of overcoming preconceived notions about persons who, by their very creation, differed from one another. Children were not born with suspicion of all whose skin tone differed from their own. They learned it from their parents.

(It was from these leads that Titus Smith was to write a daring editorial regarding "Black and White America—and Their Talking Mules"! "Dumb animals? Are mules not smarter than their whip-cracking masters? Strong, swift, and enduring, the creatures obey without question the commands of their lords in mute silence. And yet, it took a mule to *see*—a mule to open her mouth and warn of impending danger—when a man called Balaam angered his own Lord in disobedience. A man, too blinded by his own sense of superiority, failed to see the angel with drawn sword until the mule cried out the danger. How blind are *we*? How *color*-blind? Blindness can be a blessing if it is confined to differences! If blindness is to commandments, it is defying the commandments of our personal Master! 'Love thy neighbor as thyself' does not go on to say 'if he is of like skin'! I, for one, tremble at the thought.... This servant shall not rest until those signs are torn down from our public toilets: Whites Only! And until our schools stop posting the signs by separating our black people, as if they were lepers, from the white...like the sheep and the goats. Are we so blind, so mute, so *dumb* to their needs?")

Marvel went on to tell Titus about the impending scholarship—just what it would mean to her, the heavy assignments, class meetings, and discussions already concerning graduation exercises, although it was still over a month away. And then she was back to her dreams.

All the details she would have shared with her mother she shared with him, becoming—she supposed—much more personal than ever before. She did not mail the letter, however, until she could cash the check Mr. Corey handed her at the meeting. It was then that she thought of Jake.

Waving the check, she was able to catch Jake Brotherton's eye as they moved through the parade of other students changing classes as they were. "Jake, look! My first check—and for writing. Could I ask you to cash it for me? I'm never at the bank. Would you mind?"

Jake laughed. "Mind? I'd be honored. Does Mary Ann know?"

"Nobody knows—not even Mother. She stays so busy, almost like she's avoiding me. What's wrong, Jake? Is it Daddy? I should know—"

Jake had a good face, so open, so honest. He was the kind of bright, forthright young man who was sure to be a banker's choice, Marvel thought for the thousandth time. Nothing evasive about him ever. And today was no exception. He looked squarely at her before speaking.

"Yes—yes, you have a right to know." He pushed at the stubborn cowlick on his forehead impatiently. "No matter how much brilliantine I use, I still look like Buttercup in the funnies! It's precious little help I can be. All I know is what Mary Ann said."

"That's enough!"

"Just that her Uncle Dale wasn't snapping back the way he ought after the bout with pneumonia. She's not making much sense these days, worried as she is over her own folks—what they'll do—what *I*'ll do."

"What *will* you do, Jake—not to change the subject?"

He paled. "I'll stay put. I have no choice, Marvel. I'm lucky, just plain lucky, and have sense enough to know a good thing when I see it. That's how I got *her*. Mom and Pop are staying to work in my Uncle Russ' hop yards in Oregon—doing right well—but understand about me. I'll get the scholarship—I *know* I will. And, oh Marvel," his eyes lighted the pale face, made him almost handsome, "I can swing college and still work on holidays, vacations, weekends—*anytime* at the bank, with a little pay. And," Jake inhaled jerkily and let his sentence run on, "I have the promise of employment afterward! I can do it, too—can and will—just like I managed to swing both vocational training and college prep when nobody else *ever* was allowed."

"They do make exceptions, Jake," Marvel whispered, knowing that he was telling her what he longed to share with Mary Ann. Only her cousin would not listen. She wanted Jake—wanted him *now*. "Jake, I'll try to talk with Mary Ann. I'd think she would learn from Uncle Worth—"

The bell rang and they both jumped. "Oh, *please*. And listen, I'm sorry about your daddy. Just be careful—I don't think he knows."

*Daddy didn't know?*

Marvel hardly remembered Jake's hurried departure. She must have called out, "Two five-dollar bills," because that was what he shoved into her hand when they met in the hall at the end of the school day. Now she could mail her letter to Titus.

✳ ✳ ✳

Snow Harrington was on her knees tracing an embroidery pattern onto some white batiste fabric by means of a worn carbon paper. But she was alone and seemed genuinely happy to see her daughter, as if Marvel had been away for a long time. "School's out!" Marvel had called.

"Oh honey, look! Remember your friend, Erlene? She's planning something nice for you, but her mother was here today to share some patterns. I'm making a new nightie," Mother's tapering fingers caressed the material as if it were alive. "I want to have something—real pretty—when Daddy gets home. He's doing real well, his letters say—like your grandmother said he would. I still can't believe the honor!"

*And I can't believe you would deceive Daddy and me.*

"I didn't know you'd heard from Daddy or Grandmother. In fact, I didn't know Daddy wasn't well," Marvel had blurted out bluntly.

Mother's flawless skin turned gray. "I—I don't know how to explain."

"It doesn't matter how you tell me what I think I already know," Marvel said in measured tones, feeling the joys of the week fade like the light in her mother's eyes.

Mother told her then, letting the words tumble out as if they found pleasure in release. Dr. Porter found spots on Daddy's lungs. He'd be compelled to escape the dust *sometime*. Texarkana was no better, but the challenge of change would help his spirits—*not* his health. "I didn't tell Daddy or he wouldn't have gone, and not you until school's out—"

"I understand," Marvel said in calm cadence. And she did. She had known all along, hadn't she? The lovely dream was gone, the dark one back.

# 33

# The Verb
# Querer

In quick review for the weekly test in Spanish, Marvel came across the verb *querer: to wish, to want*, literally translated. But in a deeper sense, there was an implication of accepting a challenge. And beyond that, she supposed, was acceptance "in victory and in failure." Crises lay ahead, but a personal crisis for herself—a crisis of *character*. Writing words was not enough. Now she must live them, make them come alive as she had so recently spoken of color.

In that moment of revelation, Christopher Columbus came alive for her, too. Teachers had explained that Texas history justified the study of the Spanish language, history, and geography. Well, granted that Mexico and Texas were neighbors—not always in agreement over ownership of the land. But wasn't there a deeper reasoning? Columbus had sailed under a Spanish flag and with less noble purpose than some claimed. The idea, bluntly put, was to amass a fortune, go home, and find favor with Queen Isabella. But there were those who stayed long before the pilgrims—those who saw with delight the beauty of the unspoiled land, whose blood coursed in the veins of the later generations who looted the land and left the spoils for future generations to build back, while their teeth were set on edge. But the land "and the fullness thereof" was their hope, their heritage.

Buried as she was in thought, Marvel failed to hear the sound of the car or the sound of voices until her grandparents entered the house and Grandmother was scolding gently, "My, my! Don't you put those pesky schoolbooks aside even on Saturday? Well, I guess you're thriving on it. The roses are blooming in those cheeks again!"

"She's happier than a dead pig in the sunshine," Grandfather said with ill-concealed pride. "If 'Ma Ferguson' can get herself elected to be Texas governor, I wager my granddaughter here can be another John Pierpont Morgan, *the* banker!"

Grandmother Riley snorted. "Make that president, Squire!"

Everybody was smiling and embracing. Then, over hot coffee (which Grandfather always drank in spite of the temperature, saying a "good sweat" always made him fitter than a fiddle), came the welcome exchange of news. The older couple insisted on hearing about Marvel's schooling. She obliged, hurrying through details that seemed unfitting now.

"I am doing fine, just fine—am ahead of schedule, in fact. Have the required paperwork in well in advance—even material for the columns."

"Um—*hmmm*! A real Harrington!" Alexander Jay Harrington said. "Not one of those empty heads whose only social skill lies in handling a teacup like this!" And he set the china cup on the kitchen table daintily holding the handle between his right thumb and forefinger, with this little finger held comically in the air. Marvel waited for Mother and Grandmother's laughter to stop before asking for news of all.

"You're up-to-date, I think," Grandmother said without reservation. "Your mother and I talk at least once a day, and she talks with Worth's wife. The boarders are in fine shape. Fanny's a blessing, good for us all. She can handle Billy Joe, the little imp! Pesterin' her silly over trifles like 'Does God have feathers?' And the young sprout can quote all kinds of Scriptures: 'cover thee with his feathers,' 'shadow of thy wings,' 'healing,' 'as a hen gathereth'—what Fanny calls *pretend* words."

Marvel nodded. "Metaphors—like 'wings of the wind' or 'wings of the morning.' Billy Joe's blessed with an imagination, still—"

"In need of having his britches tanned," Grandfather said.

Grandmother laughed. "Which he may get. Fanny finally said, 'Now, small fry, listen here! I know you got yo'self a tow sack of problems, but ah'm fixin' t'smack you clear into th' middle of next week if you don't stop pickin' on other folks like they was a banjo!' "

"What problems, Grandmother?" Marvel asked softly when her mother went to warm her father-in-law's coffee.

Lots of perception, that one, Grandmother said. The child knew things were in a state of flux, what with his father without means—and all the talk. Not talking, more like *planning* now. Alex Jr. had written that snow had melted from the mountain passes and travel was easier now. Worth's car could make it, too, according to Jake—even Dale's.

"*Daddy's?* He—they—? I know they've talked about Oregon, but—"

"Nothing definite, certainly nothing to worry your pretty head about," Grandfather said as calmly as if discussing the monotonous wind.

Undaunted, Grandmother Riley went right on talking. *She thinks I know—and I guess I do*, Marvel thought. "Oh, Worth and Rae won't reach a decision until Dale and Snow agree. I think they all understand each other on that score. Rae would follow Worth to the ends of the earth."

"Which is just about where Oregon is," Marvel said. "If I remember, it's cold up there and it rains a lot. Is that good for Daddy?"

Mother did not look up as she poured the coffee. "Oh, we won't even consider it until you finish school, honey."

*Which has nothing to do with Daddy's health. Had they talked of Oregon?*

"How do you feel about this, Grandfather? I—I thought you— uh—might object. Daddy, too. I mean, you love banking like he loves the land. You both have dreams. I know Uncle Joseph and Uncle Emory—"

"Let me down? Yes—" and for the first time he sounded a little less sure of himself, "but I guess we can prop up our thinking with adages. So here goes: 'You can lead a horse to water, but you can't make him drink.' And the Bible warns about driving our children to wrath. Our ancestors did that for us, didn't they? Maybe bankers weren't so smart, after all. I'm startin' to think they made their bed in Wall Street and now they'll have to lie in it—misused money like farmers misused the land. Want to know what I think?"

"I've got a feeling you're about to tell us, Squire."

"Right, my proud beauty!" Grandfather told Grandmother fondly. "I think Joseph Stalin's looking over the snowy plains of Russia and guffawing.... Communism seems to be working: peasants manning tractors, mills back in operation, while capitalistic bankers here look on in awe—even try to invest there, according to rumor, and they refuse."

"Sounds like tossing confetti at the end of the war," Grandmother said. "But what's it got to do with the price of eggs—or with *us*?"

Grandfather looked thoughtful. "Confetti means celebrating—a victory. Maybe we *are* making a comeback. Things look better in the Northwest—too bad it's because of war talk. Maybe my boys *are* smarter than their old man—they always thought they were. So yes, Marvel, your Uncle Joseph and Uncle Emory are going—going up there to stay. But, thank God, if—" he blew his nose, "if Worth and Dale go, they plan on coming back."

Marvel felt as if she were caught in the eye of a hurricane—safe and secure only as long as she did not move. But eventually it would move on, sweeping her with it. Hurricanes move slowly, but this one had been lying in waiting for years, unnoticed.

"*We* will do nothing until Marvel finishes school," Mother repeated as she collected the cups.

"But Mary Ann—" Marvel said, feeling that her mouth was filled with cotton, "she has another year—"

"That's not the problem," Grandmother assured her. "It's Jake—leaving him, you know. And her attitude has rubbed off on her brother. Try to reason with her, Marvel. You have a way with her. She'll listen."

"Mary Ann's head and shoulders above the other granddaughters," Grandfather said, "but she's got a long way to go to catch up with you, my pet." His eyes sought Marvel's. "She has never learned the secret you know, that honest Abe touted: 'People'll be nigh-on as happy as they want to be.' That celebrated man made no mention of weather, none about *where* they lived—nope! It depends on the heart."

Grandmother was tapping her foot as if about to do a tap dance. "Lincoln was right. Probably took the idea from King Solomon's proverb: 'for as he thinketh in his heart, so is he.' There's so much sorrow in this sorrowful world—even right here in our own flock. But life can be beautiful, even funny, to us who have a tickle bone in the anatomy. Take the Squire and me now, we've got ourselves more problems than you can stuff in a tow sack, but we've got a good toehold on life, and we're happier than a litter of alleyway kittens. Money won't buy that!"

Grandfather chuckled. "Lots of reasons not to feel up to snuff—*if* we went looking. We get what we search for where happiness is concerned. Some say we're getting along—bah! We're right young of heart. And sure, our hotel's in need of shingling, peas won't come up and us with hungry mouths to feed, and got ourselves a mouse in the pantry that's smarter than we are. Got a litter of skunks ejecting all kinds of offensive perfumes. Somebody said to try mothballs—and they loved 'em!"

"*Your* hotel?" Mother exclaimed. "You own it? Since when?"

"*Bought's* more like it. Bank owns it still. That was to be our surprise, but my happy squire here had to let the cat out of the bag."

Marvel smiled. "*La querencia!*" she said.

Nobody in that stuffy room understood. She wasn't quite sure she understood the full dimensions of the Spanish word herself. One must put into reading as well as draw from it. It meant a medium of exchange—not totally unlike that which here in America's heartland—land Spanish explorers did *not* find five centuries before. Inhabitants had learned to substitute in order to survive—and more: loving and caring, sharing of "wealth" such as they had, binding up wounds until such time as they must leave their *querencia*, only so they could return to rebuild the beautiful.

How often Marvel was to reach into the woody draws of her heart and recall the definition, she could not know now. She only knew that she had passed a certain crisis and conquered—that there would be no need now to confront Mother, that she could conquer other crises as well—not with lethal weapons or bitter words, but with love and courage born of faith.

Her grandparents left shortly afterward. But they left behind a part of themselves, a spiritual reminder that mankind must learn to look up and see the stars instead of down to see the dust. The American dream must not become the American nightmare!

\* \* \*

A long time ago Grandmother Riley had said of her daughter, "Snow White, there is the Miers' blue blood flowing in those fragile Riley veins—beautiful to look at as purest white bisque porcelain in an art gallery, but in need of gypsylike adventure such as mine offers. Still, when the time comes, you'll measure up. You are *my* daughter, too!"

Mother was measuring up *now*. Marvel sensed it. And a new kind of understanding between them came. When Daddy's letter came saying he'd been sequestered and was "tickled pink," much as he longed for his girls, Mother smiled dreamily and said, "Do you realize what all that money can do for us?"

Then when Titus wrote: "I cannot wait to see you. *Make it soon, Lord!* I have things settled in my heart. Now I *know!*" Mother smiled wistfully again.

# 34

# Not Now, Lord, Not Now . . .

Titus' letter set Marvel's young heart soaring. Like a breath of fresh air, it came in on the wings of reborn hope, transporting her into the private world that only the two of them had explored. She took little notice that the green leaves of springtime now bled their color across a white-hot sky beneath their tree. The magic remained. This time the two were lovers, wearing jeweled matching hearts with unbreakable golden chains securing them together so long as they both should live. It was a world newly created, given another chance. And so the shadows of gloom were driven into the far corners of the earth.

When on occasion Marvel came down to earth, she "saw no evil, heard no evil" (even though the news was still dark) and (certainly) *spoke* no evil. God had given her back what she had never lost, but surely misplaced: her ability to see everything and everybody with altruistic vision. *Titus was coming home—and soon!* Blessedly, Mother had understood, or thought she did. Actually, the letter held a secret code. "I have things settled in my heart. Now I *know*," Titus had said. "Things" meant the problem he had wrestled with concerning the carrying of a gene which might account for birth defects in future generations. Now he was *free*—free to say what was in his heart: that he loved her ... loved her as he would never love another. And Marvel knew her answer!

From the bus window the view was more realistic. Leaves of the magnificent sweet gums were brown instead of green. Then overnight they were falling to be whisked away by the whirl-winds. The branches which should paint the sky with autumn-colored rainbows in the fall would never again reach out in glory. They were dead—dead like the cattle, the fish and birds. Dead of thirst and starvation. Was mankind next? Perhaps, unless people escaped. *But not now, Lord, not now.*

Of course not! Graduation lay ahead and Titus would return—his surprise no surprise at all. Marvel would be wearing the blue, and the pearls around her throat would glow like jeweled hearts. She dreamed on beneath the giant oak where the green leaves of her fantasy lingered.

It was difficult to sort fact from fiction when someone invaded her world that day—until the intruder spoke. *Erlene!*

"Oh, you startled me! My mind was a million miles away."

"Easy to see that." Erlene's voice held its usual bruskness. "Sooo, knock, knock!"

"Who's there?" Marvel smiled, playing along with the silly game.

"Letter!"

"Letter who?"

"Letter fly!" Erlene said and pulled a cardboard box from behind her in mock threat. "Open it now. I want you to have it, so no going mushy on me. Promise and I'll *letter fly* over. It'll mean more to you than me."

Puzzled, Marvel promised—only to regret it once the strings were loosed and the contents seemed to spring out like hope released from Pandora's box. "Oh Erlene—the blue dress," she breathed, caressing the silk fabric as Mother had done to the batiste.

"For your graduation," the other girl said matter-of-factly. "You don't have one, do you? Dress, I mean? I'll be eaten up by jealousy—"

"I don't have one—no," Marvel managed, wondering then why it had not occurred to her. There was the five dollars, but no time. "But what'll *you* do? You'll be graduating, too. Oh Erlene!"

"There's the reason. It's in your voice. But there's more to it. Say, how come you got out of the project, huh? None of my biz?"

"I simply couldn't afford the makings—at the time," Marvel said simply, finding herself unembarrassed. Now," and she was surprised at her sudden composure, "how did *you* manage, Missy?"

Erlene pushed at her recently permed blonde hair, and Marvel was pleased to see that she no longer wore the bright-red polish. "This devilish wind's as dryin' as lye-soap shampoo! Oh, gettin' around Miss Ingersoll was easy as fallin' off a log backward. Us girls could get by with anything these days—well, except what she calls 'war paint.' See the new me? Bare as Mother Hubbard's cupboard."

"You have a beautiful complexion—like the Palmolive soap billboard saying, Keep That Schoolgirl Complexion! You didn't make a dress?"

Erlene Gilbreath told her then that the domestic science teacher allowed her to make a wedding dress—oh, nothing fancy, sort of a plain one that could be shortened. Smart to pinch pennies these days. She and Dennis—nobody Marvel would know, came from Kansas in the CCC's—they'd make it...and without help, you'd better believe!

"I'm lucky, just plain lucky—even if we may have to move on, you know?" Erlene looked at Marvel quizzically. "Mama was over to see your mama. Guess you know? They got sort of chummy-like. Well, I'm meddlin' and that Chemistry teacher's about as tough as Mr. Angle-A-Equals-Angle-B—" She glanced at a watch on her wrist. "But I wanted you to have this dress—just in case—" Erlene saluted and was gone.

*Just in case?* The tears Erlene forbade were dangerously close. Oh no! The beautiful formal might water-spot. And those words could mean anything. Then, on sudden impulse, Marvel tenderly removed the treasured garment from the tissue-lined box. As if moved by a shimmering power all its own, the long blue dress (as heavenly blue as the little chapel's Morning Glories) sprang, wrinkle-free, into its princess shape and lay fetchingly before her eyes. "A Rhapsody in Blue"...No, Marvel smiled, Titus' "beautiful lady in blue." Lovingly, she traced the pleated-ruffles of the girlish bertha, repeated at the ankle-length hem and saw herself moving slowly down the aisle of the church. But the music she heard was not that of graduation's "Pomp and Circumstance," but the reverent notes of Mendelssohn's "Wedding March" in the "Midsummer Night's Dream" that would link two hearts together with love's golden chain.

It seemed fitting that Mother should be playing her beloved violin when Marvel reached home that late-May afternoon. The near-forgotten instrument had found its accustomed place in the dimple remaining from the long-ago time when Mother made beautiful music for them all. Only the songs were different: poignant, haunting strains from a part of Snow Harrington's past which her daughter did not know.

"Don't stop," Marvel begged when her mother moved to lay the instrument aside. "Gypsy music, isn't it?"

Mother nodded and played on. It reminded Marvel of herself, although she could not have explained why. When the music stopped, leaving only an echo in the bottomlands of Marvel's heart, it was she who sat silent instead of the violinist.

And mother found that amusing? She must have because unaccustomed laughter rippled from her lips. But that was not the reason. Instead of commenting, Mother burst out, "Daddy's coming home!"

In the shared excitement which followed, Marvel showed the blue-blue dress. Mother admired it briefly then, blushing girl-ishly, brought out her finished nightgown—how lovely and lovingly stitched, with dainty double French knots forming blue forget-me-not blossoms.

Marvel daringly grasped the soft silk format and, with one hand cinching it at her waist and with the free hand holding it to her shoulders, danced about the room. Laughing, her mother hugged the nightie close to her and joined her. It was only a moment, but it was a moment suspended in time—a moment when Mother and daughter were one, as if the child had returned to the parent's womb . . . a moment of foreverness.

Breathlessly, it ended. Mother was panting, but Marvel was remembering—remember what could have been the beginning or an end: " . . . a lifetime was spent—in one little moment with the beautiful lady in blue. . . ."

When Mother suggested that they turn on the radio and catch their breaths before snacking for supper, Marvel nodded. There was a need for catching her breath, true—and her thoughts as well. But she needed to catch up on the news, too. And for-tunately, it was on—would be, following a "brief commercial break." And a voice sounding suspiciously like Rudy Vallee's crooned (as Titus had crooned "their" song"—Was everything a reminder?):

Won't you try Wheaties?
They're whole with all of the bran.
Oh, won't you try Wheaties?
For wheat is the best food of man!

And, after heaping up generous portions of fair play and love for America (and urging red-blooded American boys and girls to build up muscular brawn and magical brains by eating the product), the announcer scooped up cooperation from parents with a sentimental version, megaphoned to the last note of *"I'm Just a Vagabond Lover."* Then the news:

Good evening, ladies and gentlemen! We view the news with mixed feelin's tonight. We're a little more skeptical now than once we were, and so we wonder: Is it too good to be true that the gloomy clouds once shrouding America from sea to shining sea are lifting? The stock market wasn't dead, after all, just sleeping? And the once destitute families have found a faint light of hope breaking through? That the shambles of the Big Crash are swept up, makin' way for business as usual? Is all forgiven, forgotten? Who paid the price—hmmm? All those installment-plan debts...the mortgaged homes lost to brokers and bankers? Bankruptcy? What self-respecting man would take that disgraceful way out? Talk about sacrifice! But none so great as the sacrifice of the murder of *self.*

And yes, it happened, folks. All the suicides we heard rumored are *facts* in that black hour followin' the Wall Street crash. Men we'd thought stable and responsible became weaklings, unable to face up to an intolerable situation. Our leaders found life unworthy of the struggle and took away what only our Creator has the power to give and the right to take away: *life*! Oh, that was 'way back when, you say? It can't happen again? Are we so blind? We're not out of the woods on *this* depression yet, no matter what the self-styled analysts on the hill in Washington and on Wall Street are claimin'. Lots of philosophers tell us we're apt to find what we look for—head-scratchin' thought. Kind of depends on whether we put on rose-colored glasses or wear blinders maybe. Me? I choose to wear no glasses a'tall—just look on what I see more than what I hear. I see want. I see need. I see unrest. I see fear.

Now, on the bright side—and we should be thankful there is one—the economy *is* pickin' up in other parts. But ours is crawlin', and no government plan—noble though it may be—can make it rain! So, don't you politicians go hollerin' that we've fixed it. And when that happy day comes, don't ask us to forget and say it can't happen anymore. The days of the speakeasies, the flask, and the back room operations are gone out of operation, together with most of the bootleggin' out in the buckeye bushes.... Gone, too, are the roll-down hose, shapeless dresses, flappers with Baby Snooks voices "makin' whoopee" while doin' the Charleston in the Roarin' Twenties. So let's hope we've learned from history—that we've learned—*not* to say it can't happen again, but that it *can*! We're making progress in some ways, gettin' more tolerant, you know, what with the 396th Infantry Band, that smart-steppin' Negro musicians' squad, blowin' away the blues on Wall Street like the winds blow ours in here....

Snow Harrington rose from her chair, stretched like a kitten, and turned the radio off. "Heard enough?" she asked. "*I* have!"

But Marvel shook her head. "Please Mother—there's something else I'm listening for. If this man's style bothers you, switch to another station—" There she stopped. Her mother, wanting to blot out unpleasantness, had murmured something about starting supper and gone into the small kitchen. Half-smiling, Marvel turned down the volume when there was an unnecessarily loud clatter of dishes.

The second newscast had more to do with American technology—at first. And then it turned into words more sobering than the previous program. Warnings concerning a dark future can be more threatening than those concerning the past.

It was good to know, the anonymous male voice said, that these United States, one nation under God, led the world in the field of technology. Those old enough could remember the courageous explorer and naval officer who triumphed over an accidentally smashed leg which forced an early retirement, was summoned to active duty, and in three short months became a hero in the world war—Victory after victory, medal after medal! Identity of the man? None other than the then Lieutenant Commander Richard Evelyn Byrd, whose adventuresome spirit soared high with his trimotored plane, as he directed the navigational preparations for the Navy's first transatlantic flight. After Armistice, Officer Byrd commanded the Naval Unit Expedition in Greenland, and in 1925 went to the North Pole without mishap. In 1927, he flew from Roosevelt Field in New York to Paris, but zero visibility forced the fearless pilot back to sea where he brought the craft down safely in the surf. In 1928, he led an expedition to the Antarctic, proclaiming it "Little America"—the only man to reach both Poles by air.

Marvel listened with interest to the man's accomplishments (some of which came before her time) and, in her own way, identified with him. At the same time, she wondered what the announcer was leading up to. She was soon to find out:

All this is but background, a review to most of you. But the news today is this: Thrice-retired Rear Admiral Richard E. Byrd is safe! A rescue party, headed by Dr. Thomas Poulter, reached him and brought him back safely to our now-established base, his "Little America"! So secret was Admiral Byrd's mission that not a word was leaked to the media—And so hazardous that the much-admired man refused to allow his men to accompany him on the important assignment. And so it was that he went to live in a nine-by-thirteen hut, buried 123 miles due south of our base, to spend six months in total isolation. Purpose of this important mission was to observe weather conditions. Nobody, including himself, could have foreseen what was to happen— that he should be stricken with slow monoxide poisoning. But with the courage so much a part of him, once more Admiral Byrd refused to imperil the lives of his comrades and issued no call for help. Providence must have prompted the equally commendable doctor who found the victim and brought him to safety. And now comes the *Why?* of all this. Our educated guess is that only our federal government knows! And we can rest assured that we are to hear more in the unpredictable days ahead. *Why* should America stake claim to a glacier? As an air base? *Why* an air base—and there? Unless—

Marvel, too, had heard enough, but she lacked the will to turn the radio off. Her thoughts were beyond the spoken words. Another depression could never happen, profiteering brokers assured a world crying out for good news, and had managed to prop up spirits with a revival of the "Happy Days Are Here Again!" theme song of Teddy Roosevelt's blighted campaign. Shoppers went wild, invested all, and Wall Street came tumbling down—again. And now another Roosevelt was busily proclaiming: "Our boys will never be sent overseas!" But *here*, Mr. President—if a trimotored plane could go from pole to pole, could war happen *here*?

Even the announcer was saying something about the *why* of the defense plants. Were we swallowing the soothing syrup of "friendly coalitions" between helpless countries and ruthless, more powerful ones who coveted their natural resources? Would there come a time for "friendly takeovers"—for the price of a crust of bread, softened in a cup of blood? There were isolationists who said it did not concern us. But what had the League of Nations promised? Protection—even if it meant wiping the aggressor from the face of the earth.

*Oh, dear Lord, not now—not now!* Marvel's heart cried out again. Daddy was coming home tomorrow. Soon graduation—and Titus! Mother was right. Don't listen! But before Marvel could shut out the startling questions, the newscaster was mentioning the nation's unpreparedness, and then swung back to technology. DuPont was experimenting quietly with improving rayon to make something called *nylon* as a replacement for ladies' silk hosiery. The trade agreements were to balance our export of scrap iron and Japan's export to us of silk. Even now, a ship from the Orient had docked and unloaded in port. Had we swung back to technology? Perhaps tied together would be more accurate, she thought with alarm and paused. It was during that pause that she heard the words which would echo in her heart forever: "Hope is a wonderful thing to cling to, until it becomes a delusion!" It was the second time she had heard of nylon. Important?

\* \* \*

The next day Marvel was able to speak only briefly with Mary Ann, and then with Duke. It was Duke and his younger brother,

Thomas, who had prompted her to listen so carefully to last night's news.

"Daddy's coming home tonight," she told Mary Ann, only to discover that it was no news to her cousin. Uncle Dale had written to her father, too. "And you know what they're thinking of doing?"

"We'll talk about that when we know for sure, and do what we have to. I just thought you'd be happy for us—" Marvel tried again.

"Happy? Bah! I know already. And I'm having no part in it!"

It was then that Marvel saw Duke shouldering his way toward them. He smiled, and Marvel noted how fit he looked. "Hello, our handsome boy cousin! My, my! You've muscled out like a wrestler." And when he spoke, the crack of adolescence in his voice had yielded to manhood's command.

"Grandfather's declaring war unless we surrender to the family tyrant's order for a Harrington caucus—wants us all together one last time. You know, before me and Tom Thumb get word from Her Majesty or called in this new conscription deal, or—or enter ROTC, Reserve Officer Training, before they nab us. Hard speculatin'. Anyway, before we leave for the Northwest. We're going *now*—us and Uncle Joseph's bunch."

\* \* \*

Dale Harrington's welcome home would have melted the coldest of hearts. The fabulously beautiful wife and daughter whom he'd described to fellow jurors now devoured him with kisses. They made this sometimes-ugly world into a place of shining beauty, and made him a better man, he had said.

In an effort to hide the tears that rimmed his eyes (Marvel knew because of his voice), Daddy was saying, "Hey there, you two! What are you up to—trying to rid yourselves of me permanently? Whatta way to go!" And the three of them burst into laughter.

The evening meal was festive. Snow Harrington surprised her family with a daintily fixed meal, the makings for which she had hoarded from her mother's gifts before the departure of her loved one. Could those women in Texarkana beat *this*? Well no, her husband teased, "But it's the *way* they serve it! You know, like

the Chesterfield ad says, 'So round, so firm, so fully-packed!' "
Mother pretended to pout prettily. With a playful wink at Marvel,
Daddy hugged his wife and singsonged: "Sure as th' vine twines
'round th' stump, you're my darlin' sugar lump." Jazzy, huh?
Something he picked up in Texarkana from a joshing jazz group.
No fun being locked behind bars for security when jurors were
sequestered—pretty doggone lonesome. They were not allowed
to call or write, and mum was the word, even to the jailer. But
they did all they could to make the jurors comfortable: decent
food, even the all-black jazz band from New Orleans! Dale Harrington had a rapt audience, needed to talk, and made the most
of it. Yes, all would have been perfect temporarily, had he been
less hoarse and interrupted less frequently by the brassy cough.
Mother was too enthralled to notice. Neither did she notice when
her daughter tiptoed away to let the two of them be alone.

When did it all change? One moment Mother and Daddy were
vowing never to allow anything short of death to separate them
again—not even a summons to fulfill his "citizen's responsibility." Dr. Porter would have filed a medical excuse—gladly and
with just cause. The next, her parents were quarreling bitterly in
low, angry words.

"You have to be out of your mind, Dale. You don't mean what
you're saying—you *couldn't*. Tell me I misunderstood—" Mother
begged piteously.

But she had not misunderstood. "You knew, darling. You
promised—"

"I did not promise any—any such thing—not for now. You
know what's important to me—what counts more than anything
in my life."

"I'm afraid I do!" Daddy was angry now, and the coughing was
worse. "You didn't want to move here, and now you're refusing to
leave. It's this house—*any* house. A house means more than
Marvel—or me!"

Mother's voice came muffled by a pillow which would be wet
by hot tears. "Lower your voice, please. You know that's not true.
Why do you make me suffer? I'll never forgive that—when—
when you know it's for you I promised to go, and for her that I
have to stay until—"

Marvel shrank as if she had been struck. She'd eavesdropped
unavoidably and then unashamedly, knowing it was herself who

came between the parents she had promised God she would honor and respect. If only He had given her some sign. But of course He had. If I believed in signs of the secular world, I would say I was born during a total eclipse, Marvel thought desperately, because I chose darkness rather than light. Her heart filled up with remorse. And some faraway part of her confused mind wondered if Mother, darling Mother, wore the batiste nightie.

The conversation was out of control. "How do you *know* Oregon's climate will be better?" ... "Mountain barriers—" ... "If faith can move mountains, it can build 'em!" ... "You're behaving like a child. I'd say go anyway. We can have gardens. I'll find work" ... "Not now—*not until Marvel finishes school.* I'll go hungry first—" Silence and then: "It's now or never. Here's my check. There'll be no money then." Marvel waited for the words she knew would come: *"We'll let Marvel decide."*

# 35

# *The Agony of Farewells*

The school year had ended.

Unexpectedly and prematurely, it had ended for Marvel Harrington. There would be no graduation for her—no fulfillment of the dreams she had so believed in, dreams too numerous to count. Only one stood out now, for only one thing mattered: *Titus would not be back.* How could she tell him of the agony gnawing at her heart? She couldn't. Titus must be spared the hurts of departure. He must never know of the agony, the despair, the hopelessness the year had brought. Only their shared dreams and everlasting faith that God would bring them through—together—had made the indignities bearable. Many times, Marvel realized now, she would have preferred the tortures in faraway lands she had only heard whispered about: to be kicked in the face by hobnailed boots, stripped to the waist, beaten. Yes, that was better than the whiplash of words, the daggers of begging, borrowing, cowering, and crawling while Daddy's captors sneered. And she and Mother went on pretending not to notice. Bloodshed would have brought a kind of relief that unshed tears could not.

She was a little girl hurt—hurt too deeply for mirth or song. And yet, she must go on pretending with words even now for the sake of others, never revealing that her dreams lay dead at her feet—corpses which could not be carried away to the Harringtons' verdant world out yonder....

Marvel had tossed and turned long after the crack of light beneath her bedroom door disappeared and there was silence. *Marvel will decide.* The words rose out of the darkness mockingly. Wasn't that always the way? Then she put the thought away, knowing it was unworthy. It would have been only too easy to affix blame on her parents—the way of the old deluder, Satan. But Mother and Daddy were not responsible for the troubles of the Depression, the Dust Bowl conditions. Once upon a time they had been two young people, deeply in love, committed to each other for better or for worse, believing, *knowing* in their simple faith that "things will look brighter in the morning." Morning had come. Nothing had changed—except themselves. They were different people—a young couple grown older and, if not wiser, at least wide awake to stark reality. The simple ways of yesterday would no longer work. It was sad. Their hope lay in her hands.

Exhausted, Marvel rose to face the dreaded day—the day she'd dared hope would never come, childishly thinking "It will all blow over." But she had known. Deep in the enclaves of her heart she had known.

The stuffy kitchen was heavy with tension and steam when she went in. The ignored kettle shrieked for attention. "Easy, kettle—down, boy!" Marvel scolded, lightly personifying the metal utensil.

Her parents looked pitifully relieved. So Marvel hadn't heard, after all. "Hello, Sunshine!" Daddy said affectionately, and Mother echoed a greeting as she hurriedly moved the kettle to the side of the wood stove.

Marvel wasted no time. "Do take one look at the beautiful sunrise, you two!" she said by way of diversion. And, sure enough, the outside world was splashed with vermilion. "Don't tell me Texarkana could outpaint *that*. But what about Oregon, Daddy—brighter yet?"

"I—I thought—I thought you might have questions," he gulped.

"I do," she said with sunrise brightness. "When do we leave?"

Mother stared at her in disbelief. "Marvel, honey, you mean you—you're willing to give it all up, make the sacrifices I'd have died to spare you—agree just like that? Look at me. I can tell—"

Marvel forced her eyes to meet her mother's. Words vanished, but she managed to nod. Daddy reached out and touched her hand. "Marvelous—my precious Marvelous—it will take a little time—but—"

The words came then. Woodenly, but words all the same. "I understand. Each day takes its toll. Every minute counts—and every penny." She felt that she was cheering for some sort of victory for which she had no enthusiasm. Foolishly, she wished the kettle were still shrieking to drown out her words. Surely she could do better.

"Wait!" she said, suddenly inspired. And, rising from the breakfast she had left untouched, Marvel walked to the front door and picked up the clutch bag she had laid on top of her schoolbooks. The snap of its flap-top opening amplified tenfold in the silence. "Here is *my* contribution! Five dollars, earned by my writing!"

Daddy's reaction surprised her. He brought his fist down on the rickety table in frustration. "And now you'll have to give up this too. Oh sweetheart, last night I thought I could ask it. But I can't!"

Snow Harrington stared at her husband, as if they were meeting for the first time. And she was biting her lip, impervious to the pain, while tears coursed down her cheeks. You—you turncoat—you traitor," Mother blubbered. "Last night you had this all—all mapped out. And now—"

"Don't cry, Snow, don't cry. Last night was different. I thought I could ask my family to make this sacrifice. And now I—I'm not man enough for *that*!" Clumsily, her husband tried to mop up her tears. But his handkerchief was wet with his own tears.

There was much to say, but it must be left unsaid. Sentimentality must be stripped ruthlessly from reality. Last night Marvel had slipped away unnoticed. But today was different. Today she was a part of this—a vital part. It was she who cast the deciding vote.

" 'The time has come, the walrus said, to talk of many things . . .' So, isn't anybody going to thank me for my mite? Who says I'll give up my writing? I've seen nothing of the outside world. Isn't traveling supposed to be educational? It's all decided, and we've a lot of planning to do. Just promise me one thing," Marvel paused, not trusting her voice, then continued, "let's not go beyond the family with this—not until I can break the news—to—some others in my own way."

Her parents promised, worshiping her with their eyes. They said a few other things, but Marvel could no longer bear it. Planting a kiss on the forehead of each, she fled, only to turn at the door to call over her shoulder: "Love one another as I have loved you..."

And she knew they would. The wound would heal—eventually.

* * *

Marvel stood before Mr. Phillips, outwardly calm. "Yes sir, you heard correctly. Something has come up unexpectedly. Forgive me for not telling you. I didn't know we would be leaving at all—certainly not before school ended."

Her underlip betrayed the heartbreak behind her feeble smile. The Math teacher, who served as principal, must have seen. "Won't you be seated, my dear? Let me get used to the idea. And excuse my intruding, but I must ask you this: Is there anything I can do?"

"You mean to change my mind? No sir. You see, it's circumstances. This is hard for me, but there's nothing I can do—nothing anybody can do. Well," she hesitated, "there is one thing, sir. Is there a way—a way I can leave—without the agony of farewells?"

This would present no problem, Mr. Phillips assured her gently—not in her case. She had contributed so much to Culverville High School that nothing was too much to ask. But did Marvel realize just what she would be letting slip through her fingers?

Numbly she had nodded and then realized that, no, she did not realize the full scope of it all.

"Students are not to know this, but Marvel, you were to receive scholarship offers from three sources. You would have had a choice of colleges and universities."

Remorse flooded her body, robbing her of reason and control of her emotions, and taking away her breath. A voice Marvel did not recognize as her own whispered, "Is there a way in which I could accept—for use in another state?"

Regretfully, he said, scholarships were restricted to the state of her residence. She would be compelled to attend an institution of higher learning in Texas. "Maybe," he said thoughtfully, "we could contact a college where you locate and recommend you on high scholarship. I will do everything I can. You know that."

Yes, she knew, and knowing cut another path through her heart. Everyone was being so kind, so understanding. This man deserved a partial explanation. "Mr. Phillips," she hadn't known this would be so difficult, "I think you will appreciate—knowing that—that my father must get away from the dust. So it's largely his health—"

Mr. Phillips clasped his hands behind his head and leaned back, a gesture so totally uncharacteristic that the scarred swivel chair squeaked in protest. From that vantage point, he was able to probe into Marvel's very soul with his sharp, penetrating dark eyes. "I can understand—in part. One day, I suppose, we will all face that. I can foresee a mass exodus." There he stopped, righted himself, and assumed his usual businesslike manner.

Mr. Phillips supposed Marvel would wish to know who offered the three scholarships?

Yes, Marvel would.

There was an offer from the newspaper, which was to be expected, he told her. Another from the Baptist Convention, headed by Dr. Holt, local pastor—Marvel remembered him? Only slightly—she'd met him through Titus, she recalled now, but it came as a surprise that the minister would see her as some missionary in a foreign field. What on earth prompted *that*? She must have given voice to the question, as Mr. Phillips was explaining what an impact her columns had (and those of her colleague, for yes, the school took pride in young Smith's accomplishments, too!). Marvel had to force herself to concentrate after mention of Titus' name. I must, I *must* devote tonight to writing him, she thought, although the task ahead wrung tears from her heart.

"The scholarship would be to Baylor University, Marvel—an honor indeed, considering how difficult it is to gain admittance there."

"Oh Mr. Phillips," Marvel whispered in disbelief. "If only—"

It was easy to see that the principal did not wish to pursue that avenue again. In his position, it was important to hide emotions, which may have accounted for his disclosure of a matter he had not intended to mention. Hurriedly, he told her that she might find it surprising for Dr. Porter himself to offer to pay her way through an equally prestigious institution—that of medicine!

"Dr. *Porter!*" she gasped. "Why—what? I don't understand—"

"This should have come from the doctor, Marvel." Mr. Phillips mopped his brow with the back of his hand. "I would ask that you see Dr. Porter in person, if time allowed. You will be unable to accept anyway, but it seems that it's his opinion you have the potential of being an excellent nurse and—" he stopped, at a loss for words.

"Yes?"

"Marvel, this is confidential—"

"Of course, sir. You can trust me."

"Completely. And perhaps you *should* know. It could make leaving easier to carry away some nice memories along with the not-so-nice. You have been helpful, Dr. Porter says, to his daughter. And knowing you, I am convinced that you expected no reward. But Kate Lynn's father saw it differently. He wants his daughter to attend Tulane—"

"Tulane!"

Mr. Phillips coughed uncomfortably. "I stand corrected," he said a little tartly as if to cover his embarrassment. "This *would* take you out of state—to New Orleans, of course!"

Of course. Marvel carefully guarded against a smile. *Of course, you hadn't intended telling me. But now that you did—*

"And I would go with her—be a stabilizer. I think I understand. But Mr. Phillips, I have a feeling that wasn't the third scholarship."

He sighed, consulted his watch, and laughed. "You have a great deal of insight—an uncomfortable amount. But you are right, my dear. The other one is so small by comparison that it looks pale—something to be issued in a breadline, a government dole."

"Those fill a need," Marvel said, feeling color stain her cheeks. "Please don't apologize for—for anything. This all means so much."

It was the studied opinion of every member of the faculty that Marvel Harrington would be an ideal teacher, he told her. Usually one or two differences arose—not so in her case. Support had come from all including—*ahem!*—one instructor whose tests of students he found to possess a "spark of genius" amounted to near-torture.

Marvel shrank from the memory. *Mr. Caldwell!*

\* \* \*

Marvel left Mr. Phillips's office with a new kind of hope. It was as if he had singled her from the huddled masses who were searching—as Americans had always searched—for happiness, in fervent belief that somehow, somewhere, somebody had a chance for a better life. Maybe Mother and Daddy were right. But the torch the principal lighted for Marvel went beyond one man's family—some nice memories along with the not-so-nice, he had promised. Yes, she would always remember and remembering would remind her just how much influence one person could have when one chose to serve—to lead, not to follow, other than in the way the Lord planned. Enticing as the scholarships were—and who could deny the honors were exciting?—they served more as reminders to her of her lifelong commitment to service, wherever it led.

Somehow it seemed fitting that Editor Corey would leave a note pinned to the bulletin board that Marvel Harrington would please drop by the newspaper office at her earliest convenience. This would be her last day at school. Mr. Phillips would arrange to have teachers turn in temporary grade sheets early in order to see how many were to graduate. So that had been good-bye. The next one came close on its heels. She must report to the domestic science cottage and manage to behave normally. Then she would drop by to see Mr. Corey on the way back.

All went well. The other girls were all atwitter. "Miss Ingersoll's weddin' date is set. *Sh-h-h-h....* We've slipped around to find out what she'd like for a present—uh, one we could afford—and guess what! We can chip in and buy it—the whole set, that bein' custard cups made out of *glass*—glass guaranteed not to bust in a hot oven!... Individual custard cups—for steamin', you know—cost just five cents.... Now, if somebody can't scrape up a nickel... and don't tell! It's a surprise."

Marvel could afford a nickel now. Nobody noticed her leaving then.

Just moments before Marvel's arrival, A. Thomas Corey had sighed and settled back in the worn cushion of his chair. The newspaper was crawling on its belly, in need of a quick fix to forestall a disappearing act like the Durant of the early 1900s. Confounded automobiles didn't have capital for proper roads back then (and, hang it all, still didn't!)... confounded cars smelled up the countryside, and noise—gee-whillicans! Scared chickens into molt... cows—and owners, too.

But on sight of Marvel Harrington, the editor brightened. "Ah, here you are, Marvel, like an answer to prayer."

"Have you been praying, Mr. Corey?" Marvel smiled, seating herself in the chair the editor indicated. The untidy office reeked of ink.

He blushed. "Can't rightly make claims to that. But I should be—praying for the soul of this newspaper. If it fails to show a profit this year—prosperity *wasn't* just around the corner, was it, no more than 'way back yonder—" and he told her about the Durants then.

But who knew? Maybe this would be the pivotal year for Texas. It seemed to be happening elsewhere. Now if the newspaper could hit the market with something revolutionary—take that continued story—

"Mr. Corey, I—I will be unable to do the story or the columns—or anything," Marvel said regretfully. "I will be leaving—unexpectedly. Thank you, sir, for the scholarship offer, but I can't accept."

He waved away further explanations. Mr. Corey was a kind man, supportive and appreciative. But Marvel had never doubted his shrewdness. Already he was miles ahead on the journey West. "I had an inkling," he said drily, looking at his ink-stained hands. "Tell you what—" and he proceeded to outline a plan whereby she would write details of experiences en route. *Then* she would write the serial, destined to be a book.

*Yes, yes!* The agony of farewell became the torch of victory—a new American dream. Go serve the huddled masses, then *come home*!

# 36

# "Then Sings My Soul..."

Mother and Daddy seemed content. It was good to have everything out in the open. Now that the climax had come, they actually welcomed it, if one could judge by outward appearances. Marvel decided it was better not to dig deeply. They would have preferred that life be kinder. But since it must be this way, they would accept it.

Marvel wanted to rub her eyes in disbelief when she caught sight of their near-happy faces. If she believed in apparitions, the change in her parents would have supported that claim. Surely they were ghosts! Only last night there had been hatred in their low-pitched voices. Those voices told the story of faces so grim and hard-set they would never smile again. And now the anger was gone, replaced by the spark of hope that had lain smoldering in ashes of what seemed to be a dead love.

It was hard to keep from singing the words she said: "It's done—I'm finished. Your prodigal daughter has come home to stay!"

Both of them rushed to embrace her. "Oh darling, you didn't—"

"Yes Mother, I did! And you know what? I'm relieved. You'll need my help. We'll work together—make this into one grand adventure."

"Oh honey!" Daddy sang out. "If that window were big enough, I'd throw myself right through the pane—gain release from this prison." Mother interrupted him at that point with a peal of laughter that startled her as much as her husband and daughter.

"And cut yourself to pieces!" she said. Which reminded her, Mother continued. He was to see the doctor before going one step further.

Daddy moaned. "No way do I need a sawbones. I'm afraid!"

" 'Fraidy cat!" Mother jeered cheerfully. "Afraid of what?"

"Not what you think—nothing Doc Porter'll find, unless it's *good*! If he says I'm sound, you my Snow White may say we stay!"

Mother looked thoughtful. "The die is cast. But see him you will, my love. He's coming *tonight*. I called him and he volunteered."

*Tonight?* Marvel realized then that keeping her departure under wraps was impossible—no, not if he listened to her. She would have no chance to tell about today either, but would it help? Not really. It was just as well that she reserve such matters for sharing with Titus. She would write to him tonight, even if she missed another night's rest....

Dr. Porter was warm and cordial as always. He asked Daddy a few pertinent questions, and then felt his pulse and listened to his chest. "It's good that you're going, Dale—real good—and the sooner the better. I want you to check in with another doctor periodically. You'll stay, I'm supposing? I envy you, but you did love the land—"

Daddy inhaled deeply, coughed, and then said something very surprising. "I couldn't if I wanted to—not now. Everything we loved is gone, caught up in the whirlwinds of—of old folly. However, I won't lose the place. It's like an old umbrella I tried to lose at school when my mother made me carry the sissy thing with me, and the teacher kept bringing it back! Same with the place. The banks don't even want it anymore, say it's worthless. Loan? Forget it!"

Not come back? Daddy's love of the land had died? His will, like his muscles, had atrophied? *No! We will not surrender!* Marvel's protesting heart echoed the imagined words of brutally beaten soldiers, robbed of everything except their faith. She longed to scream out her frustration. It would be so easy to cross over that invisible line her parents had taken for granted and be willful, disobedient—defy them and flatly refuse to go. And for the first time, Marvel Harrington understood her cousin's protest, her refusal to leave the object of her deep love. "Forsaking all others" was a part of the biblical command. She closed her eyes and squeezed—squeezed hard and ever harder—and prayed with equal fervor. God heard.

"We will let the land lie fallow," she heard herself saying as if from another world. "That's in keeping with the original law—a sabbath for the land every seventh year. The ground needs rest."

"Exactly," Dr. Porter nodded as he snapped the lid of his black bag in place, "like the body. Doctors can only lend nature a hand. The rest is up to the patient. He has to have the will to live, and something to live for. I've patched you up, old boy, like—what's his name?—Jake. Kate Lynn told me—the fellow who fixes cars."

Marvel nodded, pleased that the doctor had said what he did. "Yes sir, Jake's his name. And Daddy *does* have a lot to live for. The Bible had more to say about that. Land's not supposed to lie fallow forever. We'll come back and restore it. I—I want to thank you about the offer."

The hurt was back, and Marvel found herself unable to say more.

"Thank me? I *meant* the offer to finance your college. You show potential, and doctors never give up hope. I still want to talk about it."

If only Mother had waited, talked with her. But that was history. "There will be no time, Dr. Porter. Today was my—my last day—"

The doctor's eyes sought Mother's, and the black case dropped onto the kitchen table with a clatter. "You didn't tell me—"

Mother was wringing her hands. "I—I didn't know it mattered."

"Professionally, no—well yes, it matters. It's best for the patient. But," he sighed, "personally, it matters very much! Marvel, my dear, how can I show my appreciation? Kate Lynn and I planned—"

Marvel's response came quickly. "You owe me nothing at all, as I told you before, sir. Kate Lynn didn't need me then, and she won't need me in Tulane. What she needs is more confidence, and I hope I gave her that."

"May the patient interrupt here?" Dale Harrington broke in. "I have no idea what you two are talking about. No, never mind telling me right now. I just want to say that whatever my daughter— she's pretty special, I agree, my *Marvelous*," his voice was tender, "but let me say that whatever she did—frankly, doc, well, by

George! she saved my face. And you did, too—never made me feel I was accepting *charity*! Sooo, isn't that pay for whatever Marvel did to—uh, help *you*?"

"An overpayment!" was the doctor's quick reply. "So forget it!" He picked up the bag and began shaking hands in farewell, obviously shaken.

But Marvel detained him. "Dr. Porter, please wait. There *is* one thing you can do. Please don't reveal to anyone when we're leaving."

He looked surprised. "There's no reason. Does that include her?"

"Kate Lynn? No sir, just ask that she not repeat and she won't. I'll write to her. We've become good friends. I'll write, I promise."

"Do!" Marvel heard tears in his voice as he hurried away.

Mother and Daddy did not inquire about the doctor's reference to financial aid he had offered. But then Marvel had not expected them to.

\* \* \*

My darling Titus: (Marvel wrote, when she was alone at last) "You can read my words but not my heart," the old adage claims. In this letter, you will be able to read both, because my heart will be in my words. But I guess there is nothing revolutionary about that—between you and me. The message will be different, for how can I ask you to understand what I do not understand myself, torn as I am between the world I know and love and the world I think I was pledged to serve before my birth? It all seems so sudden, so unexpected, when in reality it has been unfolding before me all the while. The awful truth is, my darling, that I am leaving . . . leaving *now. In fact, I suppose I'll be on my way to Oregon before you are able to post me a reply. And Titus, you cannot reach me as I'll have no forwarding address. But I can write you*—and write you I will, *every day*!

Marvel paused then, both to gain control of her emotions and to decide just how detailed her explanation need be for the sudden departure. Her parents deserved privacy. And the Harrington family was noted for pride to the point of obsession. So she would not violate the rules. It was all right to be "genteelly poor" if one did not discuss (or, in truth, *disclose*) the matter. Frayed cuffs were preferable to the flashy "new money" of ill-gotten gains. Titus understood. He, too, was among "the poor." Like herself, he was of "gentle birth," but depression had changed all that for the Smiths.

"Blessed are the poor in spirit; for theirs is the kingdom of heaven," Jesus had proclaimed in his Sermon on the Mount. So yes, Marvel decided, she would include the Beatitude, saying only of their leaving that it was largely because of her father's health.

Picking up her pen, she went on to tell the details of her last day of school, freely describing the agony of each good-bye, the excitement of the scholarship offers, and explaining why she asked permission to be spared further suffering. If Mr. Phillips would just allow her to disappear quietly and without fanfare. And he did!

Except for Mr. Corey, who *ordered* me to the newspaper office, Titus. And, oh wait until I tell you! Never mind the scholarship (much as I appreciated and, yes, *need* it!), the man is most impressed with what you and I have contributed. And he wants the columns you do continued. But I will still be a part, providing, of course, that you want it that way. I was supposed to ask you, not take it for granted as I'm afraid I'm doing. It's only because I'm so excited. My assignment is to take pictures with my eyes and write about my experiences, send it all back, and you two take it from there. Do I sound excited? That's a pale word. I feel like I've been running uphill! Oh Titus, one day, darling, the editor wants us to go ahead with the novel—you know, the writing we discussed, tying fact and fiction together the way Defoe did (Never mind "Friday," it was acceptable to have slaves then—and Robinson was a kind master). By the way, did you know the author worked for a newspaper and sold his *facts* for a copper per line in England, until he turned his writing to "true fiction"? You are familiar with the others who made use of their prose-writing licenses: Hemingway,

Whitman, and now I read that John Steinbeck's putting together a book based on his research articles about the Dust Bowl. One day he'll get the recognition he deserves. I have a strong feeling that people will feel embarrassed, guilty, and responsible for the crash, the Depression and (God forbid!) another war if it should come. That being the case, the next generation may never know their heritage. Here I go dreaming again... for, sad as I am, still there's joy—the kind that God sends down, enabling me to go on singing the wonderful old hymn and meaning every word: "Still Sings My Soul."

Marvel wiped at her eyes at that point. She would not cry. She would *not*. Titus must not open a letter splashed by tears! Her mind gleaned the day for other subjects, knowing that this was no time to write about *feelings*. It found what it sought—a thought so jolting that it was unbelievable.

*I have not taken my final examinations!* No finals, no high school diploma. No diploma meant no college. But what solution was there? None, except prayer. Only God knew where circumstances would lead, if school would be in session, if she could gain admission....

What was the word she heard Chemistry students toss back and forth like a basketball once they had discovered it? *Atom*, wasn't it? Marvel had asked curiously what it meant, and Mary Ann had said, "Oh the smallest particle of any element—so tiny that it would take a lifetime to pour a thimbleful out. Yep, invisible but explosive. Wow!"

That was exactly how Marvel Harrington felt of herself at that moment. And yet, from that small particle came an illuminating light. She knew then how *The White Flag of Triumph* should be presented. And, although it was unplanned, she picked up her pen and wrote to Titus:

I feel that I'm only beginning to learn how important feelings are. They're everything, aren't they? I once supposed that each of us is shaped by experience—and, in a sense, I guess that's true. But which is more important, Titus? Our experiences or how we *feel* about them? I'm referring to our someday book, of course. We'll need true-to-life characters who go about facing very real situations together—relating, understanding those like us or unlike us ... people we know and love or those we do not know and may never meet, but love and respect because we've learned to communicate, to live together, explore one another's feelings—and admit our own without fear of being "found out." Our generation has seen so much and, as you and I have said, we're undoubtedly destined to see more. How do we survive in a world that is changing constantly and where valuable ideas conflict with other people's valuable ideas? We tend to think in terms of what's happening *now*—and we have to—but there's a timelessness we mustn't ignore. Oh, wouldn't it be a triumph to make readers forget the authors are more than products of the Dust Bowl era, restricted to the heartland—more specifically, east Texas—but anywhere, anytime, and common to us all in our search for peace "that passes all understanding." We have to look at the past, the present, and the future. How far have people progressed with their *feelings*? How far can they go—without help, and God's? Readers who expect a crime-a-minute like Edward G. Robinson committed in "Little Caesar" or a slinky Blonde Bombshell as Jean Harlow was called in her steamy movies will be disappointed, as I envision our writing. You will understand if I am communicating my own feelings, for feelings can build bridges....

And then, without pausing, Marvel opened her own heart, admitting to Titus how much, how *very* much, she was going to miss him. How much he had come to mean to her—so much that nothing could alter her feelings. Genetics were of no consequence, except as they affected his own thinking. She was glad he had resolved the matter. But for his sake only. "As my beloved Fanny would say, 'Law me!' for it would have made no difference to me." From there, without reservation, she told him of the Harringtons' plans to travel West in a caravan—*not* to seek a fortune (Very few, like Daniel, could have both gold and God!). They were forced by Daddy's health—and to put food on the table. "But my roots are here, Titus. I belong to this land. So, God willing, I will be back. But like you, I have promises to keep—

other causes to serve. In doing so, I will grow from this experience, collecting sweetness from even the bitterest herb for us— *all for us*. A part of me dies in this good-bye. So keep the part I leave with you alive." Your Marvel.

Quickly she sealed the envelope. She would not reread it, because the words needed to be said. Neither would she weaken and say the words she longed with all her heart to have *Titus* say: I love you.

Marvel thought she had suffered as much as it was possible to suffer—in every way. After so many layers of pain, one ceased to feel additional ones. How little she knew about feelings, after all, she was to lament the next day. There were all kinds of love, yes. But all kinds of sadness? This face of sadness was a stranger.

"Package for Miss Marvel Harrington!" her father said cheerfully when he returned from the mailbox. "Please return to sender in case—"

He was squinting, reading words that were not on the wrapping. But Marvel was in no mood for games. "Please, Daddy—"

Immediately handing over the package, he turned attention to an envelope in his hand. "Snow, our first letter in two weeks. So let's have a look. Hey! what's going on here? A letter from my own father? Since when did he get so formal—and why not use the 'phone?"

Mother left her sorting of kitchenware and hurried in. In her rush for the privacy of her bedroom, Marvel pushed hurriedly through the maze of cardboard boxes, and heard little of the letter's contents—just enough to know that Grandfather Harrington "requested the honor of the presence of his sons and their respective families" to join...

The package was postmarked in Austin, as Marvel had somehow known it would be, although she had expected nothing. Most people could not afford to buy gifts—and certainly not struggling college students. But the oblong box held an undreamed-of gift: a pair of the finest of black kid gloves, so fine and so beautiful she hardly dared touch them. In awe, she made an effort to read the accompanying note: "My darling: The five-dollar bill for the column belongs to you, so here is something to keep both your hands and your heart warm until we are together, and I have another chance to warm them with words."

*Oh, darling Titus, you've made my heart sad... but my soul glad....*

# 37

# The Gates
# of Hell

"Some secret—our going," Marvel whispered to her mother as the two of them sorted out what they considered to be only the essentials for the long journey. The men had agreed that there would be no trucks or trailers. Such large vehicles would have trouble crossing the steep mountains. Others had reported problems with cars, too, if they were overloaded. It was safer to travel light...sell off what they could (precious little market) ...store a few items maybe for later shipping. Surely no Harrington would come crawling back. *No, that would be a long crawl.* But when Marvel's eyes met her father's a look of understanding passed between them. And they smiled....

"It wasn't possible to keep quiet, what with all the 'phone calls back and forth," Mother, wiping a sweat-soaked strand of ripe-corn-colored hair from her forehead, whispered back. "I didn't think you'd mind too much, sweetie—except at school, and you handled that."

Mind? No, not really. Actually, it was better this way. People surrounding them...everybody talking at once...bringing food ...and helping efficiently. And from the gathering of caring friends there came a new sense of identity, a realization of just how important Dale, Snow, and Marvel Harrington were to them. Their rural world revolved around the small family. How could they carry on? What was to become of them now? The community would die down again: no church, no women's groups, prayer meetings, singings, baseball games. And they would be lost completely without Marvel's newspaper columns. Even their names would fade away and people would forget there once had been people in this valley of dry bones. Maybe God would look away in scorn and forget them, too. That was too much for Dale Harrington to swallow.

"Oh, come now! Some sort of send-off you're giving us! What do you mean God will forget? That's news to me—that our Creator has a poor memory. You know better. What'll Brother Grady say to *that*?"

Brother Grady *is* coming back? Honest engine! He *is*? Oh swell!

Marvel was proud of her father at that moment, proud of him in a new way: his strength born of their weakness. Boldly, he said: "Brother Grady Greer is indeed returning, and with the new wife you've known and loved as Mrs. Sutheral—"

A cheer went up. But Daddy hadn't finished. Raising a grimy hand for silence, he finished with a startling promise. "And *we* will be back, too. That's a promise!"

The tide had turned. The mourners were now the comforters. Mother and Daddy were in charge of their own emotions and called to lead others who had come to depend on them. A festive atmosphere filled the overcrowded shack, with excitement enlarging like a bottled-up genie released from captivity and puffing out like a rain-filled cloud.

"What an adventure! We're downright envious of y'all—travelin' like that, seein' th' world only uh few of us what's blessed with uh memory like God's (So God had regained his memory, Marvel thought with a smile inside) rec'lect from gorgraphy books ever heered uv. Oh boy!"

In the midst of it all, Mother honored the frequent requests to play her violin. She played victoriously and with such fervor that some of the composers would have failed to recognize their compositions.

Her audience loved it and joined in as she played "Bringing in the Sheaves" in near-ragtime, turning then to the old folk songs she knew they enjoyed: "Little Brown Jug," "Turkey in the Straw," and "Dixie."

So much had happened that Marvel was hardly surprised when a familiar voice called from the front door: "How 'bout you play 'Carry Me Back to Ole Virginny' for me, Miz Snow, hon?"

Fanny!

The group sang, Fanny's throbbing, hauntingly beautiful voice rising above the others. Had the women seen her ancestors' homeland ever? Or hadn't the black folk done a better job of passing on to their children reminders of their African heritage than their fair-skinned European brothers? Marvel wondered then about the yellow race. The only Oriental with whom she'd had the slightest contact was the ultra-polite boarder of her grandparents. Chinese, wasn't he? And weren't they at odds with the Japanese to whom America was exporting scrap iron? Ugly thought! When our country knew it would be forged into the weapons of war? In spite of the warmth in the gathering twilight and the merriment of those around her, Marvel shivered. She had remembered a quote she had forwarded to Titus regarding the last war: "It took the horrors of war to bring a depression to its unmourned end. One could say what started with a crash ended with a boom." And that was before *the* Depression started by *the* crash. Oh no, surely not... not to end in *the* world war, the second—maybe the last one! What a price to pay! One always paid a price. One always did, at any level. This prosperity in California and Oregon—was it worth the price of tranquility? But the die was cast, like Mother said. There was no turning back.

Preparations moved more rapidly after Fanny's welcome arrival. Everything went into boxes or crates with few questions from Fanny—and equally few explanations. "Yes'm, your gran' mamma done sent me—Yes'm, th' Duchess is countin' on y'all being there come tomorrow."

Tomorrow—that would be Friday. Good timing, as the Harrington caravan was scheduled to leave before dawn on Monday morning.

Methodically, Fanny listed what each container held and turned her attention to hand-washing intimate garments (carefully measuring water brought along from the hotel) and folding them into suitcases which would be roped onto the top of the old but "purring like a kitten" (according to Jake) Essex. All was in readiness except for packing in the feather bed, pillows, and quilts—and yes, the three-of-this and three-of-that for meals. Fanny smiled with satisfaction.

*Oh, bless her!* Fanny's heart was broken, Marvel knew, saying good-bye to people who knew her and her family—these wonderful "whites" who accepted them as equals. Fanny hungered for love even more than for bread. Love was harder to come by. But still she sang:

> Carry me back to ole Virginny—back where th' cotton, th' corn an' 'taters grow—
> Back whar th' birds warble sweet in th' springtime,
> Dat's whar dis darky's hart am long to'go.

"Oh Fanny!" Marvel cried out, suddenly overcome with emotion. "I'm going to miss you. You're family. My family and yours are one."

The familiar ebony arms wound about Marvel tenderly. And, as if she were a child again, Fanny—one hand still clutching the feather duster—rocked her to and fro. " 'Hush, li'l baby, don' say uh word, Daddy's gonna buy you uh mockin' bird....' Course we'se—we're all fam'ly—all God's chuld'ern—children. You and me's gonna make us uh promise, askin' th' Lawd—Lord God's blessin' I, Fanny, swear to keep on readin' th' Word. Now, be hushin'—me an' you knows that t'be th' tie what binds. 'Sides, Missy, Mr. Dale's comin' back—like—" Fanny's pearly-toothed smile was radiant, "Ole Black Joe. Me, I'm dependin' on you, honey chile, t'see yore papa keeps dat—that—promise. Makes no matter iffen—if his head's hangin' low as de ole song says 'bout Ole Joe. Make sure, baby, Mr. Dale comes home. Hear?"

Marvel heard—and heard what her heart said as well. For a plan had taken shape—one that must be discussed with Mother and Daddy—and none too soon, as circumstances were to prove.

Meantime, her mind carefully stored away a thought for the uncertain future: "We *are* the same family, the same coin, each of us an emblem on opposite sides, to complete that circle. Trapped, so to speak, both of us—trapped by the world's expectations and by our own expectations of ourselves—being what we are allowed to be as opposed to what we *ought* to be. But we can glimpse into each other's souls and find our own—see in them the 'other self' we never see in ourselves, just *feel*. But God knows and understands."

The conversation left Marvel feeling herself to be a character in the one-day book. What had begun as a shared dream was now being lived out. First, she had stepped into Fanny's shoes. It took only a single step forward then to step into her mother's and a single step back to fill her grandmother's. Now she could listen to them, learn from them, in a new way. The whole world lay illuminated in a new person, a Marvel she had never known before. The end was an unfinished symphony, depending on more than love's young dream. *Titus!*

She folded away the souvenirs of their past, filled up with bittersweetness: shy notes and more personal letters—in chronological order—along with with countless newspaper articles, Titus's sentimentally gentle valentine, and finally the elegant gloves. Had she left anything out? On impulse, Marvel placed the pearl necklace gently on top of her other valuables. "Thank you, Uncle Fred," she whispered. "You wanted me to wear these for that special man in my life. You were right. Pearls are not for tears, they're for love." Pearls and a blue dress Titus had asked her to be wearing for their next meeting. Quickly, she closed the box.

"Finishing, honey?" Mother called from the bedroom door. "I left my violin for last. We may want music. And what do you think we should do with the furniture? There are so many marble-topped and claw-footed pieces, outdated but valuable maybe—in memories. So?"

"Keep them!" Daddy's crisp voice was like a command. "They're from the old house that I call home. Mother Riley has offered."

Grandmother had offered so much, including copies of *Stretching to Survive* for ladies who shared Depression recipes. That meant everybody had extras to take along. For certainly there had been no increase in population in the community of Morning Glory Chapel. Instead, there was a steady decrease—something nobody talked about.

Moving the pieces, obviously precious to Daddy, would present no problem. "Cap" Bumstead had offered use of his truck. Mother suggested that the Bumsteads be given the wall telephone. Fine, fine, Daddy agreed. The time was now. Marvel made the bold suggestion then that Fanny should have the radio. Others could gather there. Who knew?

Her parents had no chance to respond. Suddenly the house was surrounded with friends—friends from the surrounding neighborhood and, miracles of miracles, the bottomland folk! Surely they had scrimped and saved for this—maybe deprived their own families. But sharing was God's law and theirs: watermelon-rind pickles, persimmon preserves, wild blackberry jelly, and home-baked bread! The date labels for "putting up" the spreadings had been conveniently stripped away. And nobody asked questions. They simply "dived in" as invited and "made pigs of themselves." Marvel listened to their quaint sayings and smiled.

These people were virtuous and giving, as well as being acceptant. What she thought of as the "other self" of her realized now that understanding was a two-way road. The neighbors had once considered the Harringtons their betters, but had come to accept them, as they were accepting Fanny's family—no more "uppity folks," "po' white trash," or "niggers." And tonight, under the most trying circumstances, sadness was gone from the farewell.

When Fanny brought a platter of meat "straight from de smokehouse," stuffed with the last of "de sweet 'taters," the crowd devoured every last crumb. It very well could have been a 'possum "treed" by one of the several lanky hounds. Fanny's face glistened with sweat—or was it joy? Laughingly, she said, "Wake up, Uncle Hezzie!"

He, like Old Ned, had dozed off with watermelon-rind preserves drizzling down his chin. That's what it would be like someday—someday before the Dale Harrington family could return. These two, like Grandmother and Grandfather's boarders, would doze off, with samples of their "Last Supper" on their fronts, and snooze away peacefully until God gave them a wake-up call—sad, but beautiful, all of it!

Mother's eyes were misty, but Daddy said in a little aside to Marvel, "Give these people *anything*, Precious—anything but the family Bible. And come to think of it, we just may enter their names in it!"

Marvel felt herself drifting far out on an ocean of love when the guests formed a circle around their hosts and sang, "Blest Be the Tie That Binds." She floated farther when there was a sudden shuffle of positions in order for all to crowd around when presenting their gift. How lovely! A friendship quilt top, every person's name embroidered on a square of unbleached domestic cloth and beneath each was an appliqued morning glory blossom. All were cut from the same pattern, but none matched in color. Few had heavenly-blue scraps and so they substituted whatever they had. The result was pleasing and heartwarming, a garden of color—as different as the givers but all blending into a bright bouquet. One hardly knew whether to laugh or cry at polka-dotted and red-checked flowers.

All were talking at once. "This'll make sure you got somethin' t'remember us by..." (as if they could forget!) and "You'll hafta finish th' quiltin'—we figgered justa top would lighten the load..." (it certainly would—in more ways than one).

Mother distributed the cookbooks while Daddy spoke with "Cap," and Marvel, with Fanny. Yes, they would wait until the crowd left.

The Bumsteads readily accepted the telephone (having sold their box for a song). "I calculate it's easier gettin' th' thingamajig off'n th' wall directly—two heads bein' better'n one. Me an' th' missus here's been wishin' on this. Wife's got—where's th' claw hammer, Dale? Like I was sayin'—"

Mrs. Bumstead laughed. "Men—always doin' one job and thinkin' on another. Marvel, the Captain wanted you should have some warm gloves. I copied the idee from Sears catalog and knitted these here."

Marvel's gasp of delight repaid Mrs. Bumstead's long hours of work. "I'll treasure these forever!" And Marvel meant the words. "Imagine me with custom-made gloves—my favorite blue with *my* initials!"

The Bumsteads were happy. Fanny was different. She was a giver, not a taker, Fanny said. "Receiver," Marvel corrected gently. "We must learn to be both, even in our relationship with the Lord."

"Dat—that's a pow'ful responsibility. Hard t'live by—"

"Don't you *want* the radio, Fanny?"

"'Course I duz—I mean—"

Marvel smiled. Her tactic had worked. "You've earned it a thousand times over. But yes, it carries a responsibility. Somebody needs to carry on our tradition out here. We've put the burden on *you*."

Fanny's caramel face was vexed. "You means—you cain't mean the likes of *me*! *Me*—askin' white folks—" She paused, and the air was weighty with indecision. "I done feel like it's Chris' mas—gettin' uh gift and me none t'give back—"

"That's the way life seems sometimes, but there's love!"

"Your little friend here's right, you can know," Mrs. Bumstead said softly. "Me'n the Captain just need uh invite!"

Neither Marvel nor Fanny had noticed that they had an audience and that it included a host of bright-eyed little faces, black noses pressed flat against the screen door. Fanny took one look at those expectant faces then, when she met the eyes of the adults, her own face decorated the bare room with a Christmas star. And suddenly they were all singing with the kind of joy that winds could never steal:

> Have you had a kindness shown? Pass it on!
> 'Twas not given to thee alone, pass it on.
> Let it travel down the years, let it wipe another's tears,
> Till in heaven the deed appears—pass it on.

* * *

The day dawned bright, clear, arched in blue. And the wind had shut its mouth. But that had all changed by the time the Harringtons had gathered at the comically formal request (command really) of one Alex Jay Harrington, Esquire. The old hotel's aching bones creaked and groaned as it bent with the wind. But Leah Johanna Mier Riley, bustling about in a ruffled pink apron which matched her cheeks, said cheerfully that a gloom day did not spell doomsday. The prophecy was wrong in this case.

Grandfather cleared his throat almost apprehensively and took over. "Now that we've gathered around the table, let's ask Brother Greer to lead us in a word of prayer. Grady?"

Grady Greer rose from his place beside Mrs. Sutheral Greer. "Dear God, we praise You for this time together and for this food so lovingly provided by You and so lovingly prepared by Your servants. Guard these loved ones as they leave us, forced by need to search for a better way. But we pray that they will not buckle under to Satan who would have them believe that money is king that it makes man immortal. If we should never meet again on this earth, we would that they take with them the blessed assurance that immortality is Your gift. Forgive our gluttony— soppin' up gravy without giving You thanks for the bread. Keep us—keep us—oh, keep us, blessed Lord—in the name of Your Son. You know—Y-You know wh-what it's like to part. *Amen!*"

Grandfather's eyes were too bright, his voice unnecessarily forceful—again to cover his emotions as dear Brother Grady had been unable to do. "I had planned on speeching now—*ahem*—but these devilish winds seem bound and determined to nest in my throat. Oh well, be glad for you're undoubtedly hungry as a herd of wild horses. I see the Duchess here's just itching to bring on the wedding feast. Brother Grady'll have something to say on that, so pitch in and feed your faces!"

All eyes were focused on the blushing bride. But it was Elizabeth Sutheral Greer's new husband who handled the news conference.

"Yes," he said, "I decided the best insurance policy was to take myself a wife full of knowledge on the matter of food! And so, with pleasure, I present my *nutritious* Mrs. Grady Greer!"

Laughter and handshakes from those who could reach across the table followed. But Grandmother, a bit out of sorts at the change of plans, made an announcement of her own. "We will postpone the revelry for now. You men may kiss the bride later, but dinner's ready. Sooo, come and get it or I'll throw it out!"

Wide-eyed, obviously believing every word, Sula Mae and Casper rushed in carrying a ham surrounded by hush puppies, and then trotted back for the remainder of the bountiful meal. Each time they deposited a dish, the young people told tidbits regarding the wedding.

"Me an' Sula Mae standed!" Casper confided.

His sister looked at him in scorn. "Sula Mae and *I*." The big dark eyes rolled from Marvel to Mary Ann righteously. To Casper she continued: "You gotta learn I'm older and a *lady*—that makes me mo' impo'tant." Casper sniffed indignantly in quick exit, leaving Sula Mae to tell it her way. But he left Billy Joe in charge of eavesdropping.

Please, Marvel and Mary Ann weren't s'posed to be mad 'bout the two of them standing up with Brother Grady and Missus Sutheral... 'twas ast of 'em... on account Brother Grady just 'bout had to hurry 'n git preachin' back t'goin—what with Miz Snow 'n Massy Dale leavin' 'n all.

Other talk of the quiet no-fuss ceremony was in progress. The *why* of it was logical. The Joseph, Emory, Worth, and Dale Harringtons had enough to cope with, and since Fanny, Sula Mae, and Casper were handy, well, why *not* set the date up? Fanny, sworn to secret, had sung a solo. Grandmother had played the wedding march, and Grandfather gave the bride away. Dear Dr. Holt had come from Culverville First Baptist. The event served a nobler cause, too: brought a roomful of black and white folks together and let them talk—*really* talk—not preach, but break bread together and pray. What's more, Brother Grady emphasized, it did no harm for preachers to fellowship either. After all, the church in Culverville was sponsoring the new church here in Pleasant Knoll (too bad the Harrington brothers would miss out on the mortgage burning!). And surprise, the Southern Baptist Association had learned about Morning Glory Chapel and would be sending representatives, almost certainly for the sole (S-O-U-L, he spelled out) purpose of taking the little church under their wing as a missionary project.

"Feathers!" Billy Joe interrupted. "See, Gran'mere, I told you God had wings!"

Aunt Dorthea and Aunt Eleanore, who had remained aloof until now, looked horrified. Erin said, "Marvel, you won that silly picture memory contest. Tell B.J. there about Pegasus, the winged horse."

Marvel ignored her as Grandmother had ignored Billy Joe. But Mary Ann said enough for both. "That was mean—mean and *horsey*! You know that was a myth, and Billy Joe knows the whole story."

"And lots more," Billy Joe, encouraged, said proudly. "I know one thing for sure: There'll be no wings for you. You're no angel!"

"So why don't you grandchildren fly in here and give us a hand with the dessert—hum-m-m? Fanny baked a big cake for the wedding but saved pieces for the family—and *everybody's* favorite: buttermilk pie!"

Busy with dessert, the group scarcely noticed when Marvel asked her grandmother to excuse her and hurried to do an errand she had forgotten until now. Surely, in the noisy din of voices, the ring of the telephone would go unnoticed, too. Talk centered around last-minute planning, of course. Marvel did hear a quick, emotional exchange between Grandmother and Mother. "I'm right proud of you, little Snow White—coming through as I knew you would. It's in your blood"..."I—I guess you knew me—better than I knew myself. I *am* excited, but sad that it has to be this way—sad for those who go and those who stay. Oh Mother"... "I know, I know, darling—Mothers always know. But in a way I wish I were going, too"... "Oh Mother, come with us—" "No," Grandmother shook her head as if to resist temptation, "I remember the call of the trail, but my ramblin' days are finished—and I belong *here*"... "With the Squire?" "With the Squire!"

But Grandmother had her memories—and her present. Maybe a future? She and Grandfather owned the hotel now, so one day— Marvel put the thought aside as she had postponed plans for herself and Titus.

Using a low voice, Marvel, in the shadowy-quiet of the hall, asked Central to call the number furnished her by the sanitarium where Elmer Salsburg was receiving treatment. In keeping with her promise, she explained that she would be leaving the state and would forward an address as soon as her family was settled. Meantime, they must feel free to call Elmer's stepgrandfather. She gave the number and hurried back, hoping not to be detected. She needn't have feared that.

Grandfather was delivering his promised message. "Now, my sons, I wish I could offer each of you a birthright, like in olden days. Crippled joke, huh? Being your father has earned *me* a right instead: the right of speaking out and expecting you to listen. At this age, these legs of mine have got to be wobbly, but I'm not wobbly in the head! I can still conduct business and be proud of the fine old family name. Now, I'm asking that not one of you soils it. Brother Grady here made mention of his life insurance policy—right well taken, too, a good wife being more precious than rubies. But your father's sending along another: a copy of the Holy Bible—best life insurance policy the Duchess and I've found, and the one you boys grew up on. And I expect you all to use it. It's your bounden duty to raise up your offspring proper-like as head of your household. Give them a purpose, otherwise, they'll return to dust like this sorrowful land. You're going to find things a whole lot different where you're heading— yep! You've known about honky-tonks and speakeasies in the cities—and rotgut called moonshine bootleggin' right here in the thickets. But you boys are bound toward where the makings grow—and temptations grow bigger! So keep your wits about you. You'll need a clear head when lowlifes out yonder go treatin' your womenfolk like dishrags! Be *Harringtons*!

"Well—*ahem!*—it's confession time now. Even a Harrington can be wrong. *I* was! I tried to create you all in my own image, and only God has that divine right. 'Bankers all!' I said when I looked on each newborn with pride. So I put you in a cage, so cocksure I was right. And in a way," the somewhat sad figure, once the domineering patriarch, said nostalgically, "I *was* right, hang it all! You see, back then *God* was the customer we catered to. We bankers didn't take advantage of the poor, the needy, the widows, and orphans. We helped pull them out of the ditch—" Grandfather's voice rose in frustration then. "We were taught that if we did the right things, bank profits would take care of themselves. So we dressed fit to kill in black business suits and shirts as white and clean as our intentions. But evil creeps in where there's money, and your old dad's as sure as he's standing here today that the Almighty will stand only so much, then crash goes the market! But we all paid the high price.

"All right, in winding down here, men, shamefaced and feeling as foolish as Adam's off-ox, I grant you a freedom from slavery! You've earned it." Alexander Jay Harrington, Esquire, scratched his head. "No joshin'—maybe there's something to be said on that. Could be that we all have to become good slaves before we're good masters—reckon? You might give that thought a whirl when using discipline on your own offspring. Then they can serve *freely*. Well, that's off my chest, but I'm not finished with my own confession. I was the biggest rule-hater this vale of tears ever heard tell of—you betcha boots. Man! How I hated that old organ my mother—rest her soul—made me play. *Hated* the thing! And could *she* keep good time—not with a metronome ticking on top of the instrument, but with a peach-tree branch switching back and forth like a clock's pendulum over my head! But I rebelled. I vowed to get even, I would. And I did! Mother pushed me into playing in a church recital at our church, so I wheezed away, dropping all the flats. And I'm here to tell you that I doubt if the congregation's recovered to this day—or the collection, either!"

Everybody had relaxed and was laughing with recovered merriment. Grandfather waited for the laughter to subside to pull his black cat from the bag. "Yep! I got even. Only life has a way of getting the last laugh, always the loudest. You see, I'd give the rest of my hair to play that instrument now. But I'm paying the price of rebellion.

"But we have to find out these things for ourselves. So be yourselves. Do what you feel you're best at doing to help the Lord get this earth back on its axis—even if it means oiling the poles Admiral Byrd's making such a to-do over. I hope I haven't been so long-winded that I put you young people to sleep. You see, I want what's best for you, my grandchildren. You're our hope of tomorrow. It's an awesome world out there, with roads leading every which way. Wars and rumors of wars are a fulfillment of this holy insurance policy I'm sending along—to—to keep your eyes focused on heaven when you're about to enter the very gates of hell!"

Grandfather Harrington's impassioned speech gave Marvel so much to think about, and it was easy to see that the others felt the same. There was no time for thinking, however. Something was wrong—*very* wrong.

Tragedy had struck. Marvel knew instinctively this was so the moment Jake raced into the room, his boyish face grease-smudged from work at Newlands' Repair and a Magnolia Oil cap on backward. "Sorry," he said breathlessly, "but there's fire—and it looks bad from here!"

Fire! All raced out in panic. Where, *where*? But Marvel knew and, drained of feeling, she turned desperate eyes toward Morning Glory Chapel, where all their earthly possessions waited to be loaded. And there, in hideous glory, wind-whipped flames leaped up in fiery triumph. The gates of hell *could* gape open on earth, she supposed. Grandfather was right.

# 38

# Rumor and Reality

The crimson scarves of brightness might well have heralded a sunrise or sunset—except that colors wavered like uncertain tides, paused mockingly only to burst in another location like a fireball and send flaming debris every direction. The winds shrieked in glee and, even from a great distance, the kiln-like heat, laden with ashes and stifling clouds of smoke, made breathing almost impossible.

Nobody spoke during the nightmarish ride to what had been the Dale Harrington house—or houses. It was obvious that building after building was ablaze in the fire storm. Marvel would never recall with clarity details of the tragedy, just impressions. In a world of unreality, she was dimly aware that her father was in no condition to drive due to his convulsive coughing. One day she must learn to drive. But for now Jake Brotherton had taken the wheel and a silent Mary Ann sat beside him. Her left hand gripped Jake's forearm and her right arm encircled Billy Joe's trembling shoulders protectively. As for the others, under ordinary circumstances it would have come as a surprise that the entire Harrington clan had come along—as well as Archie Newland whom she hadn't seen for months (or was it years?).

Time, too, had lost its meaning. It was lost in a fire so furious it might well have heralded the end of the world...and the wind Gabriel's trumpet. No! Some distant part of Marvel cried out. This devilish wind could have no part in the heavenly realm. The trumpeter was Satan himself....

Marvel leaped from the car before Jake brought it to a complete stop. Daddy was coughing so violently now that Mother refused to leave him. "Roll up the windows, darling," she said to Marvel instead. "I—I'm needed m-more here—"

Which was true. It was better by far that Mother be spared the pain that would surely come when the numbness wore off. She elbowed her way through the crowd. Who were they? Where had they all come from?

"Where'd all th' bottomlanders go when they hightailed it out like scared rabbits?"..."Disappeared—plum disappeared like th' ghosts they laid claim on seein'"..."That's right," another voice yelled above the roar of the flames, "I'd forgotten their unnatural fear of fire. Goes back to that strange swarm of fires that took the old Harrington mansion. Never did get the straight of that"..."Over a hundred degrees back in town. My skin's parched, trying to do battle with this—no water, no anything but a prayer"..."Usin' that middle-bustin' plow was uh good idee—stopped th' demon from spreadin'—but this infernal wind's carryin' it. *Look*, got th' t'other buildin'—last uv 'em"..."Oh, how in tarnation we gonna tell 'em?"..."Anybody in there?"..."Sure—"

Brushfires ... three house fires ... old outbuildings ... flaming manure piles. Exploding—exploding to ignore the dead forest of once-living trees. And there they stood, ghosts of the past, now burning again in an overkill effigy of warning. It made no sense, no sense at all—and neither did the blackened faces milling everywhere.

The family was as confused and shocked as Marvel. Even her parents had joined the crowd. Daddy shouldn't be here. Nobody should....*Oh, dear God, we need You*, Marvel's heart cried as the last building collapsed. Coals spread almost to the feet of helpless bystanders, and they were driven by the intense heat. Rumors spread as fast as the fire.

Rumor 1: Folks tried to reach the poor souls who perished in the house occupied by the Harringtons— Even tried to kick the door open. 'Twas padlocked, you know. No use. They were driven back by heat. Too late ... too late ... no telling how many bodies they'd find in the ashes.

Reality: "Oh Marvel, here you are!" The voice belonged to Annie. "Thank God y'all were gone. We didn't know and I was so worried I had to go and be sick all over the place. Oh, what a prayer meetin' we'll have when this thing's over—and not a life lost—not *one*. Papa got here just a hair before me and Mama— first white person here and can vouch for that. Oh, those poor black folks, so scared their faces were bleached plum white, but they took care of your needs before their own—you know, th' ones who ran screamin' away. I'm sorry, but thankful!"

Rumor 2: A hobo had slipped in through a window. Nobody saw him because he was more afraid of being found there than of the fire. He burned to a crisp, of course. And they'd never put much stock in talk of ghosts, but now everybody *knew* they existed. His white form just came floating out....

Reality: "Mrs. Harrington, I'm Erlene Gilbreath's mother. Hard to recognize neighbors in this kind of mess, particularly poor ones like me. But I'm here to tell you we care, and feel helpless as a one-arm paperhanger stuck in flour paste. This is fierce. But sure brings out the good in folks, don't it though, hon? Take that Mercy Smith, Ruth's mama. I'd a-never took her to have such backbone. But when she heard tell there was somebody trapped in the ole building you all use for storing stuff, you know what? She up and wrapped a sheet around her, lookin' for all the world like she'd come straight from our graveyard, and went chargin' in there like 'th' charge of the light brigade.' Lucky her man heard, went in—nothin' to the rumor—and *throwed* her to safety."

*No lives lost.* Marvel, handkerchief over her perspiring face, looked around her in overwhelming relief. Never mind that all else was gone. She had asked God for help and, as always, He was faithful. Never mind either what lay ahead ... or how the whole thing began.

But, like the fire, rumors flared now from other directions.

Rumor 3: A man trying to see in that pea-soup darkness lighted a kerosene lamp and it exploded in his hands. All started with somebody claiming to smell smoke, not so, and just look what tongue-waggin' done. In this weather, sure, kerosene could explode in a shut room!

Reality: "Mr. Dale, I dunno how to tell you—I just don't. I feel lower'n a snake's belly, blind as them shaggy dogs I used to call y'all when you lined up for haircuts. I 'spect you'll have me arrested, and I'll do time knowin' there was just cause. Oh Mr. Dale—"

"Linc" Denney's pitiful voice choked in dry sobs of remorse, but Daddy's tone was soothing in spite of his brassy hoarseness.

"Go ahead, Linc, you've no cause to worry. I j-just need to know—"

"Thank you, sir. Your kind makes a feller want to go to church— 'n I will, I promise you on my mama's grave. You tell Brother Grady—and—me, *I'll* tell God. I learnt a heap. I'm s'posed to confess—'n I repented a'ready. But I hafta tell y'all *I* set off that fire. Oh, not meanin' to—I'd never do such a thing intentional. But 'member back when th' boys usta gimme qua'ters on occasion for haircuts? I blew some and bought some dum' marshmellers from th' peddler, knowin' how starved they all was for sweet stuff—hard time findin' sticks, then no way safe place *(safe, my hind leg!)* t'duck outta that wind. Would'n' you think I had th' sense God promised uh goose an' say, 'No, we cain't risk usin' Mr. Dale's house for any windbreak—no matter it's vacant.' But the devil was in me but good, and he's laughin' his fool head off now. Minute I struck uh match—poof! Shot sky-high like a bar'l uv gas."

Then suddenly Mary Ann was beside Marvel. Billy Joe had run to stand between Uncle Worth and Auntie Rae. "Oh Marvel," she whispered, "I'm sorry—*so* sorry." Winding her arms about Marvel, Mary Ann went on disjointedly. "You're shivering. Oh, I didn't want to go—you *know* I didn't. But I never wanted something like this—"

Marvel drew back. "You mean—you mean this will stop our plans?"

"Of course. I mean there's nothing left, and you have to have *something*—something," Mary Ann gulped, "to start over— *any*where."

"Including here. We don't even have this now. We have the car and a little money. Oh, I see," Marvel said slowly, "you're thinking that this would hold Uncle Worth back. You know better!"

"I know no such thing. You know Mother and Daddy would never go without Uncle Dale and Aunt Snow, and we're needed here. You always said something good comes from every evil. Our families will stay together, and we'll help like we promised. It won't be so bad—as long as—"

"You have Jake," Marvel finished for her cousin. "How could you use this—this loss to get your way? You don't mean what you said."

"Let me ask *you* one," Mary Ann answered fiercely. "How could *you* leave Titus? Doesn't he want you to stay?"

"Does Jake want *you* to? Don't be angry. None of us can handle that—not now. All I ask is that you think—and hug me again."

Mary Ann did. And Marvel was sure the wetness of her cheeks was due more to tears than sweat. Marvel's tears lay unshed within her heart. Maybe this *was* the "nightfall of the universe" some evangelist had claimed to be at hand. No! Nobody knew when the end would come. Only God held time in His hands. Mankind's job was to be packed and ready to go. *Packed and ready?* Now only stench remained of their preparations.

Rumor 4: The scent—the unbearable scent—could spell only one thing: death! Burning of flesh—animalish, wasn't it just? Yep, same smell as when the cows were slaughtered. Could be those hound dogs from "down yonder" or just could be disease-carryin' rats...flea-bitten 'possums...thirstin' squirrels...or buzzards roostin'.

Reality: "Manure piled up for fertilizing, Mr. Worth. You'll remember how those piles produce heat even in winter. Then take this heat and fire, well, conditions were ripe for this. So good to see you out here again. We've missed you," Mr. Pruitt explained to Uncle Worth. His daughter had joined Archie and they were engrossed in deep conversation. Some part of Marvel was glad that Annie was with him. The greater part listened to the most devastating talk of all.

Rumor 5: Gone—everything those nice Harringtons owned. What a dreadful shame. Everything packed so nice, right at the door ready to be loaded. That wall of fire just gobbled it up faster'n all get-out. Turned out what looked so right up and proved so wrong. Yep, blocked th' door so's nobody could get in, then served to feed the fire.

Reality: By now family members had found each other. Once they clustered, it was easy for neighbors to locate them. Now, surrounded by those who knew the truth, the Harringtons heard the most unbelievable news of the truth. The good news came with such unexpected force that it was harder to bear than the horrors.

"Right proud uv myself, right proud," Captain Bumstead said first. "Proud me 'n you taken th' phone offen th' wall. I got all carried away after y'all left—got some other fellers an' we loaded my truck"..."Hey! Give your betters some credit, too!" his wife half-teased"..."We moved what we could tote—'n Fanny and her folks—well, you tell 'em girl." Fanny? And the furniture was safe? Marvel felt that she was astride a carnival hobbyhorse whirling faster and faster, unable to dismount, until a pair of familiar arms wound about her middle. "Oh honey-baby," Fanny was soothing, "mah precious baby—but ole Fanny heah done tole yuse— you—sorry, my tongue gets all syrupy-like when ah's excited. Onct—once I he'pped Sula Mae and Casper. Now they can pay fo' their rasin'—when you git—get gone. But I got mah radio, too. Playin' us some sermons a'ready—'n what's mo, I cleaned out all them other houses, soon as I made mah kind to understand *he* had'n' come back—that fire-settin' demon—'cause he was cast out an' bound up in chains. Ain't I right, baby?"

"Right enough, Fanny. Oh, my dear, dear Fanny, you're wonderful!"

Questions and answers came from all directions as all sought to believe that the impossible was possible, after all. "That's how it is with God," a new male voice said. It was familiar, but unrecognizable—until the wind, still dissatisfied, puffed new life into a heap of embers. In the brief glow, Marvel saw the speaker's face.

"Dr. Holt!" she exclaimed, "I had no idea—"

"That I would be here in time of trouble? Several Culverville deacons are with me, as this gives the men a better picture—"

"Picture? That's my department, pastor! I'm one of your newest converts. Remember me? Corey's the name, editor of the newspaper." The two shook hands as others clustered around the minister. Editor Corey used the situation to his advantage and pulled Marvel aside.

"You must be exhausted, Marvel, so I'll make this short and sweet. I shot a roll of film soon as I could reach the scene. Doubtful if many turned out by the artificial light of the fire, but worth a try. Your mind probably photographed it all better. Write it all: history of the place, all the human interest stories, facts. I don't need tell *you* how to handle it. Get names—newspapers like 'em. *Savvy?*"

*"Savvy,"* Marvel half-smiled, using the colloquialism that was half Spanish and half of unknown origin. It was good to speak of the fire objectively—something in which she, Mother, and Daddy had no part.

A. Thomas Corey talked on in jerky, hurried sentences. *The News Review* was getting a late-model camera for him. Marvel would please take his vintage box-type Kodak, shoot these rolls of film, and send them C.O.D. to his office along with the stories she wrote of the trip West. Did she need instructions on how to use the Kodak? No sir. Well—was she listening? Her eyes appeared to be taking pictures already.

Marvel smiled, for the editor was right. She *was* looking around her in surprise. For there was Mr. Wilshire, whom she'd not seen since leaving Pleasant Knoll School . . . and Dr. Porter! How had he heard? When Dr. Holt shouldered his way to stand beside the doctor, she realized that he must be one of the deacons. Hadn't Grandfather Harrington said the committee would consider Morning Glory Chapel as a missionary project? But the kind doctor would have come anyway. He had his black bag, the trademark of his profession. Dr. Porter saw her and waved.

Listening? Yes, she was listening all the while. But Mr. Corey's next statement caught her by surprise. "I brought a gift from Mr. Angelo, too. You made quite an impression on that teacher. Not even in his class, I understand—and I regret that. You'd have learned the typing skill. But Mr. Angelo sent along a manual, says you'll learn—"

"How kind of him—how kind of you, too, Mr. Corey. But the manual can't teach me. You see, I own no machine—so—I hunt and punch—"

"*Didn't*—past tense. That's the gift. Culverville High had just two typewriters the first year the trades and industry course was offered, but trustees went hog-wild and bought *three* new ones. I put it in the car you came in. Whoops! Deadline time for the captions for these pictures in case they turn out. Now, you take care, you hear!"

He all but ran to his car. Better for them both. Neither wanted an emotional parting. How sweet the man had been—and how dear of him to bring the gifts. But the greatest gift the editor had brought was news that he had met the Lord, the most faithful friend of all. She turned and looked over the crowd, wishing it were possible to show appreciation to these wonderful people. In their humility, all would have said, "Why, 'twas nothin'— nothin' a-tall." That's how it is with saints, Marvel thought humbly. They never know they are saints. And little could she know that she, Marvel Harrington, was considered among them. . .

Then they were on their way back to the hotel, another change in plans. "We saw it all today," Marvel said in quiet awe, "a preview of hell—and a glimpse of heaven."

"Miracles still happen," Jake said with equal quiet. "I saw more than I can count on my fingers."

Billy Joe was relaxed now and more than a little helpful. "Don't try, Jake. We're not supposed to count on our fingers."

"Or talk so much, young man!" Mary Ann said with a warning in her big-sister voice. "Marvel, I see what you meant—and I understand now. Good can come of evil, if we let it. I see, I truly see *reality*."

Never had the sanctity of life been revealed quite so clearly, its binding force between the spirit and the flesh. Preservation of lives, then added to that, preservation of material needs—and needs of the heart. God had known the importance of them all and satisfied each. A part of Marvel would have died had she lost the precious box of souvenirs: Titus' letters... the newspaper clippings... the valentine... and the pearls. Yes, most of all, the treasured pearls. And Mother had her violin, Daddy, his baseball and the money to take them away. There were some things irreplaceable, of course. A column took shape in Marvel's mind:

There but for the grace of God flee we. The worst wildfire in east Texas history... over 1,000 acres of once-fertile land charred... houses destroyed. Years of drought turned one small community to ashes. When the blistering winds whistled throughout the Dust Bowl, it only took one infernal spark. Let the obliteration of beloved landmarks—a tree, a fence— sound a warning: Next time we could lose *people. This must not happen again!*

# 39

# The Bad Years
# Are Over!

"The future looks good now that the worst has happened!" Alexander Jay Harrington declared in convincing tones. "I was proud of you—all of you—the way you walked away from that trial by fire. Not one of you looked back. I was counting heads."

Grandfather leaned over the cake of ice in the ice chest where he was readying a place for the "mess of bully-beef" purchased from a meat peddler. "Looks larpin' good," he said with approval. "These refrigerated cars are something! I hear tell now that Frigidaire's coming out with electric ones, the kind that make their own ice. But seeing is believing. So will somebody hand me a newspaper to lay tomorrow's feast on? Not the funny page. I haven't read 'Mutt and Jeff' or 'Andy Gump.' We'll all be busy tomorrow, so best all eat here again."

His attitude was contagious. Daddy said he felt like he'd been in a baseball game in which his team was scoreless, absolutely "skunked"—and then, wow! He had knocked a homer and the umpire yelled, "Home safe!"

In the big kitchen, Grandmother hummed as she scrubbed imagined dust from the shining white oilcloth covering the table. Would anybody mind snacking out here without the company linen? Lots of leftovers—and it *was* late. Nobody would. "Nobody" included the two boarders, the Greer newlyweds, and two Harrington sons, Worth and Dale. "Somebody" would come tomorrow night when Uncle Emory and Uncle Joseph's families rounded out the clan, Marvel supposed tiredly.

Uncle Worth had joined Daddy's banter. "I feel like I'd been fishing again, like when our lakes were brimming full, without luck. 'Til all of a sudden the cork started bobbing and I got my catch all of legal size, so no threat from the game warden. Oh boy! Those Oregon streams are said to be teeming with fish—no dynamiting *ever*!"

Mother and Auntie Rae chatted as they joined Grandmother. "I know exactly what the men mean," Auntie Rae said. "I was glad, actually glad, for the first time that you had no canned goods to lose—"

"Oh me, too! Just seeing food destroyed would do me in. And I realized just how fortunate we are to be heading for that land of plenty—that is, as soon as I found we were all safe. But fresh fruit, *umm-m-m*! Remember how much we used to put up, Rae?"

"I remember," Mary Ann said softly. "Oh Marvel, here's Jake—"

Marvel nodded, half hearing. Her tired mind was remembering, too. Again she thought of the bright, shining jars of whole, sun-ripened tomatoes, shelled green beans, spiced beet pickles, and Mother's special green tomato relish splashed with rings of red chili peppers. How fresh they looked after their water baths in the giant copper kettle, how reassuring. One could almost hear them whisper, "Let winter winds blow—we'll sustain you!" Daddy always looked with pride at Mother's accomplishments and commented on her ability to avoid ugly stain on those beautiful and talented hands. Well, they would do it again.

Marvel felt a sharp pain in her back. Her legs ached with fatigue, and her head nodded in spite of herself. She fought off sleep and listened to both conversations. The women were talking about exhilarating news which outshone the fire. Yes, it *was* true—every word of it. Morning Glory Chapel would be rebuilt and, along with it, a small shotgun-style house for Brother Grady and his bride. How good that the Harrington acres were available, and so close. Oh yes, the Bumsteads offered to share their house during construction. It would be "slim pickings" for a time, but the convention had made mention of a small living-expense account. Folks would manage. They'd had experience. The world war held no real meaning for the younger generation, but their parents recalled. Strange, wasn't it, how upstart writers came down with some contagious disease that started them rewriting history every once and so often? George Washington had slaves...Columbus was a woman-hater—never had one female on the *Nina*, the *Pinta*, or the *Santa Maria*. So big deal! Christopher Columbus sailed the ocean blue with an all-male crew. Villain, that's what he was, nothing good about him, just putty in the hands of—aha, a Spanish *woman*! How would history judge this generation—as a bunch of numb-numbs who plundered land like the new history claims *he* did? Or as victims of their times who made do with what they had? There would be those young smarties who class survivors of the era as ignorant know-nothings, the whole shebang—unless somebody tells it like it is while it *is* happening...some good, some bad, but God-fearing.

"We *are* doing it!" Marvel wanted to promise. But some part of her held back. The ladies, so dear to her heart, were right. But so much depended on Titus—Titus whom she was leaving, unless he stopped her.

Through the haze of her fatigue, Marvel turned her other ear to men-talk. The healing process had only begun. Each would handle it differently. Recovery would be slow. Look at the economy!

"Sorry you'll be unable to rent the house, Worth," Grandfather was saying, "but I guess you couldn't expect that. The migration has wiped this place off the map—some heading for California, most never heard tell of Oregon, and others staying put. Young folks get married and live with their families and pray *not* to have what we used to pray *for*. But then, who could blame them? Another mouth to feed, another mind to educate...all for what—cannon fodder? I know the signs!"

Could be, his sons agreed. But things had changed a lot since plastered-down hair, turtleneck sweaters, and bell-bottoms—well, except in the Navy. Everything did hark back to preparedness, after all. Most of California's recovery seemed to hinge on that, but there certainly was little hope for farmers—at least for now. Uncle Worth agreed with Daddy. He would give the world to hear cowbells and see sleek cows coming to the salt licks, their strutted udders swinging to and fro, or hear the snorting and pawings of their ring-nosed mate. Downright opposed to monogamy, that critter, and not much of a papa either, but that bull did his part in replenishing the earth! Okay, that was yesterday, back when farmers could promise sweet peanut hay and water in exchange for high-butterfat production of milk. Couldn't be edited out like Clara Bow's moving pictures. Trashy—speaking of which, it would be nice just to catch a whiff of those "barnyard stinks" or the smell of the old compost heaps where all the corn shucks and pea vines went, along with peelings from the apples and peaches the girls used to put up. What happened anyway? Man produced too much and the bottom fell out of his market, and his family went hungry.

"If I could answer that one, I'd be wealthy enough to *buy* you boys a bank," Grandfather grunted. "Still, I'm feeling about banks—well, as disillusioned as you boys feel about farming. Bankers got greedy and got caught napping. Big-eyed economists ignore the folks in agriculture now, claim they're not consumers. Well, who trusts bankers anymore either? How many rotten apples does it take to rot a barrel? One swindler can cause the world to see all bankers as rats, mites, ticks, wolves—all put together, still in white shirts but sticky-fingered, fish-eyed and flint-hearted. So, even though this roof will cover us all, you've a yearning to stand on your own—"

*As long as you can. The war will take you soon enough.*

Marvel could not bear to hear her grandfather's possible proclamation of a death sentence. The day had been too draining, too packed with grief and emotional swings for a single day to hold. Too much ... too much. Too much for her to find her way home through the conflicting mazes surrounding her body and soul. Her race was run. Now—*now* the tired muscles and jangling nerve endings of her makeup demanded their just toll. She would lie down—oh, only a moment, just lie down—not for sleep.

Slipping into Grandmother's bedroom, she kicked off her shoes and wriggled her toes within the now-soiled anklets. The dress was dirty, too, but she was too tired to pull it up over her head.

With a sigh, Marvel dropped onto the featherbed—and slept.

The slender girl, curled in a little fetal ball, with one blue-veined hand tucked childishly beneath the roundness of her cheek—now flushed with sleep—did not hear the soft footsteps of her mother. For a moment, Snow Harrington looked down at her "baby." For a nostalgic moment, she hesitated, as if longing to take her then-vulnerable daughter into her arms, soothe her, tell her everything would be all right. Instead, she tenderly touched the soft truant curls at her forehead in wonder and whispered,"Oh, my darling, how I wish that we could spare you this. I know—Mothers always know—how much the move from your childhood roots is costing. You have every reason to rebel, but you are too pure of heart. How did God decide to entrust you to us? I don't know what I would do, sweetheart—I honestly don't know—if *I* had to leave the man I love. And my heart tells me you're doing that."

Marvel stirred slightly, and her mother hastily pulled a light coverlet over her bare legs. They were scratched. Oh, that awful fire!

It was Mary Ann who awakened her. "Marvel, wake up—wake up! So much is happening. Jake came, you know, and we talked. Then along came Archie—honest! He's downstairs, says he absolutely *has* to see you. I tried to stall him off, but he's stubborn as Adam's off-ox. You're not moving. Oh, please pile out—*now*!"

"I *can't* move," Marvel groaned, trying to fight off the weariness.

"Here!" Mary Ann handed her a wet washcloth and a hairbrush. "Give yourself a lick and a promise, and make haste! I—I need to talk to you, too. I need your advice. It's important."

Taking the washcloth, Marvel wiped her hot face with the cool cloth then looked at it. Even in the dim glow of the floor lamp that her cousin had turned on she could see the washcloth was covered with soot. She used the other side and ran the brush through her hair. It was no surprise when ashes floated down. Mary Ann took no notice. She was engrossed in talking what sounded like nonsense to Marvel—not that she could hear all that well. The radio downstairs was running stiff competition.

Gentler folks in the rural areas find all this war talk disturbing. The mood of America's pre-war values still prevails in smaller towns of church-goin' people. And a fig for the Roarin' Twenties. . . . Gentle people took no pride in that era. And who's to say they're wrong? The only thing that worries 'em is the unholy emphasis put on the almighty dollar instead of the Almighty Himself! Money and God don't mix any better than water and oil. Well, they can take comfort that they've got themselves some mighty

powerful allies out there layin' claim on the same values.
... Yep! Take the Baptist churches and Methodists likewise
who're packin' 'em in all over the country—urban and
suburban alike.... Evangelist Billy Sunday's still poundin'
his pulpit like he did against strong drink, taking sides for
once with Methodist Bishop Cannon, both up there sluggin'
away in the ring together against the common enemy,
Satan. Too little God and too much money, they say, and
man can't have both. Maybe not, Aimee Semple MacPherson fires back, but *woman* can! She robs the rich and heals
the poor who pack her temple. Well-named, huh? Well, this
world needs healin'—but by an unordained and vicarious,
"Robin' Hood"? MacPherson's doing *something* with a flair,
and until charges of hell-bound frauds are proved, so be it.
But the whole thing worries our president, opposed as he is
to war and knowing the American people look to him for
fixin' things without war—like he promised. Can't be easy.
Still, we gotta look at Europe and Asia....

"I don't want to look!" Mary Ann was protesting. "Have you
been listening to that guy or me?"

"Both—and not liking what either says," Marvel admitted.
"But as to advice, I'm giving none. Count me out on this one.
We're not children anymore, Mary Ann, and grownup decisions
are hard. Have you all talked: you, Jake, Uncle Worth, and Auntie
Rae?"

"No, because their minds are made up. And now *you* don't
understand either—"

Marvel inhaled deeply. "More than you know," she said.

Downstairs, Jake and Archie waited. Archie, Marvel observed,
had scrubbed his face raw and wore a clean white shirt. But his
eyes were unchanged. The expression was still that of an adoring
puppy. She regretted coming down. Her appearance would only
encourage the well-meaning young man. All she could feel was
pity.

In her sympathy, Marvel made a false move. "How nice you
look, Archie. Forgive my appearance. But I'm glad to see you—"

*And tell you how much we appreciate all you did today,* she
had planned to finish. But Archie interrupted. "Oh, I'm glad you
said that!" And immediately she knew her words had renewed his
hope.

Prompted by a need to set things straight once and for all, Marvel did not protest when Archie suggested that they sit in the porch swing until he could "explain some matters." *Poor Archie.*

When the two of them slid through the group, nobody noticed. All ears were on the newscast still in progress:

> So, question here: Do we rebuild our Navy, arm ourselves, give pause to the whisper of something called a one-year draft, somethin' like what we used to call conscription, I'd say . . . a preparation time for young men? Or do we play "ostrich" and hide our heads behind the skirts of protest? You know what Wall Street's sayin': "We're sick to death of hearin' all this doomsday stuff. . . . What this country needs is to focus on our economy . . . invest for the future." What future? But, of course, Americans *do* have enough to deal with here at home, and we're a peace-lovin' nation. Well and good, we *don't* want to involve ourselves overseas. We've been there once, so "Walk on the sunny side of the street" and keep hopin' this continent *is* safely out of shootin' range . . . for now—

For a moment Marvel felt the world spin around her. What was the answer to all this? But if nobody else knew, how could she hope to answer her own question? The news was making her physically ill. That was it: the dizziness, the unaccustomed heartburn, and now the embarrassing rumble of an empty stomach.

"I'm sorry," she murmured faintly. "I—I forgot to eat tonight."

"No wonder," Archie said sympathetically. "Here, hon, sit down. I cain't tell y'all how sorry about th' terrible thang—"

Gratefully, Marvel let herself be seated in the cozy comfort of Grandmother's big, poufy feather pillows. *Feathers*, she thought, smiling. Nobody must let Billy Joe know what the stuffing was.

"Yes," she said quickly, "it *was* terrible. Strange thing, for awhile I felt removed—*far* removed—like I was in the firing fields—"

Again, Archie interrupted. "That's what I come t'tell yuh. So see whatcha think. I'm a whole lot smarter'n folks gimme credit for. Leastwise, I'm gettin' wised up 'nuff t'listen. Them men in

Washington's smart else they would'n be there, so when this
letter come—" he fumbled in his pocket. "Oh, for lan-sake! I
dashed off 'n left it on th' cook table. But maybe Mary Ann's told
'bout it?"

"No—not really—only that Jake was moving out—coming
here?"

"Right! An' that's 'cause of my plans—an' well, his, too. He's
got a right bright future, what with that bank job an' his book-
learnin'. Now's *my* news. I'm gonna foller th' gover'ment's advice,
take me some grammar classes to talk proper, an' enlist! See, if I
pass that big test, I can go in with a kind uv ratin'. What with my
background in th' CCC's 'n all that drillin', my future's bright,
too!"

"Oh excellent!" Marvel said with enthusiasm and relief. Maybe
the news was Archie's reason for calling. Oh, she hoped so. In the
sudden turnaround of feeling, Marvel was caught off-guard. What
was he saying? *Oh no!* her heart cried out at his words.

"So you'll be willin' t'wait?"

"W-what are you—you saying, Archie?"

"I—I thought—"

"You thought wrong, Archie dear—if this is a proposal?"

"Yes'm, it sure 'nuf is. I'll be a heap more suitable now. It'll all
be dif'rent—me, all educated, an' havin' a sure income."

"It's not that. You—you should know better. I've tried to make
it clear that you will always hold a special place in my heart, but
only as a friend—a very *dear* friend. Nothing more."

From the corner of her eye, Marvel saw him drop his head in
his hands. Seeing his awful misery made him all the more dear.
But dare she reach out and comfort him? No, she resolved, she
must not.

Instead, she said tenderly, "I'll never forget all the fun we have
enjoyed, Arch. Nobody can take your place. We were children
together." And then her heart broke some more, for the boy was
weeping!

"Archie, don't! I—I can't bear this—"

Archie awkwardly wiped away his tears and blew his nose.
"But you used t'love me. I can make you love me agin. Gimme uh
chance!"

"I'm sorry if I misled you, Archie. I never loved you *that* way. If I
had, the education and the rating would have made no difference. You know that has nothing to do with real love. I'm proud of

you and want the best for you, so you have my blessing. I urge you to go back to school and apply for the rating if that's what you want. And Archie, I want what's best for your heart, too. You deserve that!"

"If I just knew whatcha wanted, I'd do it or bust! Yore sayin' there's not uh single shred uv hope—nothin' I can do—"

"Yes," Marvel said slowly, "there is something you can do—something that will bring me happiness, Arch. And it will bring you happiness, too, even though you may not believe it now. Just know that we're not children anymore—that we've changed. The whole world has changed. But memories don't change so hold tight to those memories, and don't spoil them now."

"I want t-t-to hold *you*—"

"That's out of the question!" she said curtly. Then, seeing his hurt, she continued in a softer voice, "Just let me find my own way. There's something out there that I need to do, too. The Lord uses us in His way, and I'm learning to listen, too. Now—"

"Then there's nobody else standin' between us?"

Archie needed the truth. In trying to spare him hurt, she had only hurt him more. "I didn't say that, my dear friend. There *is* somebody else now. My heart is committed to him. You'll know what it's like someday and be glad you waited."

"I a'ready know," he said sadly. "And it's not Ruth, or Annie neither. Come on. We gotta git ya'll uh bite in that stum'mick!"

\* \* \*

Marvel's eyes searched the big room for Mary Ann. If she had played any part in this in an effort to hold her here, used her as a pawn to hold Uncle Worth and Auntie Rae in check— But Marvel's suspicions died of shame. How childish to entertain such thinking. Uncle Worth remained with the other men in discussing the likelihood of seeing young America in uniform again. Even Billy Joe, now playing a grown-up role, sat with his head cocked to one side as if he understood it all. Grandmother and Mother rattled dishes in the kitchen, but the clatter failed to cloak the sounds closer by: Mary Ann and Auntie Rae's voices engaged in a low but fight-to-the-finish conversation. Where was Jake?

The sound of his voice answered her question within moments. Jake was talking with Archie on the front porch. "Better

stay for the president's fireside chat. He'll square with us"...
"Nope, I ain't up t'listen'in', mood I'm in. Women! One beggin'
t'stay 'n th' other hell-bent on goin'. Plan on holdin' her here,
don'cha, pal?"... "No!"

Marvel drew back as if struck by a blow. Jake wasn't in favor?
Life was strange. No wonder people from other countries found
Americans a peculiar lot. And, to her surprise, Grandfather was
saying the same thing in different words. "Wouldn't you think
*everybody* would listen tonight? War talk thick as molasses in
January, but they've got more interest in boxing! Peculiar, don't
you think, a colored prize fighter thinking on climbing Jacob's
ladder into the ring to take on that Max—what's his name?—
Schmeling? A *German*! Both need some schoolin' on how to
speak English!"

"We Americans could do with some coaching ourselves,"
Daddy laughed. Then, seeing Marvel, he motioned her toward
him. And, holding onto his hand, she readied herself for the
golden voice of Franklin Delano Roosevelt:

> My friends: (Marvel, listening to the calm, resonant
> voice, envisioned the president seated in the Oval Office,
> hands gripping the arms of his wheelchair but a coura-
> geous smile on his face in case a photographer for "Time
> Marches On" newsreel were lurking nearby) I hope you are
> listening throughout this wonderful land over which flies
> the flag of freedom! And, God willing, it will stripe the sky
> with red, white, and blue of our land of the brave forever-
> more. That is a prayer...and that is my promise to the
> American people. Whatever else may be said of this admin-
> istration, let it be said that this president was a man of his
> word. On taking oath of office, I promised a sacred promise
> that most banks would reopen with your help, my friends—
> if Congress would act quickly and effectively to reorga-
> nize...and you would fight off phantom fear...pull savings
> from beneath your mattresses...have faith...and not
> be stampeded by rumors. I have kept that promise and,
> although we continue to drift from the goal, we *will* reach it!
> Together we cannot fail! Through the New Deal, I kept that
> promise, and I now repeat my next one: *Your sons will never
> be sent to fight some other country's wars....We MUST*

*remain neutral.* So I ask that you put those ugly rumors to sleep and do your part to reduce poverty here at home, and let us continue foreign trade. It is the hungry or the greedy who wage wars. *The worst is over!*

# 40

# So Long As We Both Shall Live

Today might well have been any other—except that it wasn't. It was the last day of togetherness for the Harrington clan remaining in Titus County, Texas. Over them hung the cloud of farewells unspoken—silver-lined with hope, to be sure, but a cloud all the same.

Everything was loaded for the journey. The men had taken care of that. "Woman's place is in the kitchen," Daddy had declared with a teasing pinch of Mother's cheek. His reward had been a wrinkle of Mother's nose and a playful push from the quarters to which he had sentenced her.

And now with the makings of the meal done, except for the finishing touches, they had gather 'round for Grandfather's suggested "sweet hour of prayer, followed by food, fun, and fellowship."

"Is there time for a walk?" Mary Ann asked the group-at-large.

"Oh certainly," Grandmother smiled. "You young people need to exercise to *groan* on, and that presents no problem—seeing that Mr. Bumstead called. Bless his heart! Fanny wanted to come and missed the last load, so I thought we'd wait for her. 'Twould warm her heart."

"And mine!" Marvel said with a sudden burst of emotion. Just how much time was to tell....

But for now, the Harrington grandchildren rose in unison. "You'd think they were responding to 'All in favor, say *aye*'! And I need to talk with you—alone," Mary Ann said fiercely.

The others needed to talk, too—talk and escape. The decision had been made. Right or wrong, there was no turning back, but all had private feelings of ambivalence they were sure in their youth that parents and grandparents did not understand. This was a new generation.

"This wind—I hate it," Cindy moaned, busily tying a scarf over her head. "There, I look like an old crone."

*"Refugee!"* Billy Joe put in. "Just like over the ocean."

"Don't say that word," Mary Ann almost pleaded, "not after the news—"

"But I thought it was good, the president's speech—what part I heard," Erin said. "There won't be a war, I heard him promise."

It was Duke's turn. "One man can't promise that to the world and you're right, you didn't hear it all—none of us did. Static's bad and parts faded away. Something else worries me: his health."

"It's Uncle Dale's health we have to think about, Duke," Mary Ann said to Marvel's surprise—Mary Ann who vowed last night not to go!

Her mind went other-directional now. What if—just what if the troubled nation *should* lose its leader? Oh, if she could only talk with Titus, hear from him—*anything*! He would know the answers. But of course, given a coveted minute, they would not talk of such possibilities. *We'd talk about our love—put it into words.*

Marvel forced her mind back to the present. Both Duke and Thomas were talking. Duke had decided to try for the Royal Air Force, after all. England was preparing for war, just in case. Not that American volunteers in the R.A.F. would see action—just money and training, in case something *did* happen here. One had to read between the lines, realize the situation President Roosevelt was in, trying to hold down war panic among Americans knowing what panic did on Wall Street. At the same time, he was sort of preparing them. It was like Dr. Porter's practice of feeling a pulse. Exactly, his younger brother was agreeing, but it would be awhile for *him*—too young, they claimed. He would enlist when he graduated—maybe even have a rating by then. Could be, huh, Duke? Yes, could very well be. Did the girls know the government might build an armory in Culverville or close by? Until then, reserves were training how to march and clean their guns in the old abandoned bank building at the county seat. The boys would transfer to wherever they went.

Thomas spotted two other boys, vaguely familiar to Marvel, but it had been a long time since she was in touch with most of Pleasant Knoll.

"They're leaving here, too, and I want to see if their transfer papers came through in good order." With that, Duke and Thomas clicked their heels and did a clumsy salute. "See you at dinner— pronto."

"Well, *sick 'em!*" Cindy said in disdain. "They give me a pain."

Erin giggled and clicked her heels in mockery. Marvel noted absently that the younger girl was wearing heels—not that she needed the height. "Me—I'm not paying any mind to their prattle. Let's go back. My feet hurt, and you wanted to stop by the family plot."

"Not me!" Billy Joe said, rolling his eyes. "That's where *dead* people live. I'm going to Gran'mere's and listen with Monica. Fanny's coming and she knows about ghosts. Hurry up, I'm starving." And with that, he hurried away.

Moments later, Mary Ann and Marvel—as if by mutual desire— turned toward the house left vacant by the Worth Harringtons. Together, the cousins looked wordlessly at the ruin to which it had fallen. The porch was sagging, one doorstep was missing, the paint was peeling, and the roof showed signs of neglect. It looked so sad and lonely.

Mary Ann's voice sounded as if she needed to swallow. "Let's sit here—here on the porch—just a minute. Nothing left in there but ghosts of the past, lots of memories for me—but they can't be packed."

"They'll go with you, Mary Ann—with *both* of us. I lived there, too."

Mary Ann nodded. "We have so much in common—you and me. Same houses . . . I'm not apt to forget I lived out yonder either. And to tell you the truth, the land got in my blood, too. But that's a whole 'nother story. I meant to say, we've got the same birthday—twins kinda—and twins *think* alike, uh, even more than they look alike."

"Sometimes," Marvel murmured, still wondering what happened to change her cousin's mind. Obviously *something* had.

"Oh Marvel! I hurt bad—so bad—way down deep where other people can't see."

"But feel, Mary Ann. I can feel your hurt because I hurt, too."

"We were born in the wrong generation—"

"Or the most challenging," Marvel tried to soothe, but the ache in her own heart was too great. Like ironed-in wrinkles which clung stubbornly until the next wash, the past begged for the wash of tears.

She stole a look at Mary Ann and saw fat tears on her cheeks— tears the other girl wiped away with an impatient hand. "I'm trying. I honestly am trying to accept that, for I know you're right. But it's harder for me than for you—and oh, it was awful—"

"Last night?"

Mary Ann's shoulders were shaking. "Last night—yes. But I can't talk about it, and I've *got* to. Oh Marvel—" Her voice broke then.

Reaching out, Marvel embraced the shaking shoulders. "Would it help if I—I told you how *I* feel?" At Mary Ann's nod, she went on. "All right," she said, realizing that the words surprised her as much as her cousin, "let me tell you that I'd give the world to have a second chance—go back and relive those precious moments that I—I let slip away while I lived a—well, it's a blunt word but the truth—I lived a *lie* pretending to be so brave for the sake of others. And if God would give me a chance I'd kick, I'd scream, I'd rebel—wage a different kind of war! I'd *throw* myself at Titus— never mind what other people thought. I'd—I'd say the first 'I love you!'"

Mary Ann shook her wealth of shining black curls. "It won't work, Marvel—it won't," she said in resignation. "I tried it."

And suddenly they were in each other's arms . . . understanding. And, for the first time, Marvel felt the welcome wash of tears.

It was easier for Mary Ann after that emotional moment. She hadn't realized that Marvel was human, but now Mary Ann knew her cousin was flesh and blood like herself. But, like Marvel said, they were spiritual, too—yes, *more* spiritual. Maybe that's what God did when He created man in His own image and breathed spirit into those dust-made bodies! And Marvel was right about lots of other things, too, Mary Ann blurted.

"One was when you said God had authority but gave our parents *earthly* authority. We are commanded to obey their rule. I guess I up and revolted, like Satan. Mother and I shouted terrible things. I've never seen her mad before. The room Jake's going to rent is big enough for two, but you'd think my mother thought I meant like a—a—common, cheap— Oh, never mind! Then in came Jake, and I asked him to make it clear. And he did! He—he—betrayed me. Said yes, he would be glad to make it clear that I was *not* staying—"

Marvel patted her shoulder. "Jake's a gentleman and has a good head on his shoulders. He's looking to your future. You'll be back."

The pupils of Mary Ann's eyes enlarged. "Oh, Jake won't wait *that* long. He's coming when I graduate and he gets settled. I—I guess I'm coming down with a bad case of wounded pride. We talked and it's happy-ever-after now. I still don't want to leave him, but I know that I need Mother and Daddy, too."

"And they need *you*. So does God. Remember?"

Mary Ann laughed—actually laughed. "How can I forget with *you* around? We have to stop feeling guilty, learn to love ourselves, and quit trying to justify ourselves. It would be so easy for me to hate Mary Ann Harrington, but God doesn't hate me. He knows and justifies—"

Marvel felt a lift of her own spirits. Mary Ann said *that*? Her favorite cousin was feeling her way slowly. God would do the rest. "Yes," Marvel said slowly, "I'd have felt the same way if I'd rebelled as I wanted to. And I'd have told God, without trying to justify."

Mary Ann nodded. "That's what I have to do with Mother. That's where the rub comes in—where I need help! Oh Marvel, what can I say?"

"Just put your arms around her. Mothers understand."

"Race you home—bet I can still beat you," Mary Ann said, leaping to her feet. "No shortcuts. 'A straight line's the shortest distance...' *No shortcuts!*"

Marvel stood, too. "There *aren't* any to salvation!"

Mary Ann sobered momentarily. "No, we have to grow.... But Marvel, you've been a brick, listening to my woes while you hurt. And you know, I have the strangest feeling about you and Titus—"

"So do I!" Marvel said, feeling her heart give an unexpected jog. "So—*one, two three*, GO!"

Bright-eyed, wind-blown, and rosy, they arrived at the hotel at the exact moment Captain Bumstead's truck lumbered to a stop. Fanny jumped out, taking no time to use the running board. Mr. Bumstead had left the engine running, his way of saying, "Enough good-byes." In like manner, he quickly handed several packages to the waiting Fanny.

"Ah'm much obliged to y'all, suh. Ah—I 'preciate it—"

"Forgit it. An' don' go sayin' you'll make hit up. You don' that long time ago. I had t'stop by, too. Take this, girl—an' scat!"

Fanny, her ebony face wreathed in smiles, accepted an envelope, plunged it deep into a pocket of her worn red sweater, and waved him on. At the signal, Mr. Bumstead, eyes averted, tamped his pipe and clamped his teeth down on the stem as if he held a grudge against it.

Marvel and Mary Ann stifled giggles when the truck roared away like an angry beast. In the whirlwind of dust left behind, it would have been difficult to say which created more smoke: the pipe in the driver's mouth or the pipe of the faulty exhaust.

* * *

Dinner was over. All the men sat in overstuffed silence, comfortable but regretting seconds on chicken-fried steak and all those tempting buttermilk biscuits sopped in cream gravy. They were indulging occasionally in some "remember when's" now that grist for the mills of memory was nearing the bottom of the bin. The male boarders—Abe Lincoln John, Paul Jones and Chung Foy Su—had joined them, scooting down on the terminal end of their spines to listen, only to doze off now and then.

In contrast, the ladies, having tired of their martyrdom roles for the benefit of the slave-driving men, now chatted freely as they stacked dishes and put away leftovers. Fanny and Billy Joe refused help with the dishes. Fanny was determined to pay for her meal, and boldly hung up a sign, lettered by a giggling, mischief-prone boy: No Mo' White folks 'Lowed! right over the kitchen door. His partner-in-crime would pay, of course—the medium of exchange being tall tales of things that only Fanny had seen. Auntie Rae cast some concerned glances at the forbidden territory, fully aware that inevitably all the tales were about haunted houses and departed souls. She relaxed when for the first time ever Fanny said, "Now, y'all lis'sen, small fry—'n tote 'dis truth 'long wid—with y-yuh—y'heah? Thar—there's only one ghost, an' dat gwinna be de—th' *Holy* One. Res' is in de mind. Hard t'believe, though, what wid all ole Fanny heah dun seen, but hit's gospel!"

Any minute now Grandfather would remove the treasured gold watch—his private "ghost" of the past—and announce that tomorrow would begin early. So best "fly up to roost" at a decent hour. And so would begin the "sweet hour of prayer, fun, and fellowship," the *food* part now past and jolted down. The bulge in one girl's pocket became impatient....

This was the opportune time. And Marvel Harrington drifted out.

Fanny had lovingly delivered Mother's violin, not trusting another to bring the instrument. And, of course, the caring woman had taken Marvel's souvenir box to insure safekeeping—well and good.

But more precious than any of these, there remained the envelope Mr. Bumstead had found in the rural mailbox—postmarked State Capitol, Austin, Texas, U.S.A. *Titus!* Marvel had hidden the letter away so fast that even Mary Ann had failed to see. She *just had* to be alone before opening the sacred seal. And now here she was back in Grandmother's room, her hands trembling like the few leaves remaining on the surrounding oaks. Marvel did not turn on the light momentarily for fear of being discovered. In an effort to gain control, she looked out on the roofs below over which an eerie half-moon cast a feeble glow.

Well, soon—all *too* soon, in one way—they would be leaving this dust. And her father's cough from downstairs reminded her that there was no choice. Bravely, then, she snapped the light on and tore the envelope open—not so much as feeling the cut of the flap's sharp edge.

Titus's letter was brief, she thought in disappointment. The next moment all disappointment dissolved in a river of joy. How many words did it take to change a person's life forever? *Exactly the number in his note...*

> My darling, my own: I cannot believe this—and I am totally unprepared. You see, I thought we had more time. Nothing was going to stop me from seeing you graduate, *nothing*! Not my job, my future, my promises to myself, *nothing*! How does a man propose—ask the girl of his dreams to wait—when the future looks so bleak? I guess I'll simply blunder it out—the way I would have no matter how much I

practiced. Oh Marvel, my *Marvelous*, I—why I—I *love* you. With all my heart, soul, and body, I love you! Question: How long is a girl willing to wait? *Dear God, let this reach her in time....* Your Titus forever.

Later Marvel was to wonder if she touched a single step as she ran down the stairs and into the dimly lighted hallway. There she called Western Union. Her heart was pounding so furiously, she was compelled to ask the anonymous voice to repeat his answer to her question regarding rates of a telegram to Austin.

"Did I understand you, sir? A quarter for how many—12 words? Yes—and immediate delivery. You mean *now*? Oh, thank you, sir. I'll call right back!"

As Marvel replaced the receiver in the hook of the wall telephone, her mind was already doing a word count. Yes, she had it—that was it. But wouldn't it be nice to share with Mary Ann?

Hardly aware of her motions, Marvel moved through the group which was beginning to congregate around the piano. Grandmother had seated herself like a queen on a throne and behind her bench stood Grandfather—together as they should have been half a century ago. The talented Chung had awakened and, his moon-face beaming with pleasure, was tuning Mother's violin...Fanny and Abe were plotting something...Mother, Daddy...Uncle Worth. But Mary Ann? Of course, right beside Auntie Rae, both looking subdued but at peace. Dare she interfere? But even as Marvel hesitated, her aunt squeezed Mary Ann's hand and moved over to squeeze the hand of the man God had given her.

"Come!" Marvel whispered urgently. And her cousin obeyed.

Wide-eyed with wonder, Mary Ann observed as Marvel called Western Union again. "I have my message now. It should read as follows: SO LONG AS WE BOTH SHALL LIVE STOP I LOVE YOU TOO DON'T STOP and," above the gasp behind her and the amused laughter at the other end of the line, "sign it, 'Marvel.' You may make the charge to my grandfather's telephone here at the hotel. Yes sir, that's right. I'm Marvel Harrington."

It was Marvel's turn to gasp as the man exclaimed, "Of course! The Squire's granddaughter. I remember you—th' little thing purty as a Georgia peach and smarter'n a whip—Dale's daughter, aren't you? We all go back a long way and how! My, my! The good turns your family's showed me. Like to tell you young'ns more about that some of these bright days—"

"Thank you, sir. I'll tell them if I may have your name?" Marvel tried not to sound hurried, but the family *was* waiting—

The man chuckled. "They'll know—an' there's no charge! Best wishes an' God go with y'all. When your daddy's better, here's hopin' we meet again. And, Mar—Miss Harrington, my best wishes—lucky young man. Reminds me of back when— never mind—*no charge*—"

There was a click and the line was dead....

* * *

Brother Greer had finished his prayer and was pronouncing the benediction: "'The grace of our Lord Jesus Christ be with you. My love be with you all in Christ Jesus. Amen.'" Oh yes, Paul's words—

There was a chorus of *Amens*, and Marvel and Mary Ann smiled at each other in triumph, for not one cousin remained silent. Neither was there any hesitancy at joining hands and voices in singing "Sweet Hour of Prayer." There was a kind of glow in the room—or was it the glow in her heart, Marvel wondered, that allowed her to see in others what she saw in herself? The clouds had lifted and heaven bent low.

Alexander Jay Harrington, Esquire, rapped the floor smartly with his cane. "At ease!" he said grandly, as if a troop of recruits had saluted. "We will now sing the songs dear to all generations. Music, ladies—first, my request: 'Let Me Call You Sweetheart.' Remember?"

With his hand swinging in three-quarter time taught to him in singing school, he tuned his voice with a *do-ra-me* of the diatonic scale, then sang out masterfully. And the others sang with him:

> Let me call you sweetheart,
> I'm in love with you—
> Let me hear you whis-per
> That you love me too....

Giddy with happiness, Marvel felt no surprise when her Grandfather's hands came down to rest on her Grandmother Riley's slender capable shoulders. Blushing like a schoolgirl, she chimed, "My turn!"

> I'll be loving you—al-ways,
> With a love that's true—always.
> Days may not be fair, that's when I'll be there—
> *Al-ways....*

Uncle Joseph was older. He'd seen action in the world war. It was he who suggested: "Katy, K-Katy, B-Beautiful Katy...."

Then, giggling like truant children, Fanny and Abraham Lincoln John-Paul Jones asked hesitantly for a "specil s'lection." Granted!

> Make mah bed an lite de lite—
> Ah'm gonna 'rive home lat t'nite,
> 'Bye, bye, Black-bu'd....

All made it fine through the roundelay. But who could fault them when, at the lyrics of "Beautiful, Beautiful Texas," eyes went misty? Marvel herself felt wedged between a blissful dream and stark reality. Yet in the enclaves of her heart dwelt everlasting love—and love waged war against the gloomy surveys. Yes, *love* which bore all things and believed all things. So she would be back to Titus. He would wait, as the land would wait like an abandoned toy which inevitably a child reclaimed. And meantime, with God's blessing—and Grandfather's—the Harringtons would make adventure of their departure: laughing, sometimes crying, but drying one another's tears. They would stumble and fall to their knees, but prayer would pick them up. And, together, their hearts would unite in a song known only by those who love.

# HARVEST HOUSE PUBLISHERS

For the Best in Inspirational Fiction

## RUTH LIVINGSTON HILL CLASSICS

Bright Conquest
The Homecoming (mass paper)
The Jeweled Sword
This Side of Tomorrow

## *June Masters Bacher*
## PIONEER ROMANCE NOVELS

### Series 1

1 Love Is a Gentle
  Stranger
2 Love's Silent Song
3 Diary of a Loving Heart

4 Love Leads Home
5 Love Follows the Heart
6 Love's Enduring Hope

### Series 2

1 Journey to Love
2 Dreams Beyond
  Tomorrow
3 Seasons of Love

4 My Heart's Desire
5 The Heart Remembers
6 From This Time Forth

### Series 3

1 Love's Soft Whisper
2 Love's Beautiful Dream
3 When Hearts Awaken
4 Another Spring

5 When Morning Comes
  Again
6 Gently Love Beckons

## HEARTLAND HERITAGE SERIES

No Time for Tears
Songs in the Whirlwind

## ROMANCE NOVELS

The Heart that Lingers, *Bacher*
With All My Heart, *Bacher*
If Love Be Ours, *Brown*

## *Brenda Wilbee*
## SWEETBRIAR SERIES

Sweetbriar
The Sweetbriar Bride
Sweetbriar Spring

## CLASSIC WOMEN OF FAITH SERIES

Shipwreck!
Lady Rebel

## *Lori Wick*
## A PLACE CALLED HOME SERIES

A Place Called Home
A Song for Silas
The Long Road Home
A Gathering of Memories

## THE CALIFORNIANS

Whatever Tomorrow Brings
As Time Goes By

## *Ellen Traylor*
## BIBLICAL NOVELS

Esther
Joseph
Moses
Joshua

---

**Available at your
local Christian bookstore**

---